THE
RADICAL
GENERAL

THE
RADICAL
GENERAL

SIR RONALD ADAM AND BRITAIN'S NEW MODEL ARMY 1941–46

ROGER BROAD

First published 2013
by Spellmount, an imprint of

The History Press
The Mill, Brimscombe Port
Stroud, Gloucestershire, GL5 2QG
www.thehistorypress.co.uk

British Library Cataloguing in Publication Data.
A catalogue record for this book is available from the British Library.

ISBN 978 0 7524 6559 3

Typesetting and origination by The History Press
Printed in Great Britain

CONTENTS

LIST OF ILLUSTRATIONS

ABBREVIATIONS

AA	anti-aircraft
ABCA	Army Bureau of Current Affairs
AC	Army Council
ADGB	Air Defence of Great Britain
AEC	Army Educational Corps
AG	Adjutant-General
AT	anti-tank
ATS	Auxiliary Territorial Service
Bde	Brigade
BEF	British Expeditionary Force
Brig.	Brigadier
Bty	Battery
BWP	British Way and Purpose
Capt.	Captain
CB	Commander of the Order of the Bath
CIGS	Chief of the Imperial General Staff
C-in-C	Commander-in-Chief
CO	commanding officer
Col	Colonel
DCIGS	Deputy Chief of the Imperial General Staff
DDMO	Deputy Director of Military Operations
DGWE	Directorate-General for Welfare and Education
DSO	Member of the Distinguished Service Order
DSP	Directorate for the Selection of Personnel
ECAC	Executive Committee of the Army Council
ENSA	Entertainments National Service Association
F.-M.	Field-Marshal
GCB	Grand Knight Commander of the Order of the Bath
Gen.	General
GHQ	General Headquarters

GOC	General Officer Commanding
GSC	General Service Corps
GSO	General Staff Officer
KCB	Knight of the Order of the Bath
LLD	doctor of laws
Lt	Lieutenant
Lt-Col	Lieutenant-Colonel
Lt-Gen.	Lieutenant-General
Maj.-Gen.	Major-General
MC	Military Cross
MLNS	Ministry of Labour and National Service
NAAFI	Navy, Army and Air Force Institutes
NCO	non-commissioned officer
OBE	Member of the Order of the British Empire
OCTU	Officer Cadet Training Unit
OR	other rank
OTC	Officers' Training Corps
POM	potential officer material
POW(s)	prisoner(s) of war
PSO	Personnel Selection Officer
RA	Royal Regiment of Artillery
RAC	Royal Armoured Corps
RAEC	Royal Army Educational Corps
RAMC	Royal Army Medical Corps
RASC	Royal Army Service Corps
RE	Royal Engineers
RFA	Royal Field Artillery
RGA	Royal Garrison Artillery
RHA	Royal Horse Artillery
RSM	regimental sergeant major
RTC	Royal Tank Corps
Sgt	sergeant
TA	Territorial Army
UNA	United Nations Association
UNESCO	United Nations Educational, Scientific and Cultural Organisation
WEA	Workers' Educational Association
WO	WAR Office
WOSB	War Office Selection Board
YMCA	Young Men's Christian Association

BRIEF CHRONOLOGY

1885 (30 Oct.)	Ronald Forbes Adam born in Bombay
1898-1902	At Eton College
1903 (2 Sep.)	Entered Royal Military Academy, Woolwich
1905 (27 Jul.)	Commissioned as 2nd Lieutenant in Royal Artillery;
1911 (May)	Lieutenant, posted to N Battery, Royal Horse Artillery, India
1914 (Sep.)	Regiment sent to France
1915 (Mar.)	Captain, second-in-command, 41st Bty, 42nd Bde, RFA
1915 (Oct.)	CO, 58th Bty, 35th Bde, RA
1917 (Jan.)	Major, CO, 464th Bty, 174th Bde, RFA
1918 (Mar)	Brigade major, RA, XIV Corps, Italy
1918 (Oct.)	GSO2, RA, XV Corps, Italy
1921 (Dec.)	GSO3, WO
1923 (Jan.)	GSO2, Staff College; temporary lieutenant-colonel
1926 (Mar.)	CO, 72nd Field Bty., 16th Bde., India; brevet lieutenant-colonel
1932 (Oct.)	GSO1, Staff College; colonel
1936 (Oct.)	DDMO, temporary brigadier
1936 (Nov.)	Commander RA, 1st Div,
1937 (Sep.)	Commandant, Staff College; temporary major-general
1938 (Jan.)	Deputy CIGS; temporary lieutenant-general
1939 (Oct.)	GOC, III Corps, BEF; lieutenant-general
1940 (Jun.)	GOC, Northern Command
1941 (Jun.)	Adjutant-General to the Forces
1942 (Apr.)	General
1946 (Jul.)	Retired from army
1945-53	Member of Council, Tavistock Clinic, London
1947-53	Director General, British Council
1948-67	Council member, Institute of Education, London University
1949-67	Member of governing body, Birkbeck College, London
1957-60	Chairman, UK Branch, UNA
1982 (26 Dec.)	Died at Faygate, Sussex

1

THE PUZZLE

After his release from a Japanese prison camp in 1945 the sci-fi-writer-to-be J.G. Ballard spent the holidays from his English boarding school with his grandparents. He recalled that, 'They were obsessed with the iniquities of the post-war Labour government, which they genuinely believed to have carried out a military putsch to seize control of the country, using the postal votes of millions of overseas servicemen.'[1]

This was an extreme example of the sorrow, bewilderment and anger felt by many in Britain and abroad when Winston Churchill, the inspirer of resistance to tyranny, had on the morrow of victory in Europe been cast aside by the electorate with a landslide majority for the Labour Party. Against an unexpected and unwelcome reality many find reassurance in a scapegoat. The reality in this case was that the electorate did not believe that Churchill was the man to lead a peacetime government. As the wartime Coldstream Guards captain and later military historian Sir Michael Howard wrote, 'However great our admiration for Winston Churchill, few of us saw any reason to be grateful to the Conservative Party for its management of national affairs during the 1930s.'[2]

Others closer to the centre of public affairs than Ballard's grandparents also needed a scapegoat to explain this unpalatable truth. Some blamed the voting outcome on the Army Bureau of Current Affairs (ABCA), which had issued fortnightly discussion pamphlets for the troops. In fact, few of the 118 pamphlets issued were controversial. One was suppressed before publication; that on the Beveridge Report on social security was withdrawn in favour of a more closely supervised version. Nonetheless, the Royal Army Educational Corps (RAEC) was pursued for years by the gibe that its only battle honour had been the general election of 1945. This charge had a small element of truth, for there was Left-wing influence in the army's educational service, although its extent is debatable.

Who was responsible for this? Apart from Sir James Grigg, the war minister – a very conservative figure – and parliamentary undersecretary Lord Croft – even more so – the soldier in overall charge of army education (among many other responsibilities) was Gen. Sir Ronald Forbes Adam, Bt, Adjutant-General (AG) to the

Forces in 1941–46. In modern usage he was the army's director of human resources. Did he, wittingly or unwittingly, orchestrate the Ballard grandparents' 'putsch'? If so, why and how?

Despite holding the second highest post in the British Army for five years at a crucial time, Adam is little known compared with Britain's other generals of the Second World War. Those flamboyant in style – such as Montgomery, Slim and Alexander – are famous, as is Alanbrooke. Such others as Auchinleck, Browning, Horrocks, O'Connor, Leese, Paget and Hobart have featured in history books and memoirs. Other widely recognised names are Gort and Wavell, who suffered eclipse through personal misjudgement or military or political mischance. Percival is remembered for surrendering Singapore. Battles lost and won are stirring stuff and their outcome overtly affects history. Yet without competent organisation, adequate supplies of *matériel*, and enough men trained for warfare, all the battlefield generals' plans and campaigns could have been the reverse of glorious. Without Adam's achievements as AG in 1941–46 the British Army would have been in little better shape later in the war than the disasters from 1940 to mid-1942 showed it to be. Without him, many of those of battlefield renown would not have achieved success or gained acclaim. It is not that Adam's role is forgotten; more overlooked: organisation and administration are usually regarded as boring stuff.

TWO PRE-WAR TASKS

On his appointment as AG in June 1941 Adam had been a soldier for nearly forty years, rising steadily if unspectacularly until, in 1938, he was appointed to the new post of Deputy Chief of the Imperial General Staff (DCIGS). Here, within the financial constraints and the policy vagaries of the time, he made a major contribution to getting the British Army ready for war. That it was still not ready enough was outside his control. Apart from this official task he took on the unofficial role of maintaining peace between the Chief of the Imperial General Staff (CIGS), Lord Gort, and the Secretary of State for War, Leslie Hore-Belisha, who barely spoke to each other. He then, for seven months in 1939–40, commanded III Corps of the British Expeditionary Force (BEF), held mainly in reserve. As the Allied forces in the north of France crumbled, Adam was ordered by Gort, now commander-in-chief (C-in-C) of the BEF, to establish a perimeter around Dunkirk, a move that – along with much courage, German errors and sheer luck – enabled 340,000 British and French soldiers to escape by sea. This reinforced Adam's reputation for solid competence. Then for a year he commanded the land defence of north-east England against the expected invasion.

After a brief euphoria in the latter half of 1940, morale in the army slumped – much less so in the navy and air force, which had visible successes. This was not helped by the army's selection of men for duties fitting their abilities being haphazard and inept; the picking out of men for training as officers was arguably even worse. The problems of creating a modern army of soldier-citizens, motivated and with high morale, had not been faced in the years of peace.

By the time Adam left Northern Command to become AG in June 1941 he had learnt much to convince him of the need for three major reforms. The first in time was putting the selection and training of officers on to a scientific basis, including the employment of psychiatrists and psychologists to help judge the quality of potential leaders. This upset conventional minds, political and military.

Next came another change that was deeply upsetting to traditionalists: initially bypassing the individual regiments and corps by sending recruits through the same basic training, during which their intellectual capacity, psychological balance, existing and potential skills, combatant temperament and leadership qualities could be judged, again using scientific methods. Only then were they posted to a regiment or a corps for further training that tried to reconcile the army's needs, their abilities and, if possible, their wishes. Many of Adam's fellow officers believed this undermined, in particular, the infantry's regimental system.

Finally, apart from improving morale through better welfare provision for soldiers and their families, Adam believed that to motivate the citizen-warriors of a democratic state, they needed to understand the nature of the war and the enemy they were fighting. So talks and discussions on the war, on the aims of British policy and other current affairs became an integral part of army life. Faced with an enemy promoting a fascist ideology of dictatorship and intolerance, the Army Council (comprising Britain's political and military leadership) agreed that Britain should promote its own ideology of democracy through its main weapons: open discussion and debate. But encouraging the common soldiery to think about and to discuss public affairs disturbed some. 'Theirs not to reason why, theirs but to do and die', was an attitude with many sympathisers almost a century after the Charge of the Light Brigade at the Battle of Balaclava in the Crimea. Yet the days of obedient cannon fodder were over.

With the War Office Selection Board (WOSB) Adam introduced science and objectivity in place of hunch and prejudice; in the General Service Corps (GSC), analysis and reason in place of tradition and sentiment; with ABCA, open discussion and debate into an organisation based on hierarchy and obedience. All three reforms ruffled feathers, but there can be no doubt that without them the British Army could not have made such a valuable contribution to final victory. Adam was fortunate in having solid support – particularly against Churchill in his more wayward moments – from Sir Alan Brooke, the CIGS from 1941 onwards, and from Grigg.

NOT THE SUMMIT

Was being AG during those dramatic years the summit of Adam's achievements? In having direct command over men and matters it was, but it was far from being the sum of his life. After leaving the army in 1946 at the age of 60 he continued to show great energy and initiative. During the next decade he was chairman and director-general of the British Council and an executive board member and chairman of UNESCO. He chaired a Board of Trade enquiry into the linoleum industry; he also chaired the Library Association and was on the council of the Institute of Education at London University. He sat on the boards of Birkbeck College and the Tavistock Clinic, and was principal of the Working Men's College. A leisure interest led to him being president of the Marylebone Cricket Club (MCC; the world-famous cricket club at Lord's). Concern about international dangers took him to the presidency of the United Nations Association (UNA) and to co-operate on a book on nuclear disarmament. Not until he was 84 years old did he give up his public responsibilities. He lived another thirteen years, and died in Sussex in his 98th year, his mind and handwriting still clear, and taking a long daily walk.

Adam is the exception that proves the rule of the 'Peter Principle' that in a hierarchy an employee tends to rise to the level of his incompetence.[3] His capacity for detail and hard work took him through a rising variety of staff jobs, made him an excellent DCIGS, a fine corps commander, an able general officer commanding (GOC) at Northern Command, and an outstanding adjutant-general. But the very qualities that suited him so well for these roles make it unlikely that he would have made a good CIGS or a theatre or army commander. He was a very good number two to the army, and there is nothing shameful or to be regretted about that. He rose to the level of his *competence* and flourished in it. The only occasion when he might have risked this achievement was in May 1940, when he was ordered to join a Franco-British force to try to break out southwards across the German thrust to the Channel. Events foiled this, and Adam was deprived of the one chance to prove or disprove his capacity in an important battle command.

Yet it remains a puzzle as to how a man of conventional enough background to achieve high army rank, who in a very conservative institution rose steadily with a reputation as a capable administrator with a shrewd diplomatic ability – 'a safe pair of hands' – should suddenly, when given the need, the opportunity and the authority, start to tread on official toes, kick not a few shins, and break up some of the War Office's most elegant and revered Victorian furniture, with admirable effect. And, notwithstanding criticism from Churchill downwards, Adam succeeded in most of what he set out to achieve, even though his successors backtracked on his more imaginative reforms. The British Army and the British people were fortunate in having a man of such judgement as 'Bill' Adam at their service in so many roles, over so many years.

2

FROM INDIA TO INDIA

For several generations India was the birthplace of many British soldiers. During the Second World War they ranged from Terence 'Spike' Milligan, gunner and Goon, to Percy Hobart, armoured warfare expert and developer of 'Hobart's funnies' for D-Day – amphibious and flail tanks, flame and mortar throwers, armoured bulldozers. Spike's father was a quartermaster-sergeant, Hobart's a senior official in the Indian Civil Service. Soldiers, administrators and judges were the formal core of the British Raj. The informal underpinning was provided by engineers, teachers, missionaries, doctors, the occasional journalist such as Rudyard Kipling, and businessmen.

Among the last was Frank Forbes Adam. Born in Scotland in 1846 and educated at Loretto, the then recently established Edinburgh independent school, he went out to India at the age of 26 as a merchant, a description he continued to apply to himself in later life. He prospered as a partner in Graham's Trading Company, carrying on Britain's imperial trade. In 1883 he married Rose Kemball, the daughter of a Bombay High Court judge. Later in the decade he reached the apex of the Indian west-coast business world as president of the Bank of Bombay and of the Bombay Chamber of Commerce, and membership of the Port Trust. He was also part of the formal structure of the Raj as a member of LegCo – the Legislative Council, the nominated body consulted by the governor about provincial matters. His prominence in the business community and his public service were recognised by his appointment in 1888 as a Companion of the Indian Empire and a knighthood in the same order two years later.

On 30 October 1886, at the cool hill station above Bombay, the Adams' first child, Ronald Forbes, was born. Because of the high mortality rate among European children, it was common for the infants of the prosperous to be sent to Britain early on. Ronald went to England at 3 years old to the care of relatives. Fortunately, Frank Forbes Adam, unlike his contemporaries in government service, had some control over his own career, and this separation did not last long. In the following year, Sir Frank and Lady Adam returned to Britain with their second and third sons, Eric Forbes, born in 1888, and Colin

Forbes, a year later. Where the Forbes name originated is uncertain, although it was initially used as a further given name. The family settled in Cheshire, at Hankelow Court, in the village of that name. The house is described by the architecture historian Sir Nikolaus Pevsner as a 'brick, black and white house from 1870s, enlarged 1901'; in short, mock Tudor.[1] Sir Frank began a second phase to his business career in Manchester, then the world centre for the textile trade. In 1896 the family's fourth child, Hetty, was born.

The family's return to Britain meant that the boys, apart from Ronald for a year, were spared the fate of many of their Indian-born contemporaries of being sent 'home' when very young to stay with relatives, at boarding school or even with foster parents, and not seeing their parents for years until rare home-leave brought them back to Britain. For mothers particularly this caused much anguish; for many children it caused lifelong psychological trauma. However, Ronald and his brothers did not escape boarding school at a young age. In the 1890s British schools, both private and state, were with few exceptions based on the precept 'spare the rod and spoil the child', certainly in spirit, frequently in practice. This applied at Ronald's prep school in Sussex, Fonthill, which his brother Colin described as having been in Ronald's time something of a 'Dotheboys Hall' (à la *Nicholas Nickleby*), although improved in his own days a few years later. Colin assigned his brother's reticence and taciturnity to the treatment he received there.[2] One attribute Ronald did acquire at Fonthill was the very precise and clear handwriting that he kept all his life. Once at Eton from September 1898 until December 1902 he was, according to a 1976 interview, 'very happy', and is recalled as saying, 'I made up my mind pretty early that I would go into the army'.[3] His brothers outshone Ronald academically. Both were King's Scholars at Eton, and both went on to King's College, Cambridge. Eric joined the Foreign Office, dying at 37, and Colin the Indian Civil Service until ill health forced a return to Britain a few years later. They were the family's sprinters, with Ronald the long-distance runner, in achievement and longevity.[4] Hetty lived to age 81, Colin to 93; Ronald outlived all his younger siblings. Considering that, in the view of the military historian Basil Liddell Hart, 'the Army was the vocation of the sons who were not likely to shine in other professions', Ronald did well.[5]

'THE SHOP'

Ronald wanted to join the Royal Regiment of Artillery (RA), which meant entering 'the Shop', the nickname for the Royal Military Academy at Woolwich, where gunners and engineers trained. (Cavalry and infantry trained at the Royal Military College at Sandhurst.) To prepare for the entrance exam he was early in 1903 sent for six months to Adams and Millard, a British-run examinations 'crammer' in Freiburg, Germany. He mixed with very few Germans and learnt no German. But those months in Germany helped get him into the Shop as a 'gentleman cadet' at the age of 'seventeen years, eleven months and three days', as the records meticulously detail.[6] His own recollection was of scraping in bottom or second to bottom in the entrance list; the Woolwich records are a little more generous: thirty-third out of thirty-nine. In Freiburg, Adam had gone to a fencing master who also taught him the sabre, with which German students fought duels (although Ronald never did). At the Shop new cadets had to provide a display for the seniors: 'box or fence or sing or dance or do something […] a sort of initiation rite'. His swordplay helped establish his credentials with his seniors. Otherwise Woolwich provided a general education, regular riding school, general drill and gun drill. It was a strenuous course physically and – some assert – intellectually, and the position in which the cadets were placed at the end usually affected the rest of their careers.

But, according to the biographer of Noel Mason-Macfarlane (Adam's future brother-in-law), there was an 'undemanding mental climate' at Woolwich. Mason-Mac's more intellectual approach was looked upon as something of an oddity, 'an attitude which, as far as his brother officers were concerned, was to pursue him for the rest of his military career'.[7] Sir Frederick 'Tim' Pile, a contemporary of Adam and who, in the Second World War was GOC AA Command, found that his:

> two years at Woolwich were the greatest possible fun […] the education at the Shop was a general education with a leaning towards military affairs. One thing they did not teach you was anything about one's job as an officer. One learned quite a lot about field engineering. One great military campaign was studied and no doubt the cadet could have won that campaign pretty easily. One learned to dress smartly and to sit on a horse with reasonable security, but what happened when one took one's battery on parade was never revealed.[8]

Aged 19 years, 9 months and 27 days Adam passed out, once again placed exactly thirty-third out of thirty-nine, and was commissioned as a 2nd lieutenant. Woolwich graduates could go three ways: the 'top slice' went into the Royal Engineers (RE) for further study and better pay, the remainder to the Royal Field Artillery (RFA) or, if placed very low, to the Royal Garrison Artillery (RGA). As Adam put it, he 'managed to get posted to the Field Artillery', on 27 July 1905. After a month at the School of Gunnery at Shoeburyness, in Essex, he returned to Woolwich for four months at the Ordnance College. Posted to the 54th Bty of the 39th Bde, RA, he spent three years at Shorncliffe, in Kent, and then as long again in Edinburgh.

A tall, handsome young officer with the seemingly obligatory moustache of the time, there was more to his life than drill and gunnery: his photograph album for the late 1900s recorded shooting parties, polo, fox-hunting, balls and country house parties when on leave in Cheshire.[9] In early 1911 he started to keep a diary: January is blank, February and March had sparse entries; from then on the daily entries were fuller. In September there was a seventeen-day gap, just with an entry, 'Shooting diary'.[10]

The entries for the spring months recorded military life in Edinburgh: parades, orderly officer duty, musketry and gun drill took up the mornings. Almost every afternoon and evening Adam was out riding, or playing rugby, polo, hockey, cricket or golf, or billiards in the mess. At night (sometimes well towards dawn) he went to plenty of parties and balls. On 13 February he met a Miss Redford: 'Very pretty girl and nice; must get some dances with her first opportunity'. That opportunity came three days later, when, after sitting out three dances with a Mrs Arbuthnot, he 'danced the rest with Dulcie Redford [...] an excellent dancer and prettiest girl in Edinburgh'. Early in March he is dancing mainly with her; on 21 March he had twelve dances with her. On 11 April he, 'Danced all except 2 with Dulcie. Grand finish to grand day.' She appears again on 25 April, but following the receipt on 13 May of orders to India, he said goodbye to her five days later. The diary recorded the letters he wrote to family and friends, showing that after a weekly letter to his mother and a frequent one to his friend Audley, Dulcie was the addressee most often noted. On 31 December 1911 the diary ends: 'My first year's effort at keeping a diary, fairly useful but find it rather a d–d nuisance'. There's no more diary; no more Dulcie.

BACK TO INDIA

The posting showed that Adam's achievement in getting into the RFA was only a first step. Now a lieutenant, his Indian posting was initially at Ambala, 125 miles north of Delhi. A few months later he was posted to N Troop, Royal Horse Artillery (RHA) with the Secunderabad Cavalry Brigade in south India. Just as the RGA was considered the boring end of the RA, so the RHA was its elite. It customarily used the cavalry term 'troop' for what was officially a battery. N Troop had appropriate Indian links as it had originated in 1811 as the First Troop, Horse Brigade, Bombay Artillery.

The RHA traces its origins back to the early seventeenth century and was firmly established during the Napoleonic Wars. Its role was to provide mobile battlefield support for the cavalry. Unlike the infantry and cavalry, where the purchase of commissions lasted until the Cardwell reforms in the 1870s, advancement in both the Royal Engineers and Royal Artillery always depended on ability; courage and dash were not enough – and even less, wealth and position. Gunners always held that they were special, in a scientific arm. To be picked out for the RHA was an extra distinction. For all ranks, driving a 1 ton gun and limber across country under fire was extremely difficult and required a high level of skill and training.

And, of course, there had to be those slight differences of dress that so delight soldiers: the RFA wore flat buttons, those of the RHA were rounded, artillery officer Harry Siepmann noted.[11] Another distinction he recalled was that the RHA had, 'the privilege of advancing at the trot and going into action at the gallop, whereas we field gunners were supposed to advance at a walk and go into action at no more than a trot'.[12] The RHA's historian Shelford Bidwell stressed that this was, 'a service in which every man had to be alert and had his special part to play, in which the slightest mistake might cause a bad accident or, worse, deprive the infantry or cavalry of fire support when it was most needed'.[13]

The requirements regarding horsemanship and gunnery were the same as in Wellington's day, although the weaponry had evolved with more accurate breech-loading guns and more deadly ammunition. The skills required meant that the RHA was in demand for tattoos and similar ceremonial displays, and it retains that role in the twenty-first century. Adam may not have been placed high in his class list but he had other abilities that were recognised, horsemanship among them. Yet he had not learnt to ride as a child; it was the army that taught him.[14]

In these relaxed Edwardian years the army was undergoing desirable although inadequate change. The Conservative government had tried to get the army to accept the lessons of the Boer War but it was too close to the vested interests. As with the earlier reformers Cardwell and Childers, it took a Liberal war minister, Lord Haldane, to impose change. His legacy was the Imperial General Staff, the Territorial Force (later Army; theoretically only for home defence), and the Officers' Training Corps (OTC) at public schools and universities to provide a reserve of partly trained officers or to prepare some for military careers. These reforms laid the basis for the British Expeditionary Force (BEF) of 1914. Although the Liberal government was generous to the navy (and responsive to populist press campaigning) in financing dreadnoughts and other modern ships, it was parsimonious towards the army, spending less each year between 1907 and the start of the war, although it did increase the budget to cover the creation of the Royal Flying Corps in 1913. There was not enough money to increase pay or pensions, replace old weapons or provide ammunition for a long campaign.

'BROOKIE' AND 'GEORGE'

In India, Adam met a man who would become a lifelong comrade-in-arms and friend, Alan Brooke, two years his senior. At Woolwich, Brooke probably worked too

hard, his biographer wrote. He dropped back two places and failed to get into the
Royal Engineers – for his and Britain's benefit, for sappers rarely reach the highest
ranks. Adam, named by his parents 'Ronald', was known to his army friends as
'Bill'; even more obscurely, 'Brookie' always called him 'George'. For young officers
life in India was comfortable and enjoyable, the demands of drill – 'We prided
ourselves on our gallops past', Adam recalled – and duty being compensated by
leave and opportunities for sport, notably polo and shooting. N Troop comprised
six 13-pounder guns. The officer complement was a major, a captain and three
subalterns, with 205 British other ranks and 234 horses. On a duty rotated among
the junior officers, Adam spent a year in command of the battery's ammunition train,
with Indian non-commissioned officers (NCOs) and soldiers. In Britain, an Army
Service Corps (ASC) contingent of 108 Indians manned the train, with 137 horses.[15]
The Indian personnel were more numerous and their animals more varied.

There was a great deal more to gunnery than a smart turnout and spectacular
gallops. It was, as noted, a scientific arm. Just as gun technology had in Adam's
young days moved on from 1815, it had moved on even more dramatically
since its earliest days. Nonetheless, many things remained the same. In 1588
Cyprian Lucar translated and published Niccolò Tartaglia's 1537 treatise on 'The
properties, office and duetie of a gunner':

> A Gunner ought to be a sober, wakefull, lustie, hardie, patient, prudent and
> quick spirited man, he ought also to have a good eyesight, a good judgement,
> and a perfect knowledge to select a convenient place in the day of service,
> to plant his Ordinance where he may doe most hurt into the enemies, and
> be least annoyed by them, and where his Ordinance may not be surprised by
> the enemie.
>   A Gunner ought to be skilfull in Arithmeticke, and Geometrie, to the end
> he may be able by his knowledge in those artes to measure heights, depths,
> breadthes, and lengthes, and to drawe the plat of any peece of ground, and to
> make mines, countermines, artificiall firewoorkes, rampiars, gabbions or baskets
> of earth, and such like things which are used in times of warre to be made for
> offensive or defensive service.[16]

Tartaglia prescribed eight other paragraphs of advice and instruction to a Gunner,
including that, 'A Gunner ought also to procure with all his power the friendship
and love of every person'. This must have been a difficult ambition regarding an
'enemie' to whom a Gunner is trying to 'doe most hurt'.

Adam's army record shows that he reached Higher Standard level of proficiency
in Hindustani, the lingua franca of the British military in India. He also studied
Persian in the afternoons, when the weather was too hot for other activity.
Why he undertook this study is not recorded. It could have been a possible
career move: southern Persia was within the British sphere of influence and

a British company was starting to exploit the oil resources. Or, perhaps it reflected a need for mental stimulus in the then philistine atmosphere of the British Army.

THE DURBAR: PARADE AND PAIN

During his first tour in India Adam took part in the Imperial Durbar of 1911 when the new King-Emperor George V visited his Indian domains. After a thirteen-day march (on horseback for the RHA) the brigade spent fifteen days in Delhi in early December. After four days of rehearsals, the troops lined the streets for the monarch's arrival – 'got absolutely weary of sitting on horses […] got back worn out and leg very sore', the diary recorded. The leg kept him off duties for three days; he had earlier had a sty and a boil on his face. Although in the 1970s Adam recalled the magnificence of the Indian princes' parade with elephants, at the time he was understandably unappreciative of the imperial splendour, the silk-lined ceremonial tents in the great temporary city to house 250,000 visitors, the bejewelled maharajahs and rajahs, and the 2,000-strong military band. Yet his suffering seems to have been in a good cause for the honour of the regiment. The *Times of India* was wildly enthusiastic:

> The Royal Horse Artillery went in like the wind, the horses ventre-à-terre joyously tugging at their traces, the guns leaping after them like things of life. In a sense it was almost a matter of regret that the horse gunners were in the van: the spectacle they provide is so superb that everything else suffers by comparison.[17]

When the King-Emperor George V started back to Britain, the gunners had a thirteen-day march back to barracks.

ON SHIKAR

During Adam's time in northern India he and some other subalterns went big game hunting, an occupation very attractive to the British and Indian elite in an age when the concepts of conservation and endangered species were embryonic. A bullock or goat was tethered at a particular spot, with the hunter in a platform in a nearby tree; an electric light could be switched on when a tiger, panther or other predator approached and seized the prey. On Adam's first time out, a tiger was too far away from him and was shot by another officer. Another time he wounded a panther and had to follow it across a ravine for the kill. On another occasion, in southern India, he got two panthers, which were skinned and turned into rugs that he kept for many years. This time there were no trees and he was hiding behind a rock. While there had been little danger when he was in the tree, if a panther had come at him from behind this time in this exposed position, 'It would have been too bad'. Asked by historian Peter Liddle a late-twentieth century question as to whether he had any remorse at killing such 'magnificent beasts', he gave a robust early-twentieth century reply: 'Well, a panther is really a most awful nuisance to the villagers because he takes their goats. Lies up and captures their goats as they are driving them back in the evening and it is a real menace to the countryside.'

A pointer to Adam's character is that the 1911 diary contains precise notes on various aspects of army life in India, such as a diagram of 'wireless apparatus', notes on the frequency and composition of horse feeds, and a list of the clothing, equipment and supplies needed on shikar. He also recorded his wage bill in barracks for his seven servants, from a bearer (20 rupees) to a grass cutter (5 rupees), a total of 66 rupees (a nominal £4.26).

Life for the BORs – the British Other Ranks – was very different. Their lot was of up to fifty men living in what was described as a 'bungalow', but was, 'more of the nature of an aircraft hangar', very solidly built, about 250ft long, about 100ft wide and between 30 and 40ft high. They were very light, very cool and well ventilated.[18] There was little privacy. Including compulsory church attendance on Sundays, there was no escaping parades. Even the two weeks leave granted each year was often spent in barracks, except for those who had saved enough from their meagre pay to escape briefly. Food was poor in quality and inadequate in quantity. Permission to marry was controlled, and warrant officers and senior NCOs had priority for married quarters. Many BORs hardly spoke to a white woman in years; association with 'native women' was strictly discouraged except where brothels were unofficially tolerated. One compensation was that there were people even lower down the social scale: the 'natives', or at least those with whom they came into contact. These provided services that British working-class men could not command (except perhaps from mothers and wives): laundry, ironing, boot polishing and barrack cleaning. And, as Kipling celebrated, there was the regimental bheesti, the water-carrier. The writer was cynical about the attitude of the British public towards 'The Soldiers of the Queen' and of the successor king: 'For it's Tommy this, an' Tommy that, and "Chuck him out the brute!" But it's "Saviour of the Country" when the Guns begin to shoot.'[19]

THE 'FISHING FLEET'

For officers, apart from sport and hunting, more recreation was to be found in the officers' mess; and in Adam's case at the Secunderabad Club. His mess there was quite large because of the field artillery brigade stationed there. Mess dress was, of course, as formal as in Britain except that in hot weather the officers wore white. The club demanded even more decorum than the mess. Only the senior officers would have their wives with them: 'it was an understood thing that a subaltern in the Horse Artillery did not get married'. There were dances where young officers could meet the daughters of the senior British officers, officials and businessmen. But it was nothing like Edinburgh. A noted feature of imperial social life was the annual 'fishing fleet', when young middle- and upper-middle-class British women, suitably chaperoned, would go out to India for a few months in the cool season with a view to finding a husband.

Alternatively, when young men were on home leave from the army, administration or business, they might spend their time meeting young women suitable as potential brides. After two years in India, Adam got home leave in 1913, during which he found himself a suitable bride, Dorothy, the radiantly beautiful daughter of stockbroker F.I. Pitman. They got engaged; the arrangement of a wedding was left for his next home leave. Brookie also wanted to marry and needed to seek permission. He and Adam decided to apply together to their CO. '"Who'll break the ice?" said Adam. "I will", said Brooke, and he did', Adam recounted.[20] Brooke was back in England on leave and got married on 28 July 1914.

Although expected at Delhi headquarters, which had cable connections to the War Office, the news of the declaration of war a week later came as a great shock at regimental level (it took three weeks for British newspapers to reach India). N Troop was mobilised on 9 August, was ready six days later and sailed from Bombay on 9 September. In Brooke's absence, Adam was back in command of the ammunition train and got the 17 wagons, 29 mule carts, 120 men, 98 horses and 58 mules on board ship. On reports that the German cruiser *Emden* was in the Indian Ocean, the ships dispersed from their convoy and met again at Port Said. Meanwhile, Brooke, posted back east, rejoined the unit in Egypt. Then, landing in France at Marseille, the troops travelled north for a three-week hardening course near Orléans. It went into the line on 5 November near Berguette.[21]

During these years Adam appears as a conventional young officer from a conventional background with the aptitudes, attitudes, tastes and pleasures of one of his time and class. Academically indifferent, he struggled to get into Woolwich and did not shine in his studies there. But his postings when commissioned suggest other qualities that registered with his superiors. Nevertheless, there is no indication of any particular concern for the morale and well-being of the ordinary soldiers that he was to display thirty years later.

So, in 1914, Britain's 'contemptible little army' – in the phrase attributed to the kaiser – went to war. The bilingual Siepmann contended that a more accurate rendering of the original German is 'an absurdly small army'.[22] If so, the kaiser's comment was factually correct when the British Army was compared with its Continental allies and enemies. But accuracy in translation offered no opportunity for the British survivors of those first weeks of modern warfare to adopt with perverse pride the title, 'The Old Contemptibles'.

Though not among the earliest arrivals in France, Brookie and 'George' were at the front within a few weeks: two energetic, eager young officers, firm friends and comrades-in-arms. Neither they nor anyone else could have imagined that, thirty years on, they would cement that alliance as Number One and Number Two in the British military hierarchy.

3

THE SOMME AND THE ASIAGO

The cavalry in general and the RHA in particular largely lost their historic roles between 1914 and 1918. These were based on an assumption of open field campaigning, without fixed battle lines and defences, apart from the occasional strongpoint or fortified town. They soon proved almost irrelevant on the Western Front. Throughout, the war horses provided the main haulage almost up to the front line, although tractors and traction engines proved essential for the increasingly heavy guns and other equipment deployed. Lorries more and more took over other transport tasks, and cars carried senior officers. Within a few months of the outbreak of war, the enduring image of the Western Front was established: hundreds of miles of trenches from which men of both sides periodically climbed to die in their thousands in fruitless attempts to break through the enemy's lines. Although the cavalry were constantly on tenterhooks to play their role when the 'big push' would break through the enemy defences, when the final, and successful push did come in the late summer of 1918 it was tanks and artillery that proved the decisive mobile factor. The cavalry did at last have a role exploiting the breakthrough, and suffered terribly from machine-gun fire.

War based on a static front line had been presaged on a lesser scale in the Russo-Japanese War in 1904–05. That conflict showed the importance of machine guns (which the Germans inevitably grasped more readily than the British[1]) and of indirect fire, by both these guns and by artillery. Indirect artillery fire, with a forward observation post passing back information on targets and their bearings to the hidden artillery, replaced the historical line-up of guns visible to the enemy. In the Far East, barbed wire had come into use to defend entrenched positions, and mortars and grenades to attack them. The importance of signals, increasingly by telephone, was recognised by the more far-sighted European soldiers.[2] Early British and French reluctance to adapt to the new world cost many lives. Protection of soldiers became necessary – steel helmets and gas masks appeared in 1915. Warfare had come a long way from the legendary eighteenth-century gallantry of, *'Tirez les premiers, Messieurs les Anglais'* (the well-known French phrase, loosely translated as 'English gentlemen, please fire first').

Late in October or early November 1914 at Neuve Chapelle, the newly promoted Capt. Ronald Adam rode up to an abandoned house to set up an observation post (OP): 'I think we were in full view of the enemy. About 500 yards from the trenches or it may have been 700 yards' – not an impossible range for a good marksman. On the top storey he installed a telephone and registered the battery on the German front line.[3] He then took his section of two guns 3 miles further south to where they could enfilade the German trenches: 'it was a pretty dangerous position because we had to sandbag ourselves properly in because of ricochets and bullets flying around most of the time'.

The accelerated promotion of wartime as armies expand and men die was already apparent: instead of the usual eleven years in the RA to get a captaincy, Adam achieved his in a little over nine, in October 1914. Another personal change was that when on leave in England the following January he got married to Dorothy, who became a 'VAD', a member of a Voluntary Aid Detachment of St John Ambulance.

It was barbed wire and trenches that did much to stabilise the front line from Switzerland to the North Sea, and cut out opportunity for strategic surprise. Much artillery fire was devoted to trying to cut the enemy's wire before infantry attacks, though with uncertain results. But artillery, a subsidiary arm in pre-war days, came into its own. The European war saw siege warfare on an unprecedented scale. Heavier and heavier guns and howitzers were brought into use by both sides in attempts to break the deadlock. This meant that the RHA became little distinguishable in function from the field artillery. The number of regular and Territorial RHA batteries went up only from forty to fifty during the war, whereas RFA batteries more than doubled in number from 404 to 876. The previously disdained RGA increasingly took its place on the battlefield to provide the heavy guns now demanded; it went up from just three batteries to 401.[4] The coastal artillery's experience of dropping heavy shells accurately on to distant targets proved far more useful in Flanders fields than the RHA's historic flexibility and speed. There was little call for smart gallops past in France. At the beginning of the war, anti-aircraft (AA) batteries did not exist; by its end there were 289. Overall, the RA nearly quadrupled from 447 batteries to 1,616. British production of artillery pieces expanded dramatically from only 91 guns and howitzers in 1914 to over 10,000 in 1918 – bringing the total to 25,000 during the war years. Gunnery of all nationalities was trying to 'doe most hurt into its enemies', in Lucar's translation.

The expansion of the infantry was even more marked – elevenfold from 161 regular battalions to 1,750 at a wartime peak. In numbers of men it rose from 299,000 when the regulars, reservists and Territorials were all mobilised in August 1914 to a peak of over two million in mid-1917 and down to 1.6 million by the Armistice. Despite the great increase in numbers of men and battalions, the number of infantry regiments was unchanged; additional battalions – in some cases more than twenty – were formed within the existing regiments. This attempt to maintain the local connections of the infantry was undermined by the increasing need as the war went on to cross-post men to make up losses in particular regiments. By 1917 the revered regimental system was effectively finished, though carried on in name and sentiment. The cavalry, with little scope for action in Europe, did not expand at all. When tanks were introduced in 1916 they were initially manned by the Machine Gun Corps. In numbers the RE were the great gainers, rising tenfold to 237,000 during the war years, a reflection of technological advance and of the use of saps (deep tunnels packed with explosives) to undermine enemy positions.

During the war RA personnel had risen from 93,000 when mobilised with reservists and Territorials in August 1914 to 549,000 by November 1918, excluding the nearly 43,000 dead and the many more thousands medically discharged. Of the fighting arms 7.6 per cent of casualties were gunners compared with 86 per cent infantrymen. It became the norm to replace men lost and guns destroyed, with postings from one battery to another, from brigade to brigade, and from division to division. Adam's own moves illustrate this. By March 1915, as a captain, he was second-in-command of the 41st Bty, 42nd Bde, RFA; in July he became adjutant to the 3rd Bde, RFA – his first step to an administrative career; from October he was CO of the 58th Bty, 35th Bde, RFA. This constant movement between units designated only by numbers shows the gulf between the artillery and the infantry, whose units were known by names of sometimes historic origin. Their numbers – the Seventh of Foot, the Sixtieth Rifles, and so on – still existed but were formal only. This difference and Adam's own experience were to prove significant when he achieved high rank and position three decades later.

DIARY

Adam was not involved in any noted battles in 1915: not at Neuve Chapelle in March, nor at Aubers Ridge, Festubert or Loos. For him, it was a relatively quiet year. This changed in 1916.

Despite the King's Regulations ban he began keeping a diary again, of which two notebooks started after Easter 1916 survive.[5] His entries during the next few weeks illustrate his routine. On 30 April: 'Fired 518 rounds plus 553 later at night. Apparently the huns did nothing.' On 2 May he went down to the infantry and 'did trench crawl as usual. Nothing interesting'. On 8 May there is the first reference to the Maxse Redoubt, the observation point named after the brigadier-general commanding the 18th Div., the XIII Corps, of which Adam's battery formed part. On 17 May his battery was heavily strafed early in the morning, with two German heavy batteries firing about 200 rounds in four gun salvos. Adam counted seventy craters around the battery and at least half of those fired were duds. 'No danger luckily but some narrow squeaks.'

Tartaglia's sixteenth-century rules did not only demand skill in 'arithmeticke' and 'geometrie' but 'knowledge in those artes to measure heights, depths, breadthes, and lengthes, and to drawe the plat of any peece of ground'. Adam showed himself adept at the last in a series of meticulous sketches of the enemy lines.[6] OP officers may have had binoculars, compasses and range finders, but for their records they relied on the eye and hand; photographs would not have been clear enough. On 18 May Adam noted: 'Did landscape sketch from Maxse.' This was to prove important six weeks later.

In his diary Adam was careful to write nothing that might be of use to the enemy, should his notebook fall into their hands. There is no mention of how many of the British shells were duds (a massive problem until well into the war), nor anything about the number or the quality of British guns, nor, except in passing, reference to any individual lost or any detailed mention of British casualties.

From 2 June Adam had a short time out of the war with ten days' home leave. He had to sleep on deck on the cross-Channel ship. In London the following day, he and Dorothy lunched at St Ermin's Hotel. Then they did some shopping, went to a comedy by J.M. Barrie called *A Kiss for Cinderella*, and had supper at The Savoy. Three days later they took a train to Bournemouth, staying at the Canford Cliffs Hotel – 'Lovely spot' – and bathing and walking until the 10th when they motored to Southampton, where 'Doff and I parted'. He boarded a ship, this time with a cabin, and two days later: 'Found battery well.' Most of his diary entries are equally terse.

THE SOMME

The following days were mainly spent at Maxse, registering guns and preparing for what was to become known as the Battle of the Somme – that 'big push' that was expected to change the face of the war. It did, although not as expected.

The army's preparations for the assault included amassing substantial ammunition: for each 18-pounder, with which the 58th Bty was equipped, 354 rounds were stocked at the guns, another 1,000 near the guns, and 250 at divisional dumps; in all, 1,604 rounds per gun. Yet Adam's own battery was a minor element among the artillery on the British sector of the Somme front, which totalled 808 18-pounders, 202 4.5in howitzers, 182 heavy guns and 245 heavy howitzers. There were 1,447 British guns in all, with 90 French guns in support.[7]

Adam's own position was in the OP, telephoning target coordinates back to the subalterns in command of the guns. His 1 July entry reads:

Day of attack up at Maxse at dawn, foggy day so could not see much of attack at first. Good view later of 21st Div, 7th Div and 18th attacking. Our special attack in evening. Saw Manchesters attack and a lot of casualties. They got Reitange and Bois Francais.

The following day he recorded that Fricourt was captured — all featured on his Maxse sketch. Sixty years later he described how his battery of 18-pounders was 'in a rather extraordinary position because we enfiladed the German trenches which turned just south of us away from the general line at right angles'. Before the offensive, the position had come under howitzer fire with shells falling all around the guns, without any of them being hit. The gun emplacements and the ammunition dumps to the rear were well sandbagged for protection.

On that first day he saw many British infantry to his right mown down by a machine gun before fresh troops came to take the enemy trenches and still the gun. His own battery could not intervene because the British troops were too close to the enemy wire and were outside his battery's sector. Frustratingly, while his battery was moving forward to occupy a captured German reserve trench, some tempting targets were missed because there was no telephone yet from his forward OP. This was his memory in his 90th year. The fog of war intervened, according to his diary: after the capture of Fricourt the battery was ready to move at 1 p.m. on 2 July and advanced two hours later via 'Happy Valley'. At Mametz he arranged and marked the position, but they were then ordered back to the old position. 'No sooner back & the teams taken away then ordered to advance.' But at least the 18th Div. achieved its first-day objectives, although at a loss of 30 per cent casualties, dead and wounded.

Eight days later, Adam noted that: 'Welsh supposed to attack Mametz wood early bombardment with no success as they never started.' The following day: 'Mametz wood attack a total failure owing to lack of push by 38th. Battery shelled all night. Gnr Kingston wounded.' The next day: '38th took most of Mametz.'

Who Gnr Kingston was — to merit a diary mention — is unknown, possibly his runner or batman. Adam named few of his fellow soldiers, with Kingston alone as one who suffered misfortune. Likewise, he told little of his own unit's casualties and, apart from the Manchesters' 'lot of casualties', nothing about the 19,000 Britons who died on the first day of the Somme, with twice as many wounded. Men became inured to suffering. In any case, each battery, company and section — and indeed each man — knew little of what was going on outside his immediate area until rumour and report brought news.

The three days that it took the 38th Div. to capture most of Mametz Wood cost it 5,000 casualties for a few thousand square yards. Mametz lies a few miles east of

Albert on the north side of the Somme. Today it is in a restored rural landscape, with fifty British cemeteries nearby. In the Somme *département* as a whole, there are 363 cemeteries and churchyards with the remains of 144,000 British and Empire dead. Another 100,000 with no known graves are commemorated on memorials, including British architect Edwin Lutyens's great arch looming over the landscape at Thiepval. In all, 575,000 British and Empire soldiers died in France; many others died later in Britain and elsewhere from their wounds.

An innovation on the Somme – attributed to Alan Brooke[8] – was the 'creeping barrage' whereby the guns, firing in salvo, are gradually elevated so that their shots, normally of shrapnel, would step-by-step sweep across no-man's-land, the enemy wire and trenches. The Germans took refuge if they could, with the attacking infantry following closely – and if with good gunnery and a good deal of luck, safely – behind the exploding shells of their own artillery. It was calculated that with an 18-pounder firing at 2,000 yards range the infantry could safely be 44 yards behind the shell bursts.[9] Of course, faulty or misaimed guns and premature shell bursts could not be avoided, and deaths from 'friendly fire' occurred.

General Martin Farndale wrote that in the British Fourth Army only the XV Corps and Maxse's 18th Div. in the XIII Corps used this technique successfully. The 18th Div. early, short lifts were from trench to trench, with the final 1,000 yards covered by:

> a genuine creeping barrage, lifting every 50 yards every 1½ minutes, and the attack was most successful, with the artillery fire being very effective and accurate […] At last there was a way of dealing with the enemy tactic of going to ground very deep and coming to the parapet after the barrage had lifted.[10]

Unlike the French and Germans the British were not using gas in this offensive. On 17 July Adam recorded: 'Poison gas shells all around the battery in evening'. Two days later, he wrote: 'Gas-shelled in morning. Made the place stink and very nearly hit guns and mess.' By the 21st, the battery had only one gun still operative and was pulled out of the line.

TRENCH FEVER

On his return to the front Adam went down with trench fever, a disease caused by body lice that affected up to one-third of British troops. Although gunners were set back from the most forward lines, their living conditions were little better than those of the infantry; personal hygiene was a constant problem. Adam's 2 May diary noted: 'Had a bath this morning.' The high point of the sickness was usually brief – an alternative name was 'five-day fever' – but it took a long time to recover. Siepmann's description read:

There is no cure, and the treatment is simply to let it runs its course. The legs, especially the shins, can be very tender, and even an accidental jolt of the bed can be agonizing. The pain seems to increase at night, making sleep almost impossible […] eventually recovered and was allowed home for a short convalescence.[11]

Adam got it worse than Siepmann. On 8 August he noted: 'Retired to bed with a high fever', and he remained there for several days. On the 15th he noted that he was up for three hours in the evening, but two days later the fever came on again. The next day he was sent to the casualty clearing station. But on the 23rd: 'Back to the battery and got as far as wagon line but too weak to get up to guns.' He spent three days in the wagon line before a relapse combined with 'inside trouble'. On the 31st he was sent to the base hospital in Rouen and, on 6 September, noted: 'Sent home to Osborne.' This was a convalescent home for officers at Queen Victoria's old residence on the Isle of Wight. The medical card dated 9 October describes his condition as 'debility'.[12] He spent ten weeks on sick leave followed by a month on light duties.

During his time away from the front, on 15 February 1917, his father (already a knight) was created a baronet, taking the title 'Sir Frank Forbes Adam of Hankelow Court in the County of Chester'. An active Liberal, he had an extensive role in public service in the north-west of England, chairing hospital boards, the council of Victoria University of Manchester (now Manchester University), which had awarded him an LLD, and the local Territorial Forces Association. He was also Deputy Lord Lieutenant of Lancashire. Subsequently, Sir Frank and Lady Forbes Adam moved to Pownall Hall, in Wilmslow, Cheshire (a Georgian property rather better favoured by Pevsner), where they lived in some opulence. The name Forbes, originally used in the family as a second given name, was now employed to form a double-barrelled but unhyphenated family name. Having entered the army simply as Adam, Ronald was known by this name throughout his army career, and later. He usually signed himself 'R.F. Adam', although occasionally after 1945 as 'R. Forbes Adam'.

After recovering from trench fever, the now Maj. Adam in January 1917 took command in England of the 464th Bty, in the 174th Bde, RFA, and on 12 May took it to France. This time he was posted further north, on Vimy Ridge, where 16 May and successive days were spent getting the guns into position. Alan Brooke was attached to the Canadian Corps nearby. On 19 May he came to tea with Adam, the first of several meetings: 'Very nice to see him again.' Military matters were rarely mentioned for some time in the diary.

More important on 13 July was: 'Received wire in the afternoon giving news of Doff's little daughter and *Times* with the announcement. Very excited. Did nothing much rest of day.' Two days later: 'Had a letter from Doff which much relieved me. Both well. Went down to wagon line. Everyone doing well there.'

During early August things remained quiet. There was much preparing but little shooting. The 15th was busier: 'Up to OP early for attack on Hill 70. Fired barrage and smoke barrage. Saw a lot of movement and guns going out. Attack a great success, and a great many huns killed. All objectives taken.' The next day: 'Rode into Arras with Roberts to lunch & tea & see sights. Went round horses back late.' The next day again was active: 'Up to OP early to strafe a house in Cité Dunord. A lot of shooting and sniping there. Got 5 huns altogether.'

Late August offered Adam a much more pleasant experience. At 4 a.m. on the 26th he started off for Arras en route to Paris for ten days' leave. He arrived at 4.30 p.m. and, 'Went to meet Doff's train but missed her somehow & met her at hotel.' Unlike the leave in Bournemouth in June 1916 there are no details; on 6 September he, 'Left Doff at hotel on completion of Paris leave'.

TO ITALY

The next few weeks were much as before, but November brought preparations for a move, revealed on 13 November to be to Italy, where forces were under heavy pressure from the Austro-Hungarians. Since early in 1917 the Italians had been reinforced initially by ten – and later three more – British heavy artillery batteries, and three infantry divisions. The French brought in added firepower and men. Both countries' forces were strengthened again at the end of the year after the Italian rout at Caporetto, when the line fell back to the River Piave, 15 miles from Venice.

Adam, now commanding F Bty of his own RHA, boarded a train at Cassel on 14 November. They reached Turin three days later to 'a great reception, flags, coffee, cigars for the men, but managed to water the horses in spite of all'. From there, they marched for a week through Mantova to Montagnana – 'Good billets and nice mess.' Then to Torrea, 'Where we had the best billets yet in a magnificent chateau with many rooms and were very comfortable (one night only)'. Siepmann too was posted to Italy in November 1917, but he presented a less straightforward account of his RFA battery's progress across Italy. Seeking good billets wherever they could was a priority, and he showed guile by taking his unit on one-day or two-day separate army depots, so drawing double rations. His account reveals not so much the fog of war on the battlefield, as its general incoherence, incompetence, muddle, confusion and contradictory orders behind the lines.[13]

On 26 November, with a rare touch of personal feeling, Adam wrote: 'General Arbuthnot round, who for once recognised me.' The following day was more positive: 'Gorgeous view today of the Asiago Plateau & the Mts Grappa & Tomba. Another mail in & heard from Dorothy which was a joy.' The plateau, 35 miles east of Lake Garda, had already been the scene of a frustrated enemy attempt to profit from Caporetto. December was spent siting OPs and digging in, while on the 11th undergoing, 'Heavy shelling by huns'. On the 20th a break loomed: 'Arranged to go to Padova next day with Col.' On the 25th: 'Soldiering had a day of absolute peace. Worked round gun pits in the morning & presented Colonel's cigarettes and wished everyone a merry Christmas.' War soon returned and the next few months in Italy continued the routine of shelling and counter-shelling so familiar from France. Adam moved on, becoming in March 1918 the brigade major RA, XIV Corps and, the following month, brigade major RA, 23rd Div., which meant he was away from day-to-day gunnery. His path to joining the staff had begun.

The early months of 1918 were fairly quiet for the British troops in Italy. Activity resumed in a major fashion in June. From 10 to 12 June there are no diary entries, but on 13 June he recorded: 'Instructions for offensive kept me busy all day.' But before the Allies could launch their attack, the Austro-Hungarians – reinforced by Germans from the Eastern Front after the Russian Revolution – caught them unawares by attacking to the south-east across the Piave, the last line before the Lombard Plain, with a secondary assault on the Asiago front. Late on the 14th rumours circulated among the British troops that an attack was coming. At 3 a.m. the next morning 1,000 enemy guns opened up. The battle report by 35th Bde R.A., 23rd Div. reveals confusion, for the enemy had pinpointed the Allied OPs very accurately and shelled them heavily. Although the batteries escaped fairly well, the main British ammunition dump was destroyed. After two days of confused fighting, much of it hand-to-hand, the line was held. The early failure to spot the enemy build-up had been a major fault of intelligence. The 'lessons learnt' report after the battle noted the 'methodical and minute observation' by the enemy by ground (not aerial) observation, and stressed the need in future to duplicate all OPs and to ensure their secrecy, and to relocate all guns immediately.[14] On 17–20 June Adam was busy resiting guns.

Among the aspects of army life denounced by Hugh Dalton, a young wartime lieutenant who served on the Asiago Plateau in the RGA in 1917–19, was poor leave provision for British troops, compared with the French and Italians. Most British men got leave only every nineteen months. In Dalton's unit, junior officers went home about every eleven months, while staff officers and lieutenant-colonels went home about every three months – as he acidly observed: 'in view of the danger of brain fag and nervous strain following upon their greater mental exertions and their abnormal exposure to shell fire and the weather'.[15] It took Maj. Adam ten months to get home, leaving on 28 August and arriving in London two days later: 'Dorothy met me looking very pretty.' They stayed at Bray, near Maidenhead, relaxing, punting and Adam finding his 13-month old daughter, Barbara to be 'quite friendly'. There followed a trip to town to see a matinée of *The Naughty Wife*, a three-act comedy with Gladys Cooper, which ran for 598 performances over eighteen months. Adam's diary recorded churchgoing, playing with Barbara and a family visit before, on 13 September, 'Doff saw me off at 3.15 at Charing Cross.'

After the enemy failure to hold its crossings on the Piave in June, the Italians resisted Anglo-French pressure to counter-attack immediately. A major build-up began. On 27 September Adam recorded that a raid was successful despite heavy resistance. They captured sixty-five enemy personnel, including five officers. Two days later, he wrote: 'Morning in the office messing about. News from all fronts excellent.' In Venice the next day he recorded: 'News of peace with Bulgaria.'

It was not until the end of October that enough Allied firepower and forces had been assembled to ensure success in Italy. It then came quickly. On 4 November, Adam's diary recorded: 'Armistice with Austria-Hungary came into effect at 3 p.m. Have started a filthy cold.' Yet despite his cold, the next day he was out with his general inspecting ammunition dumps. The next two months were occupied with similar routine, except on 27 November when the Allied troops paraded for the King of Italy. Adam's diary ends on 8 December.

Dalton was bitterly eloquent in a book published late in 1919. He recorded his high regard for his Italian comrades-in-arms for their courage and devotion, but he had scorching contempt for some British fellow officers. Of Armistice night he wrote:

> In a few officers' Messes, especially among the more exalted units, men of forty years and more croaked like ravens over their impending loss of pay and rank [...] To have been, through long and uneventful unmental years, a peacetime soldier puts the imagination in jeopardy and is apt to breed a self-centred fatuity, which the inexperienced may easily mistake for deliberate naughtiness. Yet these brave men, who hate peace and despise civilians [...] found themselves left alone to their private griefs, ruminating regretfully over the golden age that had suddenly ended, gazing into a future without hope.[16]

In later years Dalton became minister for economic warfare during the Second World War and, in 1945–47 the Labour chancellor of the exchequer.

In June 1918 Ronald Adam became a Member of the Distinguished Service Order (DSO). In June 1919 three mentions in despatches were recorded, and an Order of the British Empire (OBE) in the military division came in the king's birthday honours the same month.[17] He was posted as brigade major to No. 5 District, Aldershot Command, at Bordon in Wilshire. The Adams now had a second daughter, Margot, born in October 1918.

4

RISING STAR

Hugh Dalton's tirade boiled over from his experience as a young wartime officer among more senior regulars. But he did point to a fundamental issue facing the British Army in 1919: what was it now for? The four years of war had transformed an imperial police force of modest size into an army of 3.5 million, raised, like other European armies, by mass conscription. A year after the Armistice it was cut down by nine-tenths and returned to voluntary enlistment. Two years later it totalled only 217,000 men, or 30,000 fewer than in 1913. But could it just return to the *status quo ante bellum*? Well before 1914 the 'splendid isolation' trumpeted by late nineteenth-century British politicians had shown itself to be a dangerous delusion, and Britain had been forced to take sides in the international pattern of alliances. Rushing to defend 'gallant little Belgium' was a pretext to hide from the public the extent of the secret commitment to France and Russia. The subsequent bloodletting led, in its aftermath, to a deep popular revulsion against any thought of another Continental war: 'never again' became the watchword. The famous press placard, 'Continent cut off', summed up the British attitude.

Yet the British Empire was larger than ever, with new territories acquired in the Middle East and Africa; the former would prove vexatious for the next three decades. Besides, Britain in post-war treaties had accepted potential military commitments within Europe by guaranteeing the post-war frontiers of Belgium and France. The war had been financed mainly by borrowing, and two-fifths of the national budget in the early 1920s went on interest and capital payments (the National Debt rose from £797 million in 1914 to £7.48 billion in 1919). Drastic cuts in expenditure were made. By 1925 the army's budget was down to one-third of the 1920 level, whereas the RAF and the navy were only down to two-thirds. Defence expenditure for most of the next twenty years was in real terms less than in 1914, notwithstanding costly demands arising from developments in aviation, armoured vehicles, aircraft carriers, communications and anti-submarine warfare. Until the late 1930s defence expenditure was less in real terms than before 1914. The army was the Cinderella service: from 1926 to 1934 an average of only £1 million a year was spent on new equipment.

Popular disdain for the army was clear in the quality and the quantity of post-war entrants. Before the war, eighty university graduates had sought commissions each year; in 1924 only twelve graduates came forward for the 650 commissions on offer.[1] Recruiting to the ranks was no more encouraging; sergeants were not being recruited for the next generation of soldiers. All Britain struggled to find cause why the insatiable Moloch on the Western Front had rolled on unchecked: 713,000 English, Scottish, Welsh and Irish men never came home, and families throughout the Empire mourned another 203,000 men.[2] Many tens of thousands of families were caring for men who had survived, but who were damaged physically and mentally. In 1922 more than 943,000 men received disability pensions.

The army did not help its own cause by an unwillingness to face up to a changed world, and its parochial squabbles added to the malaise. Dalton was right in accusing regulars of regretting their years of excitement. The war over, Sir Michael Howard was to comment later that:

> the Army remained firmly geared to the pace of regimental soldiering as an agreeable occupation rather than a demanding profession [...] many officers, so far from wishing to adapt to social and technical changes, looked to the Army as a haven where they could escape from them.[3]

New ideas were often snubbed. In May 1920 Col J.F.C. Fuller wrote how tanks were replacing horses just as steam had replaced sail. His suggestions were mild: the gradual replacement of horses by tractors, the formation of divisions of twelve infantry battalions that included tanks, horse artillery, medium artillery, an enlarged cavalry component and one battalion of tanks 'for use as mechanised cavalry'. He was trying to allay conservative fears, but still provoked a strong reaction.[4] The previous year he had argued that: 'The conditions of war [...] have completely changed and with this change must the brains of the army change also, so that they may discover the new applications of the unchanging principles of war.'[5] Did the brains of the British Army change enough during the next twenty years to cope with the changed circumstances?

The renewed emphasis on imperial policing meant that the horse could retain its use, and its status. Building on Britain's pioneering of tanks would not only have been expensive: they were noisy and dirty machines and unsuitable mounts for gentlemen. 'Having a good seat' was again a requirement of an officer. Cavalry officers had two horses at their disposal, and even Royal Tank Corps (RTC) officers had one each. The British Army adhered firmly to the values and pastimes of the landed gentry, from which it still drew many officers. Moreover, there appeared to be a dilemma about tank development: should it be of heavy infantry tanks for Continental use or lighter, more mobile ones believed to be more suitable for imperial situations, notably the Middle East? Despite exploiting this issue and the return to imperial policing, the cavalry – like other arms – had to suffer big cuts. Historian Hew Strachan regarded this as a rearguard action by the cavalry against mechanisation, with the former keeping their own regiments (with some amalgamations) and a small tank regiment.[6]

Ronald Adam's own RHA shared this nostalgia. Once at the forefront of tactical thinking and action, it succumbed, and, in the view of gunner and historian Shelford Bidwell, remained static and ossified in its outlook: 'When all the ferment of tactical ideas took place over the introduction of armoured warfare the R.H.A. was in stables or happily playing polo and hunting.'[7] Not until 1936 did it begin to modernise itself. The following year it provided two mechanised regiments in the first 'mobile' (i.e. armoured) division, equipped with tractor-towed 3.7in howitzers to support the tanks. In the Second World War it regained a more reliably mobile role when equipped with self-propelled guns.

NO RETURN TO THE RHA

Adam had had 'a good war', bearing no physical scars at least, rising from lieutenant to major in four years. In peacetime, however, with fewer dead men's shoes to fill, promotion slowed. The problem was acute for gunners as the RA fell from its wartime peak of comprising 27.5 per cent of the army to below 16 per cent by 1935; conversely, the cavalry recovered from barely 1.5 per cent in 1918 to over 5 per cent, and the infantry eased up from 49 per cent to over 52 per cent.[8]

The Staff College, Camberley, offered aspiring officers a way forward and passing its course became increasingly essential for advancement to senior rank. Adam got on a course there in 1920, due to the fact that another candidate was involved in a divorce and so deemed unsuitable. Col John Dill was senior instructor; other instructors included Maj. Lord Gort. Other students in early post-war years included Lt-Col Harold Alexander, Lt-Col Alan Brooke, Capt. Bernard Freyberg, Maj. Percy Hobart, Maj. Bernard Montgomery and Lt-Col Archibald Wavell. Whatever faults Dalton had found in some regulars, Adam and such associates now had the all-important 'p.s.c.' – passed Staff College – on their records. Contacts with instructors and fellow students proved valuable in later years. After a spell at Woolwich and as a General Staff Officer, Grade Three (GSO3) at the War Office, Adam returned to the Staff College early in 1923 as an instructor, classed GSO2. Between the wars he spent six years at the college: one as a student, the remainder as an instructor and, for just three months, as commandant. Apart from nearly three years on field postings, the other years were at the 'War House'. Although largely outside the regimental structure, Adam was still affected by the promotion system. It took him four years to regain briefly a temporary lieutenant-colonelcy when GSO2. In 1926 he became a brevet lieutenant-colonel: he had the badges and some privileges but not the pay of that rank. In 1932, at the age of 47, he made full colonel, with his seniority backdated two years.

As was required of staff officers, he periodically returned to regimental duty. The first occasion was in March 1926, when he was sent to India to command the 72nd Field Bty, 16th Bde, for an unusually brief ten-month posting. In India he was posted to Kirkee, near Ahmednagar, and faced a heavy demand of ceremonial duties. Each visiting dignitary merited a different number of artillery salutes. In April, five days were devoted to a parade for the C-in-C of India; in June, a shorter time for the governor of Bombay; in July, a parade in Poona for the viceroy himself. The last, at any rate, recorded a favourable comment on the parade's turnout. There is no personal diary record on this occasion of stys, boils or boredom; only the dry report of the battery's *Digest of Service*.[9] An escape from ceremony came in September when Adam and a detachment from the battery took part in manoeuvres for five weeks at Abdulla, near Quetta. In December there was a march to Aundh for twelve days' practice camp. A week later, on Christmas Eve, Adam was posted home to be a GSO2 in Military Training at the WO, despite (according to his army record) being 'recommended for the RHA'.

He was accompanied to India by Dorothy; Barbara and Margot, now aged 8 and 7, went to boarding school and in the holidays to the care of relatives. While he was in India he succeeded as the second baronet.[10] The family expanded again on 17 December 1927 when twin girls, Bridget and Isobel, were born. 'Brookie' became godfather to Isobel, and the wife of another fellow gunner, Edmund Schreiber, was Bridget's godmother.

STICKING TO HIS LAST

What Adam thought of the army in those years is not known. His draft memoirs start in 1935. But he must have been very frustrated. As a young, unmarried man before the war he had had the excitements of India. Now his career was more humdrum, with frequent moves from posting to posting, from one location to another. Bordon, Aldershot, Camberley, Woolwich were among his UK postings between the wars. For his spells at the War Office in the 1930s he could commute from Camberley without disturbing family life. Although men such as J.F.C. Fuller, Percy Hobart, Archibald Wavell, Giffard Martell, Charles Broad and others were speaking and writing about weaponry, strategy and tactics, Adam stuck strictly and assiduously to his administrative duties. He was, according to his daughter Isobel, a workaholic: she recalls him at his papers at weekends while she and her twin sister played round his feet. He was not easily distracted when at work. The twins have happy memories of his clowning when they were young, such as falling over his sword when about to go to a regimental dinner, and making up stories in which they featured.

Adam was very intelligent but had 'no intellectual pretensions', as *The Times* was to write in an obituary over forty years later. And he was on the way up. In 1930 he added 'i.d.c.' to his record after a course at the Imperial Defence College, established in 1927. The same year he was among eighty-seven officers, from the CIGS downwards, senior officials and educational representatives at a conference on the problems of recruiting officers. One problem addressed was that 90 per cent of officers were retired at age 50. The infantry was short of seventy new officers each year, whereas the engineers, artillery and cavalry were above their establishment levels for officers, and signals and tanks were attracting adequate numbers.[11] Even when unemployment reached 3 million, recruitment remained poor for all ranks. Army pay was not enough to tempt many from poorly paid jobs or even the dole, and many of those who did enlist were of poor quality. 'Going for a soldier' was not an ambition for the respectable working class, and the lower middle class was even less tempted. Cardwell's hopes in this respect were no more satisfied in the 1930s than fifty years earlier. An institution with a rigid distinction and a great gulf between only two classes did not reflect the national society that it served, even at a time when deference was still widespread. In 1931 the army was down to 188,000 men, half of them in sixty-seven infantry line battalions on imperial postings, leaving at home fifty-nine line and ten Guards battalions, often undermanned. Sixty of the home battalions were earmarked for an expeditionary force, leaving just nine for internal security, defending lines of communication and overseas reinforcements.

THREE DISCONTENTED POWERS

As the international situation deteriorated, the threat to Britain came from three different disgruntled powers in three different theatres. Germany resented the limitations on its power and prestige under the Treaty of Versailles; Italy felt it had been inadequately rewarded for joining the Allies in 1915; Japan wanted equality with the European powers and the United States. Growing economic stress facilitated Hitler's rise, intensified Mussolini's nationalism, and consolidated the militarisation of Japanese society and state. For Britain and France, the menace was much greater than in 1914 when only Germany had sought change to the international order. The enigmatic presence of the Soviet Union terrified the Right, and loomed over the British Raj. The 'Great Game' between Russia and Britain in central Asia was now reinforced by an ideology with appeal to colonised peoples. The problem for Britain was that in the event of a European crisis it would be less possible to withdraw forces from the Empire, unlike in 1914 when Japan and Russia had been friendly. Moreover, three-fifths of the

British troops in India and in the Indian Army were already concerned with internal security, with most of the rest on the North-West Frontier. There were few Indians available to serve outside the subcontinent. The Empire as asset and the Empire as liability were closer and closer in balance: would the liability come to outweigh the asset? 'Overstretch' may not have been a buzz word in the 1930s but the British Empire was, to the perceptive, past its peak, and was struggling to conceal the fact.

With the revulsion at the slaughter on the Western Front, popular and political sentiment implicitly favoured the historical 'maritime' approach over the 'Continental' approach. Basil Liddell Hart, a former infantry officer and now the military correspondent of *The Times*, intellectualised this sentiment. War studies historian Brian Holden Reid summed up Liddell Hart's thinking: 'no matter how cleverly it was articulated or debated, [it] was based on a passion amounting almost to an obsession to avoid a repetition of the Great War'.[12] Historian Brian Bond recorded that a common view was that 'Britain had been inveigled into a total war, against her true interests, as a result of the pre-war staff conversations with the French; and also that the political aftermath had proved the four years of carnage to have been largely futile'.[13] Unlike Continental states, Britain appeared to have a choice, and it feared being dragged into another European conflict.

Liddell Hart made two notable contributions to military thinking in the 1930s. First, he urged that armies be organised on mobile lines, with both artillery and infantry carried on armoured vehicles as an attack force, aided by low-flying aircraft. British backwardness is clear from the army estimates for 1935–36, at the time when Hitler reintroduced conscription and revealed the existence of the Luftwaffe. The British Army budget was raised by 10 per cent to £44 million, of which only £772,000 was for expenditure on motor vehicles, including £270,000 for tracked vehicles of all kinds. Fuel for all vehicles was up by £12,000 to £121,000, whereas fodder for animals rose by £44,000 to £400,000.[14] Nothing could have better illustrated the absurdity of the army's priorities. It was no accident that Hitler announced his own big increase in military spending on the same day as the British estimates were published.

Liddell Hart's second thesis was that Britain should not undertake a major Continental commitment but follow its traditional policy of blockading a Continental foe, aided by the additional weapon of air bombardment. Any land contribution to a conflict in Europe should be a few mechanised units, he argued, but it would probably be best to commit no land force at all. Liddell Hart's ideas chimed in perfectly with the national mood.

Britain disregarded his first, rational thesis on armoured warfare, and by default rejected the second, more questionable one, also. It did not have the means to make any effective Continental contribution, small or large, traditional or mechanised; nor was it willing to provide any. The pledge of no conscription in peacetime was equally nostalgic. It assumed that the conditions of 1914 could apply again, with (perhaps) a small professional army and French allies holding off a German offensive, while a mass army was recruited, trained and armed. That policy had barely succeeded in 1914; a successful repetition was less likely still.

The National Government formed in response to the economic crisis retrenched all round, cutting the pay of civil servants, teachers and servicemen, and 'bowler hatting' many serving officers. The chancellor of the exchequer, Neville Chamberlain, applied a sceptical eye to all expenditure. In 1932 he stated that a request from the Defence Requirements Committee for £97 million over five years was 'impossible to carry out', as it would need a special loan, which was 'a broad road that leads to destruction'.[15] He clung to this attitude as long as he could. But the government gave muddled signals: on 30 July 1935 the new prime minister, Stanley Baldwin, told the Commons: 'When you think of the defence of England you no longer think of the chalk cliffs of Dover, you think of the Rhine. That is where the frontier lies.'[16] But when Hitler crossed that frontier nine months later Baldwin did nothing; the Italian threat in the Mediterranean appeared to be greater. Lacking even diplomatic support from Britain, France would not act alone against Germany. In any case, because of the Maginot Line policy and mentality of relying on static defences against Germany, it no longer had enough mobile forces to enforce the Treaty of Versailles. The contradictions and hesitations of British policy in the later 1930s were determined by both economic and military pressures to reduce the risk of conflict with one or other of the three potential enemies. The risk was that the bad men would combine. They did so in November 1936 when Japan signed the Anti-Comintern Pact with Germany, with Italy following on a year later. Trying to mollify the last over Abyssinia (Ethiopia) and Spain became key elements in British policy.

ADAM'S DEBT

Liddell Hart's role in this narrative is less about his strategic thinking than the contacts he had with Adam in the 1930s and the influence he had over Adam's career. Adam's 1961 memoirs make only an oblique reference to Liddell Hart and his papers contain just one letter from Liddell Hart in 1960. Liddell Hart's papers, on the other hand, contain several letters they exchanged between 1937 and 1960, and a note on Adam's 'refusal to consult' him after he became Deputy CIGS (DCIGS) in January 1938. Adam also features in Liddell Hart's diaries, when he was GSO1 at the War Office, after two years as senior instructor at the Staff College.

On 15 November 1935 Liddell Hart lunched with Adam and Col Sir Bernard Paget, GSO1, Military Intelligence. Liddell Hart noted how among 'younger men' at the WO (Adam was in his fiftieth year, Paget two years younger) there was 'a more encouraging attitude' towards his ideas. On the co-ordination of defence, he urged on them the need for a small combined general staff as advisers to a minister of defence, overarching the individual service ministries. Adam and Paget agreed, and talked of the defects of the present system. They also 'seemed to agree' on the need for a combined intelligence structure for all three services:

> I was glad, and rather surprised, to find how conscious they were of the evils of the past and present friction between the Services [...] they agreed – ascribing it largely to a suspiciousness that magnified every Air Ministry step as part of a cunning plan. The Navy was worse.[17]

Liddell Hart recorded of the same meeting that both Adam and Paget regretted that the present election had not produced a stronger Opposition. Labour had recovered quite a lot from its 1931 debacle but was still heavily outnumbered by the Conservative-dominated National Government, which included National Labour and National Liberal Party members. Liddell Hart continued:

> Adam, indeed thought that the best chance of carrying through a co-ordinated defence scheme lay in a Socialist government – largely because it would be less fettered by vested interests. He made the interesting point that nationalisation of the means of transport was a necessity for an effective defence scheme. Only by that means could we hope to short-circuit London, as might be essential in the face of the air menace; also to develop other ports at London's expense.

This is a unique indication of Adam's political views at that time, although it suggests a pragmatic as much as an ideological stance. History had shown that the Conservatives were too close to the army to take decisive action on reform, and for two generations reform had been put through by Liberals – Cardwell, Childers and Haldane. By the mid-1930s the Labour Party had to a large degree inherited the Liberal vote, if not the mantle. The remarks are the nearest Adam ever seems to have got to an indiscretion; less an indiscretion than an eccentricity, at a time when the Labour Party had only just replaced a pacifist leader who wanted to disband the army and had formed only two short-lived minority governments, the second of which had split the party. In 1935 a majority Labour government seemed a fantasy. When it did become a reality ten years later, it set up a Ministry of Defence and nationalised the railways.

ADAM AND A CONTINENTAL COMMITMENT

Although Liddell Hart's diary shows that Adam was not an automaton, a lecture he gave at the Staff College in February 1936 on the role of the British Army was impeccably orthodox in terms of the political and military strategies of the time. In his papers there is a manuscript outline of a lecture in his precise hand, as well as a fuller typewritten text attributed only to an 'M.O.I. Colonel'. It stressed that:

> The role of the British Army has been constant throughout history. It is true that we have fought on the continent of Europe from time to time. Much of the fighting was done by mercenaries, and no force was kept specifically for that purpose. Forces were collected for the emergency as it occurred and as often disbanded after the emergency had passed.
>
> If we take history as a guide, unless the war directly threatens our independence, e.g. by enemy gaining possession of the Low Countries, we shall avoid taking part. Those critics who state that the British Army is training for the last war instead of the next one, are mostly obsessed with the idea that the next war, like the last war, will be fought in Europe.

Adam firmly rejected Liddell Hart's idea that in a European conflict Britain should provide only naval and air support for Continental allies: it would appear to them as only indirect aid, and blockades work slowly and air power was unproven in a European war:

> Refusal on our part, therefore, to provide direct military assistance would inevitably be interpreted by an ally as abandoning them to their fate, whereas the arrival of even small forces will have an incalculable moral effect out of all proportion to their size. [18]

That air power was an unproven force did not prevent public alarm at its potential threat to Britain, giving a new angle to the historical need to retain the Low Countries in friendly or at least neutral hands. In 1932 Stanley Baldwin had imprinted on public consciousness the belief that, 'The bomber will always get through'. The rest of that sentence – 'any defence you can visualise today' – and his further comment that the danger would be decreased, 'if there is a possibility of retaliation in force', are usually overlooked. [19] These years saw a revolution in aircraft technology. In 1934 fighters and bombers were basically of the same configuration as twenty years earlier: biplanes with fixed undercarriages. The next few years saw monoplanes with retractable undercarriages, covered cockpits, oxygen, radios, eight machine guns and heavier bomb loads. Plans for four-engined bombers were drawn up at the end of the decade. Early experiments in radio location – later known as radar – were in hand.

Adam had depressing experience of the difficulties of inter-service co-operation; his genial nature acted to soothe sores. As the army's representative on the Joint Planning Committee, his RAF and Royal Navy opposite numbers were Bert Harris (later to achieve fame – and notoriety – as 'Bomber' Harris) and Tom Phillips. In 1961 Adam recalled a 'hot controversy' at one meeting:

> Bert Harris turned to Tom and said 'Tom, in the next war, you will be on the bridge of your flagship, and you will be attacked from the air. As your ship is hit and begins to go down, you will turn to your flag captain and will say "Flag that is a damned big mine we struck."' In view of the tragic loss of Tom Phillips when his battleship was sunk off Malaya by Japanese torpedo-bombers and he lost his life, it was a prophetic statement.[20]

As Deputy Director of Military Operations (DDMO) and a temporary brigadier, Adam was also involved in international negotiations. The first were with the Egyptians about the withdrawal of British forces to the Canal Zone. This was an urgent matter in view of the Abyssinian crisis caused by the Italian invasion of that country and by Mussolini's agitation among the Egyptians. The agreement reached was that British troops in peacetime would exercise in the Sinai but not the Western Desert, where of course any threat from the Italians would lie. Moreover, the records of tracks, sand conditions and water in the Western Desert – made after earlier operations – could not be found. The army had to rely on reports from explorers, each of whom considered their routes were the only feasible ones, although their information about water and sand conditions was useful, Adam wrote in 1961.

Adam's diplomatic skills *vis-à-vis* the other services, the Egyptians and the Turks (who wanted more weaponry than the British could or would supply) were also called on in talks with the French. In December 1935 during the Abyssinian crisis he and an RAF group captain were sent to Paris to hold discussions with the French war and air ministries (the navy having insisted that if the French wanted to talk they should come to London). 'It surprised me that such junior officers were sent but I believe this was to keep matters from the press as we were unknown and would not arouse suspicion.'[21] It also meant that the British commitment could if necessary be played down, although a gesture to the French had been made. With a military attaché as interpreter, two British colonels faced four French generals across a table. Adam was disconcerted to find that the maps in their meeting room did not cover the area south of Switzerland, and also by Gen. Gamelin's comment that he and Gen. Badoglio, the Italian commander in East Africa, had been great friends since they had served in their respective country's embassies in Brazil. 'He [Gamelin] disliked the idea of fighting the Italians,' Adam wrote. The talks achieved nothing, in Adam's view. He found Gamelin to be 'a small pleasant man with dyed hair, but not a convincing Chief of Staff' (the historian Martin Alexander takes a more generous view of Gamelin).[22] After Hitler reintroduced conscription in March 1936 Adam took part in further talks with the French, this time in London, but they 'led nowhere'.

The two countries' objectives were too far apart and had been since 1918. Although Lloyd George had won the 'Khaki Election' on the basis of 'squeezing Germany till the pips squeaked', British opinion realised that 'the Carthaginian peace' (i.e. the brutal Versailles settlement) was, in the British economist John Maynard Keynes's words, unjust, unenforceable and by the 1930s dangerous.

By the mid-1930s Adam's words in his Staff College lecture summarised London's view: 'It is clearly impossible, though the French are still loath to believe it, to keep a strong and virile nation like Germany in subjection and her reaction has been to challenge the dictatorship of the Treaty of Versailles'.[23] The French, whose war dead were 30 per cent more numerous than those of the whole British Empire and whose north-east region had been occupied and devastated for four years, were ruled by a mixture of fear and vengefulness. They had no Channel to offer the illusion of safety – as indeed events were to prove in reality.

The Italian advance across Abyssinia involved Adam in another way. He had to arrange with the Foreign Office for the defence of the perimeter of the British Embassy with sandbags and barbed wire, laying on rations and tents for the expected influx of British subjects seeking refuge, and bringing in a garrison from India.

Of his experience at this time Adam later wrote:

> The job of D.D.M.O. was pretty hard work, but I had learnt to read very fast at the Staff College when correcting students' exercises and this was most valuable. So often one had little time to read a Cabinet or Chiefs of Staff paper and prepare a brief. I have done the whole job in an hour, but it had one advantage and that was that one had to produce a short paper. Briefs were inclined to be far too long […] The only result is that your master does not read it.[24]

This is a good pointer to Adam's success as a staff officer; one of Gort's weaknesses was producing overlong documents.

FIELD COMMAND – AND FISHING

Adam's second interwar regimental posting had been for nine months in 1932, with the 13th Field Bde, at Woolwich. His third period away from staff duties began in November 1936 when for ten months he commanded the artillery element of the 1st Div., retaining the rank of temporary brigadier he had held as DDMO. He was back to active soldiering but, like his two previous such spells, for less than a year. Shortly afterwards the division (less the artillery) was posted to Shanghai, where the Japanese threatened. Adam enjoyed this break from the office. Most of the summer of 1937 was spent at practice camp in Devon, where in the evenings and at weekends Adam could get in lots of fishing. After that, the divisional artillery, which was in its first year of mechanisation, went on an exercise in East Anglia. There was some fishing there too.

On return from manoeuvres in September he went back to the Staff College, this time as commandant, where he expected to stay and enjoy his time there for a few years. No longer having a horse provided, Adam bought his own. Soon he was promoted to major-general, although still a substantive colonel. Although in 1961 he described his move to the college in bland terms, the appointment was far from easy. The previous commandant, Maj.-Gen. Lord Gort, had been chosen as his military secretary by the new war minister, Leslie Hore-Belisha, who took up office in May 1937 and started to impose his will on the army. According to Liddell Hart, Gort had suggested to the minister three names to take over the college, saying Adam was the best. But the CIGS, F.-M. Sir Cyril Deverell, favoured another. In September he sent the minister a memo with the criteria he thought necessary for the commandant:

1. He needs to be a clear and stimulating speaker;
2. He should have the gift of generating enthusiasm for study and progressive thought;
3. He should have a critical mind, since the Staff College is an educational centre, and an attitude which encourages younger men to express their minds freely;
4. He should have fairly recent experience in command of troops in order to check the tendency to develop a 'staff mind' out of touch with the ordinary soldier;
5. Above all, at the present juncture, he should have had direct personal experience of the working of a mechanised unit or formation – since all tactical and strategical methods were being radically affected by the introduction of mechanisation, and there is an urgent need to evolve new methods of command as well as a new technique of staff work to fit the changed conditions;
6. It is desirable, at least, that he should have had some personal experience of Air Force work – as this now comes into every army problem.[25]

Adam fulfilled the first four criteria without difficulty and for the sixth he could point to his experience on the Joint Planning Committee. The mechanisation of the 1st Div. RA component was not real tank experience. Deverell's stress on this suggests an expedient in favour of his own candidate, given his earlier opposition to Hore-Belisha's proposal that Percy Hobart lead the new mobile division instead of his own nominee, a 59-year-old cavalryman. The minister did not win that one: he compromised on a gunner with a tank man as deputy. However, he had made up his mind about Adam, who he considered to have 'a good and objective mind. He strikes me as being of better metal than most of those who fall in the academic category.' [26]

Once installed, Adam lunched with Liddell Hart on 25 October and told him what he wanted to change at the college. He thought the two-year courses were too long: some officers were not suitable to command higher formations, although perfectly competent in more junior positions. He put the senior division of the college to work on a study of a one-year course, after which officers would get experience on the staff and then, if suitable, return to a senior course, limited to about thirty officers. [27] By this time, the college was increasingly important in raising the professional quality of the army, the senior cohort of which had moved from being 'an elite based upon social prestige to an elite based on the kinds of management skills required by a large and multifarious organization'. [28] By 1930 two-thirds of senior officers were p.s.c. – passed Staff College. Adam was well up in this change and pushing it further forward.

The content of courses changed over the years, with studies adapted to the current military and international situation, including such topics as propaganda in wartime. Notable, just before Adam's return, was a two-hour lecture on psychology by an RAMC officer, Lt-Col Nichols, who said that Sigmund Freud shared the fate of many original minds: 'unrestricted abuse and perverse misunderstanding'. Lt-Col Nichols saw British army officers as a closed caste with limited knowledge of other classes. Herd thinking was 'very prevalent in the fighting forces', and it overrode logical thinking. An example of this was – most provocatively to an audience of soldiers – 'curious regimental customs'. But, at the same time, the herd instinct was the basis of discipline. The higher incidence of 'shell shock' among British than French troops in the First World War was attributed by Nichols to repression: 'the second name of the British […] undue repression of Fear, done in the wrong way, is the cause of breakdown and "shell shock". Express your fear, but carry on and you will never break down', he advised. [29]

In September, Adam wrote to Liddell Hart thanking him for a paper on army reorganisation, adding: 'Any paper of yours deserves the greatest attention […] Congratulations on your article in *The Times*'. Two months later Adam sent him a detailed four-page response, as 'my first and personal views'. He received a cordial reply from Liddell Hart, hoping to see Adam at the next meeting of the college dining club. [30] On another occasion Sir Ronald and Lady Adam had lunch with the journalist.

More personally, the Adam family had been struck by tragedy. They had not even moved into Staff College House when, in early October, their second daughter, Margot, fresh from a finishing school in Switzerland and recovering from an appendicitis operation, died of septicaemia within days of her nineteenth birthday.

5

STUMBLING TO WAR

To later generations Neville Chamberlain is popularly presented as a figure comical in appearance and demeanour and of pathetic ineptitude in achievement. Yet in the 1930s he was a dominating figure in British politics. James Ramsay MacDonald and Stanley Baldwin may have been prime ministers during the first two-thirds of the decade but Chamberlain, as chancellor in 1931–37, was a major determinant of policy. In foreign affairs he believed that Britain should avoid Continental entanglements, and that the principal aims of policy should be to defend Britain's shores, its trade routes and its empire. In this he had a great deal of public and political support: 'never again' to a long, bloody war was the overriding national sentiment. For some, the rise of fascism reinforced this isolationist sentiment: those unpleasant events were taking place 'over there, in Europe'. Others were favourably impressed by the dictators. Others again saw them as a threat to be vigorously countered. Many on the Left managed in contradictory fashion to oppose both fascism and rearmament.

On becoming prime minister in May 1937, Chamberlain was able to impose his views more firmly. He considered the outgoing war minister Alfred Duff Cooper too inclined to favour an expeditionary force to the Continent in the event of war. He did not question the centuries-old British aim of keeping the Low Countries out of the hands of a major Continental power: in earlier times Spain and France; in the twentieth century, Germany. But after the costly intervention in 1914–18 he sought other means to pacify the Teutonic beast. Thus, as his new war minister he appointed Leslie Hore-Belisha whom he believed would more faithfully pursue a 'limited liability' in Europe. Defence expenditure was nonetheless being increased: the February 1937 Defence White Paper proposed spending £1.5 billion over five years, averaging three times the figure when Hitler had come to power. But the field army would get little benefit, just two more tank battalions.

Along with others, the prime minister was deeply impressed by air power and accepted his predecessor's dictum that 'the bomber will always get through'. A film based on H.G. Wells's novel, *The Shape of Things to Come*, markedly affected public opinion, and the bombing by the Germans of the Spanish town of Guernica in the month before Chamberlain became prime minister reinforced the fear. A belief in the efficacy of an aerial 'knock-out blow' led the government to emphasise, on the one hand, the Air Defence of Great Britain (ADGB) based on AA guns, the nascent radar system and fighter planes and, on the other, to prepare a fleet of long-range heavy bombers – Baldwin's 'retaliation in force'. When war did come, aerial bombing was to prove devastating but not as decisive as its enthusiasts (and those who dreaded it) believed. The rein on spending meant that neither the army nor the air force had enough resources for its needs.

The prime minister knew that Hore-Belisha would be dynamic. A Liberal who had helped to persuade much of his party to support the National Government in 1931, he initially held junior posts. In June 1934 he became minster of transport, with a seat in the Cabinet the following October. He seemed just the man to shake the War Office out of its lethargy, and he depended on the prime minister's patronage. Hore-Belisha recorded that, talking to Duff Cooper, 'He mentioned that the military element might be very unyielding and they might try to make it hard for me as a Jew'.[1] Gen. Ironside noted in his diary on 30 May 1937: 'He will probably be our saving. He is ambitious and will not be lazy like some of the others were. He starts in when things are at their worst and will have to show results.'[2] Later on, few senior officers were so generous. Another reason for disparaging Hore-Belisha was that in the First World War he had served in the Army Service Corps, whereas Duff Cooper had been a Grenadier and won the DSO.

Moved to the Admiralty, Duff Cooper introduced Hore-Belisha to Liddell Hart, beginning a significant association. Chamberlain, who found Liddell Hart's views on avoiding a Continental commitment satisfying, commended his book *Europe in Arms* to his new war minister.[3] Lord Bridgeman found Hore-Belisha a man of open mind, but he, 'Unfortunately [...] took the unwise course, in bringing in Liddell Hart as his unofficial adviser, and so providing himself with two alternative sources of opinion on the same problems, and placing himself in a position where he had to take decisions which he was hardly qualified to take.'[4]

The minister was caught between Chamberlain's views and the opinion of the soldiers that the defence of Britain depended on sending as an expeditionary force if the Low Countries were to be held against a German attack; indeed, the development of air power reinforced the need to keep them out of hostile hands.[5]

Hore-Belisha had started early on to make an impact: in a note to Chamberlain he listed seven fields in which it was necessary to 'eliminate':

- the mentality that the whole role of the army is to repeat its task of 1914–18
- resistance to new developments, including anti-aircraft (AA) and mechanisation
- the Indian obsession

- sentimentality in promotion – 'buggin's turn next'
- an 'insuperable reluctance' to take decisions on, e.g., extended use of Empire manpower or accepting recruits with false teeth
- an inclination to seek such perfection of material that no 'go ahead' order can be given on any existing design
- the 'complacent assumption that events will wait until a staged programme can be completed'.[6]

Finally, the minister wanted to bring about the 'vitalisation of a stagnant atmosphere'. Hore-Belisha's first 'elimination' was a reflection of Chamberlain's views on Continental entanglements. From this perspective, the sin of the CIGS, F.-M. Sir Cyril Deverell, was that he wanted an effective field force for possible Continental deployment, although at the same time he believed that India remained a priority. Given the tight army budget, however, these aims were incompatible. The stress on air defence tightened the screw even more. Between 1934 and 1939 only 22 per cent of rearmament expenditure was on the army and that mainly for ADGB.[7]

Adam's appointment at the Staff College was not the only instance of Hore-Belisha's refusal to rubber-stamp the military hierarchy's nominations based on seniority. The minister had also wanted Maj.-Gen. Lord Gort as his military secretary, because he was impressed by his energy and zeal for reform, and he got his way in that too. In the mid-1930s, 'the senior ranks in the army were in danger of becoming a self-perpetuating gerontocracy',[8] which he was determined to change. But the minister's lack of tact did not always help. Soon after taking office he had circulated to the General Staff an eighteen-page Liddell Hart paper entitled 'The British Army: Considerations on its Scale, Form and Functions' that included comments about the excessive age of Britain's senior soldiers. Its more senior recipients were not pleased. However, Hore-Belisha won. In August 1937 he decided that, in future, generals and lieutenant-generals should be retired at the age of 60, major-generals at 57 and colonels at 55, with tenure in command and staff postings limited to three years. Thirteen generals were retired. At the end of the year – encouraged by Liddell Hart – Hore-Belisha persuaded the prime minister to also let him sack the CIGS, aged 61, and two other members of the Army Council.

GORT, PILE OR ADAM?

To be the new CIGS the minister and Liddell Hart discussed, amongst others, Gort (aged 52), Sir Frederick Pile (53) and Adam (53). Liddell Hart recorded:

In suggesting Pile, I emphasised the importance of mechanised knowledge as well as his reforming spirit. He would be able to carry through a programme of modernising the Army more than any other others. Adam was perhaps the ablest of these, but not so certain to carry out the changes needed.[9]

In mid-November Liddell Hart suggested reviving the post of DCIGS, to which the minister responded that he favoured Gort as the executive man and wanted to 'put a thinker alongside him, rather than under him. I suggested Adam as the thinker', wrote Liddell Hart.[10] By now what he called 'the partnership' with the minister was in full swing. However, the decision went against trying to have two CIGSs. Hore-Belisha saw Gort (with his VC and three DSOs) as the glamorous public face of his new model army, with the newly promoted Maj.-Gen. Adam as the brains. He thought Adam could 'concentrate on the strategic side. He has a good and objective mind. He strikes me as being of better metal than most of those who fall in the academic category'.[11] The upshot was the minister's telephone call to Adam at the end of December 1937 to offer him the deputy's post. Adam was out riding when the minister rang. On his return, his first reaction was to think it was a hoax.[12] So his tenure as commandant of the Staff College lasted less than three months.

Hore-Belisha later compiled a list of thirty-three decisions he had taken: item 16 reads: 'Adam made Commandant of the Staff College – picked out from far down the Colonel's list'; item 31 regarding the creation of the DCIGS post: 'Adam, still only a substantive colonel, picked out for this lieutenant-general's post'. Among other changes he recorded was Wavell appointed as GOC Southern Command; Percy Hobart, 'an officer with mechanized experience', as director of military training; Harold Alexander aged only 45, as commander of the 1st Div.[13]

Other measures individually of a more mundane nature were introduced. Pay, marriage allowances and the terms of enlistment were improved. The maximum age limit for recruits was raised from 25 to 30. Men with false teeth and spectacles were admitted. Such measures helped to improve recruiting numbers, although not enough: the 30,000 shortfall in manpower in July 1937 was still 20,000 a year later – 12 per cent of the establishment. Three-quarters of the deficit was in the infantry. Moreover, the quality of recruits caused concern, because as the economy recovered the army was competing with industry for skilled men. In the latter half of 1938, the percentage of one rifle regiment's recruits with poor education rose from 50 to 70 per cent – and this in a key unit in the mobile division where a high proportion of men would have to be drivers and wireless operators. Hore-Belisha wanted to go further, proposing that all men wishing to join the army should initially go into the ranks, with the most promising after a year going on to officer training. This might attract more of the middle classes, but Liddell Hart considered it might equally cause disgruntlement among men who joined in the hope of gaining a commission. In response, the minister suggested a shorter enlistment period, or that such men could buy themselves out if disappointed in this aim.[14] This too proved a step too far. In the 1930s, only 5 per cent of officers came through the ranks, and most of them were quartermasters. Over four-fifths of officer cadets were from public schools. Half of the junior officers never got beyond major because promotion depended on a vacancy occurring at the next highest rank within their regiment or corps. Now, however, promotion would come after specific periods of service. The effect of this was sharp: on 30 August 1938 some 2,500 subalterns and captains were promoted at one go. At that level in the army hierarchy at least, Hore-Belisha's reforms were appreciated.

'BIG BRAIN'

Douglas Brownrigg, who replaced Gort as military secretary, saw Adam as the perfect supplement to Gort: he had 'a big brain, a trained intelligence, and a profound knowledge of men and affairs'.[15] Once back at the 'War House' Adam started to apply these qualities. Compared with the rhetoric of Hore-Belisha's 'manifesto', with its seven 'eliminations' and one 'vitalisation', within a month of his appointment he put forward in simple soldierly terms seven concrete proposals for change. He suggested to the new CIGS and to the AG, Lt-Gen. Sir Clive Liddell, that all types of reorganisation should be decided urgently: 'I suggested that they should make up their minds and then take to the Army Council for decision those matters which we could get through in time […] and stop discussions in the Army on the changes that could not be got through before war came.'[16]

The list Adam put forward covered:

- the organisation of infantry and armoured divisions;
- reducing the size of infantry battalions and their reorganisation into companies with one scout and three other platoons;
- whether machine gun battalions should be abolished and whether AA and AT battalions should be formed and, if so, whether they should be artillery or infantry units;
- whether the reorganisation of the field artillery brigades into regiments and four-gun batteries could be carried out before war came;
- rearming the medium artillery;
- the problem that the Royal Tank Corps had plenty of instructors and artificers while the cavalry had none; 'If something was not done quickly the cavalry would not be ready for war for some years';
- reorganisation of the General Staff.

Apart from the last item and the brief mention of AA, Adam's proposals concerned a field army. This showed the tensions at the top. The previous month, the Cabinet had put the defence of the UK, especially ADGB, as the first objective, followed by two imperial roles. Co-operation in the defence of any allies came only in fourth place. This policy was embodied in a (rather muddled) Cabinet Paper printed in February, 'The Organization of the Army for its Role in War'.[17] This stated: 'On the outbreak of war defence against air attack may be the primary requirement.' Gort and Adam were doubtful about this focus as it challenged their emphasis on the field army.[18] On the face of it, their opposition was a matter of strategic analysis and a rational decision on the distribution of scarce resources. But Hobart commented to Liddell Hart that, 'With regard to A.A. defence there is still the feeling that it is something foreign in the Army, and that its claims must not be allowed to interfere with building a large field army – more subconscious than explicit, but all the stronger as a brake'.[19] This is an interesting contemporary pointer to the issue that Norman Dixon, ex-Royal Engineers and professor of psychology, raised about many soldiers' attitudes towards defensive measures: that they are seen as a sign of weakness and effeminacy.[20]

Also on 24 May, Hobart commented to Liddell Hart that Gort depended more and more on Adam, who was, 'charming to work with, and a most able man, but a great centraliser. Wants to do everything himself, so that the directors are reduced to the role of a G.S.O.1.' Adam, he added, sends constantly for the junior officer directly concerned and short-circuits his superior, so that they do not know what is being done. 'This consultation of junior officers is a virtue carried too far. If Adam were laid up or called away, the whole machine would stick.'[21]

When Hore-Belisha took office, the army's overseas plans provided for four infantry divisions and one mobile division ready for the Continent at fourteen days' notice, with the subsequent despatch of another twelve divisions. The new policy proposed that two regular divisions and one mobile division, 'equipped for an eastern theatre', be ready within three weeks, followed by two other regular divisions by forty days later.[22] External priority now focused on the Middle East. In April 1938 the Cabinet discussed the possibility of conversations with the French and emphasised that because of the strength of the Maginot Line any German knock-out blow would be likely to be aimed at Britain's industrial and other resources, 'which are especially vulnerable to air attack'. The probability of Britain being able to send an expeditionary force to France in the early stage of the war 'is so slight that Military Staff Conversations are unnecessary'. Gort reported that at most 5,000 men could be made available.[23] Nor did the RAF have any margin to be able to help in the defence of France. At the time, German aircraft production was over four times the British rate. Hore-Belisha argued that not only was there 'an obligation of honour, but also a counsel of expedience' to assist France, with Duff Cooper adding that it was 'not possible to contemplate France with her back to the wall and three million young men in this country in plain clothes'. Chamberlain replied that he had never been 'dogmatic about ultimately sending a large army to France', but that Britain should not base its plans on that possibility.[24]

As for ADGB, one of the two existing regular AA groups was in the Middle East, and AA already took up one-quarter of regular RA strength and one-third of RE manpower. In addition, there were three Territorial Army (TA) AA divisions of 48,000 men, with 600 guns and 2,500 searchlights. The new policy meant that two more TA divisions would be needed. Yet despite a recruiting campaign, the TA in the summer of 1938 was still well under its nominal peacetime strength. Boosting the TA appeared to the government a cheap and easy way to increase the army's strength. But this had its limits. The volunteers received no pay, only allowances that in many cases did not cover the travel and other costs they incurred for their duties. They were not only giving their time freely to the nation, they were subsidising its defence.

AIR–SEA–LAND FRUSTRATIONS

Adam's concentration on army reorganisation did not exclude involvement in international negotiations. He recounted how the Turks, 'whom we particularly wanted to keep friendly', wished to buy AA guns and landing craft. The British could not and would not provide these, as their use might be to attack Italian-held Rhodes or Greek islands in the Aegean. 'I was given the task of wining and dining them at intervals and making pretty speeches.' But he did press for giving the French twenty 3.7in guns to defend Paris in exchange for their equal value in infantry anti-tank weapons to fully equip the leading divisions that went to France: 'a considerable psychological value' (although the guns proved of little value in 1940). Getting landing craft for the British Army was equally difficult; a possible landing at Benghazi behind the Italian lines was in mind. But the Admiralty doubted it would have escort vessels to spare from convoy duty, while the air force considered that enemy air power would put a stop to any attempts to get ashore on a hostile coast. After considerable argument, the soldiers won their case and each service agreed to put up £20,000 for a combined operations centre at Eastney under a naval commandant. But on the start of the war he was withdrawn by the navy and the establishment was broken up, only to be reformed later. Experience at Dieppe, and in Sicily and Normandy, would show that landings on a hostile coast were possible only with full air and naval superiority, and brilliant deception plans.

The reorganisation proposals that Adam had outlined in January 1938 ran into problems. Regarding the cavalry and tanks he wrote:

> Personally, I feel that it is now or never is the time [...] Amalgamation, semi-amalgamation, or temporary loaning of personnel may be the answer. The cavalry depot is on the tapis; cost £450,000; ready in 1941. This is useless to get the cavalry ready for war. We may have to break up cavalry regiments [...] Let us do it as a definite scheme. We must however keep the matter secret until the decision has been taken, otherwise the lobbying will be appalling.[25]

But he did not win that battle. When in April 1939 the Royal Armoured Corps (RAC) was established, it gathered in eight Royal Tank Corps battalions and seventeen cavalry regiments, each of which retained its own name. The same document shows that Adam's hopes of knocking the infantry into a more rational shape had to be put on hold: 'The group system and amalgamation of depots may be desirable, but is probably incompatible with readiness for war and should be relegated to the future.' One other controversy was about the suitability of infantry tanks in the Western Desert, compared with light tanks. Adam recorded a later discussion with Gort about whether the army should hide its I (infantry) tanks in case the government told the army to stop their manufacture. In 1961 he noted: 'In the light of the I tanks' success in Wavell's campaign against the Italians, we were quite wrong in our ideas.' There was some success in getting a 2in anti-tank gun tested and into service. When the RA commander reported this, Adam told him, 'Now go and produce a 4in gun as quick as you can', but the sparse money available made progress slow.

One change affecting the whole army was to reduce the traditional marching in column of fours to three ranks, which took up less road space. But even that was resisted from those who wanted to keep fours for ceremonial purposes. Adam thought it stupid to retain unnecessary drill and recognised that the Guards regiments were the key. 'Boy' Browning, who commanded the Grenadiers, laid on a demonstration for George VI, who accepted the new drill for his next Birthday Parade. Adam in 1961 wrote that, in addition, the slope arms 'had to be abolished' – although without explaining why. Reformers thought that the army should revert to the earlier command to 'shoulder arms', whereby the rifle is held vertically close to the right side of the body, with two or three fingers in the trigger guard – the practice in the rifle regiments. Adam remembered that as a gunner he was 'not supposed to know anything about drill' and kept in the background at a demonstration parade; but he could see that some Guards officers disapproved. Most military members of the Army Council accepted the proposal, but not the AG who responded: 'Whoever abolishes the slope strikes at the discipline of the British Army'.

Gort (a Grenadier) agreed with Liddell Hart (a Leicester). The slope remained. Adam was sceptical about the value of drill: 'It always struck me that many officers considered drill as an end in itself and not a means to an end.' [26]

One successful innovation was battle dress, which was being tried out by various units to replace the service dress with a waisted jacket and puttees. The new uniform comprised notably a tunic ending at the waist and webbing gaiters over the ankles. On active service it was worn by both officers and other ranks, and was later adopted with appropriate changes in colour by the navy, air force and civil defence services. Dyed dark brown with large round yellow fabric inserts, it was also worn by Axis POWs.

LIDDELL HART COLD-SHOULDERED

Adam's appointment as DCIGS led to sudden and curious change in his relations with Liddell Hart. Following the cordial letters and meetings towards the end of 1937, the latter was shocked to receive a handwritten letter from Adam dated 9 January 1938 stating, 'I feel that I cannot now give you an opinion which must be an official one.' [27] Adam added that he hoped that Liddell Hart would still let him see his papers and that they could meet from time to time, but that he could not now give his opinions on paper. [28] The two later exchanged letters, agreeing to meet for lunch later that month, but there is no evidence of it having taken place. Liddell Hart recorded his pained reaction:

> What is the theory implied here? No one before has expressed one like it – Milne frequently wrote me at length when he was C.I.G.S., and also Deverell, as well as various of their chief assistants. It becomes less understandable <u>now</u>, when A. is aware, I am in the confidence of the S. of S [secretary of state]. This should be an opportunity to clarify relations towards the best possible co-operation for the service of the country [...] A clear understanding between us, and the clearest possible understanding of each other's views on specific questions, is important (a) because it is inevitable that I should be constantly consulted in general by Ministers and other Parliamentary leaders, (b) because I am likely to be asked my opinion by the S. of S., (c) because of the weight *The Times* carries. There is much less chance of a detrimental divergence if we can discuss each other's point of view and endeavour to reconcile them. [29]

On 12 January Hobart recounted to Liddell Hart how Adam had the previous week given him 'an explicit warning that the "Secretary of State" was going to take a more strict line about officers talking to me about what is going on, and wished to reserve communication with me to himself. Hobart asked if this meant that officers could not have their own private friends.' [30] It appears that

Adam had invoked the name of the minister as a cover for orders from Gort, for Hore-Belisha assured Liddell Hart that he had said nothing to give rise to the idea.[31] On 14 January, Pile related that 'some time ago he heard that Gort had said something to the effect that now the Army must be run by soldiers again and not by newspapermen'. Pile added that it is natural that 'they [presumably Gort and Adam] should be resentful of the man who put them there, and jealous'.[32] Gort is the key here, being jealous of Liddell Hart's influence with the minister, despite his earlier friendship with the journalist and sympathy with his ideas to modernise the army. He directly benefited from the removal of more senior men at Liddell Hart's instigation. But Gort now found the position galling and resented the role of the *éminence grise*.[33] Resentment of Liddell Hart's influence was general among senior officers; he had, after all, risen no higher than captain in his army days. Liddell Hart's own vanity was also a goad to Gort: he recorded how the editor of the *Daily Telegraph* had said to him, 'I hear you are the C.I.G.S. now', while he also overheard himself being described by a government minister as an 'unofficial C.I.G.S.'.[34] The anger of the official CIGS at such implied denigration of his position is understandable, and Adam acted at his dictate. The two men's attitudes did differ: Gort was outright in his ingratitude, whereas Adam, to the extent that he ever revealed his feelings, was reticent. Liddell Hart noted, 'Adam and Hobart show palpable signs of embarrassment'.[35] Liddell Hart recorded no later meeting with Adam, although Gen. Giffard Martel on 21 June passed on to him that Adam thought his article on 'The Question of the Field Army', 'was very good, and did not criticise it'.

In other circumstances Adam was not at all averse to receiving unofficial information. Bernard Montgomery, posted to Palestine in late 1938, was in a biographer's words 'fortunate to have an important friend' at the War Office: Adam. Adam wrote that he would be grateful for Montgomery's views on the situation in Palestine. Montgomery disagreed with GOC Sir Robert Haining's view that the Arab revolt was a national movement; he thought the insurgents a 'group of professional bandits'. Adam replied to him on another occasion that, 'Your letters are most valuable […] and go beyond the normal official stuff that we get.'[36]

Hobart's analysis of the overall War Office situation was that Hore-Belisha did not realise that he had to deal with a corporation and that, 'if he stops driving it along, it will flatten him. His stay is short, while the corporation will last. Every officer wants to get on in the long run, and does not want to be regarded as "Bolshie", will be loyal to the corporation rather than to the temporary head.' Adam was a good company man, and at that stage of his career was not prepared to be regarded as 'bolshie'.

Given Adam's reticence, reliance on Liddell Hart's one-sided view based on his careful recording and filing, is inevitable. Adam's 1961 manuscript, consciously or not, is coloured by hindsight. This perhaps explains military historian Brian

Bond's judgement that, 'Perhaps the unkindest cut of all for Liddell Hart was the way in which he was cold-shouldered by some of the officers, such as Gort and Adam […], whose advancement he had done so much to secure.'[37] But Liddell Hart appeared to bear no grudge. In July 1939 he got at the army's old guard indirectly by complimenting Adam: 'That, despite outstanding ability, he should, at the age of fifty-two, only have reached the substantive rank of colonel, was a significant reflection on the past state of promotion in the Army.'[38]

Hore-Belisha's lack of tact appeared again early in 1938 when he circulated Liddell Hart's latest paper to senior officers, despite the writer having stressed that it was for his private information (in fact, for Adam's as well).[39] John Colville (private secretary successively to Chamberlain, Churchill and Attlee) recorded how on 2 February, the minister 'delivered a panegyric on Liddell Hart's merits to an unresponsive audience of Gort, Adam, Creedy'.[40] At about this time, the minister told Liddell Hart that he had better drop out of 'the partnership' unless Gort was willing to accept his co-operation. When on 21 January 1938 the journalist lunched with Gort at the minister's urging, he found the soldier extremely pleasant, but that 'he was so insistent on how much he wanted my advice, and so close to effusiveness, as to raise a doubt.'[41] For a while 'the partnership' continued, but in a less open way. An attempt to bridge the gap was made by the minister proposing to the WO that Liddell Hart be taken on as an official adviser.

In 1961 Adam wrote of Hore-Belisha:

> He was very anxious to start research in the War Office; I think that what he wanted was to get in some outsiders, e.g. military critics from the papers but I had persuaded him to let me set up a small staff directly under me to carry out a series of studies […] I set them to work on an examination of the War Office set up as a first problem […] Jack Gort had asked me what they were doing and I took along to him the first draft of their report to see. Most unfortunately, he was going in to see the Secretary of State and took him the draft to shew him what Adam's young men are doing.

Adam then had to spend half an hour explaining what had happened to Sir Herbert Creedy, the permanent under-secretary at the WO.

Liddell Hart responded to the idea that he become an official adviser by saying that he did not want to be 'in the War Office', and raised the matter with Adam who 'asked time to think it over'. The journalist took the hint, and on 19 February wrote to Hore-Belisha that, 'the completion of the Army estimates was a suitable time to bring the partnership "peacefully to a close". I should be too happy in regaining my old freedom as a critic to feel anything but friendly to you, for an interesting experience.'[42] The preparation of the army estimates was one of Adam's tasks (as DCIGS) with the minister, who was particularly keen that his first essay in that field in March 1938 should be a success, and so strengthen the role of the army. As with his own seven proposals put forward in January, Adam saw dangers in trying to do too much, for 'we could not possibly realise these ideas in the time available and it would give wrong ideas to the Army and the House of Commons of what was practicable'. During one discussion on the estimates Adam noticed that Hore-Belisha kept glancing into a partly opened drawer at a paper – 'written by Liddell Hart I suspected'. So 'the partnership' had not entirely ended in February. Anyway, the estimates – cut down by the Cabinet by 20 per cent from the draft level to £347 million – went down so well that the minister gave his advisers a champagne dinner at the House of Commons.[43] However, the real world was moving on: three days later – while the prime minister and the war minister had been putting all their emphasis on home defence, imperial sea lanes and the empire – Hitler occupied Austria.

In 1961 Adam wrote with his usual understatement: 'Relations between Hore-Belisha and Lord Gort were becoming more and more strained and I found myself in the unfortunate position of being a go-between. I got on well with both men, but it meant delay, misunderstanding and was most unfortunate in every way.' Having got rid of one CIGS, the minister could hardly get rid of another less than a year later. From the military viewpoint the minister 'had the reprehensible habit of asking soldiers and junior officers what they thought of their seniors.'[44] He was, John Colville wrote, 'dynamic in his energy, fertile – sometimes to the extent of being ludicrous in his imagination and a reformer of untiring zeal', but he could be 'rude and overbearing', showing 'an impatient manner, an intolerance of generals or civil servants of slower mind than his own'.[45] But, Colville conceded, he could be 'lovable to those who knew him well and an irritant to those who did not'. Adam got on well with him, but whether he found Hore-Belisha lovable is doubtful, if only because that would have indicated a depth of emotion that he could rarely display. Freddie de Guingand (military secretary 1939–40) wrote: 'Hore-Belisha I found a most colourful character; initially I did not take to him much, but later I developed a great affection and regard for my new master.'[46] Quick of mind though Hore-Belisha was, Adam recalled how he had himself, 'learnt the need for patience and that it was certain that if you thought a point had been decided you must be prepared to have the whole argument all over again the next day'.[47]

MUNICH

Despite the Cabinet clinging desperately to its 'no Continental commitment' policy, within six months – which included the *Anschluss* of Austria with the Third Reich – the pretence of preparing a field force for an eastern theatre had given way to accepting reality, at least in part, for it took the Munich Crisis (provoked by Hitler's ambition to dismember Czechoslovakia) before even Gort would agree to detailed talks with the French. At these talks Adam renewed his acquaintance with Schweizguth, who at their conclusion turned to him and said: 'This is the first occasion in which our conferences have not reminded me of a football match under a strict referee [...] On previous occasions, I have always expected the whistle to go for offside whenever we were getting anywhere.'[48]

The Munich Crisis of October 1938 showed up not just the inadequacy of Chamberlain's policy of trying to appease the dictators; it confirmed the inadequacy of the ADGB. Already, in July, Duncan Sandys, a backbench Conservative MP, a TA 2nd lieutenant and Churchill's son-in-law, had criticised in the Commons the unready state of the anti-aircraft defences. During the summer Gort – to anticipate an appropriate idiom – took the flak for this: he was twice summoned before a Commons select committee and treated as a hostile witness.[49] Hore-Belisha was so preoccupied with his political survival that he saw neither Gort nor even his own military secretary Brownrigg for several weeks. Sandys was proved right the following October. The mobilisation during the Munich Crisis of TA personnel in coastal defence units and the two AA divisions revealed serious deficiencies in organisation and equipment. This spurred the government to greater action.[50] In April 1939 the separate AA Command was finally set up, initially under Brooke, then Pile: it had seven divisions, with a total of nine envisaged.

Politically, Munich led to Duff Cooper's resignation from the Admiralty and Hore-Belisha's conversion to the soldiers' view of the need for a significant field force for France. But it was not until the following February that the Cabinet formally accepted this position.

The slow progress with rearmament had several causes. There was budgetary constraint, confusion over the ADGB/field force issue, concern that an extended programme would affect industrial exports, the shortage of skilled men, and Whitehall's own procurement procedures. Hore-Belisha himself complained of the last in July 1937, arguing that the procedures provided for no continuity after a limited time and contractors could not look forward to orders over a long period. They preferred to contract with the Admiralty or the Air Ministry, which were not hampered in this fashion. The problem had not been solved by the time Adam became DCIGS: when the board of Vickers told him that once an existing order was completed they would have to disperse the skilled labour force, he was unable to get Treasury sanction for a change.[51]

Behind all this, however, was Chamberlain's conviction after Munich that he had satisfied Hitler (at the expense of both the Czechs directly and of Western power indirectly through the loss of their thirty-four divisions, some mechanised). Hotfoot from his meeting with Hitler, Chamberlain told the Commons on 1 November that 'we are not today in the same position as we were in 1914, in this respect: that we are not now contemplating the equipment of an army on a continental scale'.[52] His hope that war could be averted drained away in the following months. The government stepped up its preparations in January 1939 by launching on the radio and via the press a National Service Appeal for a register of men and women for both military and civilian service. A forty-eight-page handbook was distributed to the 20 million households in the country. But the numbers coming forward fell well below the target and most volunteers were for civil defence not military service. More men did join the RAF Volunteer Reserve and the TA but the numbers signing up for immediate regular service was still below hopes. The Auxiliary Territorial Service (ATS) began to recruit women. On 15 March the falsity of the Munich Agreement was revealed when Hitler occupied the rest of the Czech lands and set up a clerico-fascist puppet state in Slovakia. Taking the Rhineland, the Saar, Austria and the Sudetenland into the Reich could be interpreted as uniting all Germans, but absorbing the rest of Bohemia and Moravia could not.

Now even the incurably optimistic, or the most craven, had to admit that Hitler would not be appeased on any terms. Speaking in Birmingham two days later, the prime minister asked rhetorically: 'Is this the end of an old adventure, or the beginning of a new? Is this, in fact, a step in the direction of an attempt to dominate the world by force?'[53] But he was still concerned not to provoke Hitler. The latter was, of course, never 'provoked' except to stage-manage something he had already planned. Chamberlain feared that bringing Churchill into the government might be interpreted as a hostile move. Labour and the Liberals made clear they would not join a government under Chamberlain's leadership. The prime minister still feared the trade unions' reaction if he introduced military conscription, a step that they believed would be followed by industrial conscription. Chamberlain and Hore-Belisha were desperate, as Sir John Slessor, Marshal of the RAF, summed up graphically:

> suddenly out of the blue, without the smallest warning, at the end of March 1939, Mr Hore-Belisha, the Secretary of State for War, announced that the Territorial Army was to be doubled, and the Cabinet, shocked into action by Hitler's absorption of Czechoslovakia, decided to increase the Field Force to thirty-two divisions. The excellent machinery of the Chiefs of Staff and the Committee of Imperial Defence was blandly ignored. The decision was based on no careful appreciation by the Chiefs of Staff as to what sort of Army was wanted and what for; there was no consideration of whether we could afford a great Navy, a powerful Air Force, and now an Army on a Continental scale; no assessment of priorities [...] or what its implications might be in respect of the requirements of the new Army for air support. Even the General Staff was hardly consulted [...] and I well remember the look of almost credulous bemusement on the usually cheerful countenance of the D.C.I.G.S., Ronald Adam (my old Colonel of Camberley days), who had only just heard of it.[54]

In order to strengthen the defences immediately, Hore-Belisha on 19 April suggested that TA AA units be called up for six months and reservists mobilised for three. It was then realised that the declaration of the State of Emergency that such a measure required would alarm rather than reassure foreign opinion. According to Hore-Belisha, Chamberlain at first refused to believe that the TA could not combine their daytime jobs with night duty on ADGB searchlights; and the Cabinet thought it unfair that TA volunteers be required to disrupt their work and their lives while others would carry on unhindered in their civilian jobs. This time, the military were consulted and rejected the proposal as unworkable.[55]

Adam revealed his openness of mind in another direction at a time when British officialdom was deeply suspicious of anyone who had fought in Spain for the Republic.[56] He approached Sir John Brown, the director of the TA, and asked him if he could get hold of a former sergeant-major in Spain who had written a book about the effects of German bombing: 'Brown was a wonder, he knew everyone and immediately arranged a lunch at which we had a long talk about these attacks', he wrote in 1961.

It was not only politicians who deceived themselves about the dictators. Hore-Belisha recounted – perhaps with relish – that at 11 p.m. on 5 April the Foreign Office had rung him to say that Imperial Airways had reported that Mussolini was about to attack Albania. He phoned Gort, who exclaimed 'bilge': it would take a week of preparations, and Mussolini had given an assurance that he had no intention of interfering with Albania's sovereignty.[57] Two days later Albania was invaded, and defeated in five days. The Italian dictator's German counterpart having mopped up Czechoslovakia, he was not to be outclassed. Hitler was contemptuous of the British moves: on 3 April he ordered the planning of 'Operation White' – the invasion of Poland. Chamberlain's 'guarantee' to Poland, and to Romania and Greece, in time proved hollow. A further indication that matters were slipping out of British and French control was the replacement in early May by Stalin of his foreign minister Litvinov by the servile Molotov. The ensuing months saw the half-hearted Western attempts to woo the Soviets, which ended in humiliation with the German-Soviet pact on 23 August.

During April 1939 the war minister still urged conscription on the prime minister. On 18 April he recorded an 'unpleasant interview' with Chamberlain, who accused him of having 'a bee in his bonnet' about it. The political leaders in France, disillusioned by British wobbling, were seriously considering a policy of retreat, leaving Germany with a free hand in eastern Europe.[58] Among the public there was widening circulation of the defeatist canard that the British were willing to fight to the last Frenchman. Even friendly voices were demanding *un effort de sang* by the British; in short, the conscription of a mass army. Two days later Sir Horace Wilson, the prime minister's special adviser, told Hore-Belisha that it was agreed to bring it in, but that it was still secret. Significantly, the minister did not learn this directly from the prime minister. Hore-Belisha rang

Wilson the following day to insist the Army Council be told, in order to avoid a repeat of the fiasco over doubling the TA.[59] Chamberlain explained his volte-face from 'no conscription in peacetime' – last pledged on 6 October 1938 – because 'while we were not at war, it was a mockery to call the present conditions "peace", and that these undertakings did not therefore disturb him'.[60]

Adam's comments on all this in 1961 were recorded with marked understatement: doubling the TA and bringing in conscription 'produced large forces, but the problems of organisation of balanced forces were made very difficult [...] As we got nearer and nearer to war we were all fully employed in makeshift arrangements to catch up with the increased manpower'. Finding the accommodation, catering facilities, clothing, weapons and other equipment and, not least, the officers and NCOs to take on the reception and training of so many men, diverted the army from its already daunting tasks that summer. Under the Military Training Act passed in May, 240,000 men of between age 20 and 22 registered for service, and 34,500 were enlisted on 15 July as militiamen – the name chosen to link them to the historical formation. They were due to serve for six months, with three and a half years in the reserve. But such was the shortage of accommodation and training facilities for the first contingent that the second scheduled for September was cut back to 9,000, with another 18,000 due for call-up in October. It was in vain, for on 3 September, war was declared, and the National Service (Armed Forces) Act was passed.

Notwithstanding the grave deterioration of the international scene, Gort maintained his quarrel with the minister. Through June and July of 1939, Colville recorded:

... the time, strength and energies of Hore-Belisha and the General Staff were consumed by internal squabbles, although they did make some useful decisions, in particular to establish a 'Preparations Section' in the War Office, placed under Adam's authority and charged with the task of making administrative plans for the despatch of a British Expeditionary Force to the Continent.[61]

In July, Creedy retired and was replaced by P.J. (Sir James) Grigg, with whom Adam was to work closely in the following years. As Colville wrote:

There was nothing quiet nor conventional about P.J. [...] Brilliantly clever, honest and indefatigable, he was outspoken to the point of rudeness and it never crossed his mind to suffer fools gladly. He respected men for their competence and not at all for their position. If he thought ill of a Minister he served, he said so to all and sundry, including the Minister. He held truthfulness to be a cardinal virtue, tact a social affectation. He was respected by all, feared by many and loved by only a few who had experience of his more sterling qualities. Hore-Belisha, delighted by the prospect of such a dynamic successor to Creedy, had little idea of the sea-green incorruptible Tartar he was welcoming into the uneasy fold of the War Office.[62]

On the morning that war came, air-raid sirens sounded in London. At the WO Adam was meeting French officers and they all went down to the basement. 'We heard sounds exactly like A.A. guns going off and I remember saying to the French that at least we had some guns. Later I realised it was the banging of doors.' The alert, moreover, was not the Luftwaffe aiming a knock-out blow at London but a civilian light plane taking off without authorisation in Kent. That night there was another alert, this time caused by a wrongly orientated radar screen reporting night-fighting squadrons on a training exercise as incoming raiders, with each squadron sent up to intercept interpreted as further waves of the enemy. Adam was staying at the United Services Club and at first ignored the alert but was roused by one of the staff and urged to the shelter. He lost his way and wandered into the female staff quarters. 'The screams made me realise where I was and I went back to my bed to sleep.'[63]

French officers, banging doors, mistaken identities and flustered *domestiques*: Adam's war started with all the elements of a Georges Feydeau farce.

6

RETURN VIA DUNKIRK

There was nothing farcical about the war in Poland. On 1 September German forces attacked from the west, north and south. Warsaw was devastated by bombing, but it was no knock-out blow. That came when, after nearly three weeks of brave Polish resistance, Stalin joined Hitler in a fourth partition of Poland. The British and French did nothing to ease the onslaught on their allies. The RAF made daylight raids on German ports until heavy losses forced a switch to night bombing, and then much of its action was dropping propaganda leaflets. At sea, a number of German surface ships and submarines were sunk, while a U-boat's penetration of Scapa Flow and sinking of a battleship humiliated the Royal Navy. On land, the French carried out patrol activity and some faint skirmishes towards the German lines. It was the *drôle de guerre*, the '*Sitzkrieg*', the phoney war.

By a narrow decision, the Cabinet on 3 September appointed Gen. Gort as C-in-C of the BEF rather than Gen. Sir Edmund Ironside, who took over as CIGS. In 1961 Sir Ronald Adam recorded that Gort's appointment to the BEF had been a shock: he recalled a Staff College lecture in which Gort himself had said that one of the greatest mistakes of the First World War was to send the CIGS to command the BEF, for F.-M. French had taken away with him a number of senior officers from the War Office. Gort was 'as delighted as a boy freed from school' on his appointment, Adam wrote: 'I had enjoyed working with him and had come to know him very well.' He wondered whether the move was due partly to the continued ill-feeling between Gort and Leslie Hore-Belisha. Gort was comparatively young and had never commanded a major force. On becoming CIGS, he had overtaken two more senior officers, Lt-Gen. Sir John Dill and Lt-Gen. Alan Brooke, who were now to serve under him in France as corps commanders.[1]

Adam's careful planning during the summer turned into achievement as the BEF began to cross the Channel in early September. By the end of the month 152,000 men, 21,000 vehicles and 120,000 tons of supplies were safely in France. The weakness of the logistical arrangement was that, because of – in his view –

'alarmist advice' from the Air Ministry as to what German bombers could do to ships crossing the Channel further east, the BEF supplies were landed at ports in western France, with the men landing at Cherbourg. This meant that a great deal of time and 108,000 gallons of fuel were spent every day carrying supplies to the front, over a distance the equivalent of Edinburgh to London. The British Army was the only one of the combatants to rely entirely on motor transport, but much of it was unreliable civilian lorries. By the spring of 1940 there were nearly 400,000 British soldiers in France in five regular divisions and five TA divisions, three of them engaged on pioneer work and training. Some regulars were sent to TA formations to stiffen them up, for they had lacked the time to train adequately.[2]

The weapon supply situation was not reassuring. In December only 70 of the 204 infantry tanks required in France were there – barely one-third; by the end of February 130 were expected to be available, against a requirement by then of 461 – much the same proportion. By May, the BEF would still be short of 166 cruiser tanks. Only light tanks would be up to target. The anti-tank situation was the most serious: only four of the ten divisions would have enough two-pounder guns (which were to prove quite inadequate). The light AA situation was better. Although supplies of Bofors guns from Continental sources were now blocked, by June 1,000 guns were expected to have been delivered, with home production running at 150 a month.[3]

Unlike 1914, some continuity was maintained at the WO. At the minister's insistence Adam stayed in London, but with Gort's assurance that he would ask for him to command his new III Corps when it was formed. During this time Adam made sure that the awaited Canadian corps would be housed in Aldershot and not camping out on Salisbury Plain as in 1914. The period of continuity did not last long: on 25 October Adam was appointed to that command, and was pleased to be in a strong enough position to pick his senior officers. The III Corps HQ was set up at Alresford, in Hampshire, but its allocated divisions were scattered: the 51st (Highland) Div. was elsewhere in that county, the 42nd (East Lancashire) was in Northumberland, the 44th (Home Counties) in Dorset, and the 50th (Northumbrian) in the Cotswolds. At this stage all the divisions were skeleton formations. Gradually the corps took shape, despite its dispersal. Late in the year, the first militia signallers joined it – men called up in July before the main conscription act came into force in September. The corps adopted as its insignia a green fig leaf on a white square, an allusion to Adam's name.[4]

Brooke recorded on 21 October that Adam had come over to France for a couple of days. Adam thought the Germans would not attack, although they were starting masses of rumours about impending attacks. He thought they would start another peace offensive with the hope that boredom with the present conditions would induce the Allies to make peace. Brooke, on the contrary, thought that when their internal conditions became critical the Germans would be forced to start some sort of offensive.[5] This sort of speculation was typical of the phoney war.

Although it was barely two decades since the earlier BEF had served in France, there were virtually no men or junior officers in the new force with experience of European warfare. At more senior levels there was experience, but in many cases the officers, WOs and senior NCOs now promoted to cope with the expansion in personnel, had been rightly passed over in peacetime. Many officers brought back into service were out of date and, in some cases, psychologically damaged by their experiences in the earlier war.

In January 1940 the most prepared of the III Corps divisions, the 51st, was ordered to France. Adam decided to go with it, and immediately picked up 'flu from the divisional commander. After recovering he went with Brooke to visit one of his II Corps divisions that was in the Maginot Line. The opposing lines were some way apart, so that there was opportunity for patrol activity. There was not much shelling, but it was a good front for running in divisions, Adam concluded. The effectiveness of the Maginot Line was much exaggerated, as Hore-Belisha recognised when, on holiday in the Vosges before the war, he was told by the local military governor that the German defences across the Rhine were much stronger. In the event, the Line proved largely worthless, although fostering an illusion of invulnerability among the French public. Worse, it enabled – indeed obliged – the Germans to channel their attack forces further north, beyond where the line ended, south of Luxembourg.

By February, the 50th Div. had also arrived in France, to be held (like the 51st) in reserve. The sector allocated to the main BEF was a 30-mile stretch of the Belgian frontier, from Halluin, north of Lille, to Maulde, 13 miles to the east. It was later extended westward to Armentières. The BEF began to reinforce the existing frontier defences with pillboxes and other works in their sector, which ran through the heavily populated industrial zone that straddled the frontier. On the British left flank was the French Seventh Army under Gen. Giraud, and on the right, the French First Army, under Gen. Blanchard. Writing to the CIGS on 29 September, Gort noted of the latter: 'I would judge him a good soldier, will hold'.[6] Adam was less impressed with Giraud: he was 'a fine upstanding figure, and pleasant to meet, but did not inspire great confidence in his fitness for modern war'.[7] Overall commander of the Allied forces in north-west France was Gen. Georges, whom Adam knew and respected from the talks before the war.

Allied plans, dominated by French considerations, were defensive. However, in the event of a German attack on the Low Countries, they provided for the Seventh Army crossing Belgium into Holland, with the BEF and the French First Army moving forward to secure the River Dyle, east of Brussels. This itself would be a defensive move, for the French wanted to keep the conflict away from their own borders, having lost the northern industrial area and much other territory to the Germans for four years in the First World War. So an advance into Belgium, and diversionary campaigns elsewhere, would be welcome.

THE FALL OF HORE-BELISHA

Separation by 200 miles did not ease the friction between Gort and the war minister; it might have exacerbated it, for there was now no Adam to administer emollient oil. The minister came to believe the soldiers were dragging their feet over building pillboxes along the frontier, an echo of attitudes towards defensive measures that Percy Hobart had raised with Basil Liddell Hart before the war. Norman Dixon, writing a long-distance psychological viewpoint, quoted Hore-Belisha's diary of 2 December 1939: 'Ironside, after his visit to B.E.F., came to me and with great emphasis told me that the officers were most upset at the criticisms made about lack of defences […] He said Gort was threatening to resign.' Dixon asked acidly: 'Can it be that somewhere in the minds of some military commanders there lurks a natural distaste for defensive measures.'[8]

The 'pillbox affair' was the most bitter and, as it proved, the final evidence of the lack of empathy between Gort and Hore-Belisha. When the king became involved, Chamberlain decided that Hore-Belisha had outlived his usefulness. Moving him to the Ministry of Information was mooted until it was realised what a propaganda gift to Hitler it would be to appoint a Jew to that post. Against the advice of Winston Churchill (now at the Admiralty) Hore-Belisha turned down the offer of the Board of Trade. He left the government in early January and held no subsequent wartime office. Apart from his disregard for military protocol and pride, the fact that he was Jewish certainly played a part in his unpopularity among the British elite. Not all senior soldiers were critical. Maj.–Gen. Sir John Macready observed that Hore-Belisha, on joining the War Office, had shown that he was no rubber stamp, and had gained the gratitude of many lower down the hierarchy by his reforms. His 'display of energetic inquisitiveness was a shock to many of the older school of military thought […] that the army should not be tampered with by civilians'.[9] He is not ranked with his Liberal predecessors as a great army reformer, if only because his reforms were swallowed up by wartime changes. But by appointing Adam as DCIGS he had created a great agent for change at a crucial time.

Gort, who also owed his rise to Hore-Belisha, both as military secretary and CIGS, wrote nothing about the resignation. Colville defended him:

> He had never disguised his dislike of Hore-Belisha, and had been deeply affronted by the aspersions that 'The Pill-Box Row' had appeared to cast on his competence as commander-in-chief […] Gort was distressed by the suggestion

that he, a soldier owing allegiance to the Crown and its delegates, should have been instrumental in procuring Hore-Belisha's fall from grace and power.[10]

Adam was succinct, and just, in his opinion: 'Any reformer becomes unpopular, but the Army was in better state by August 1939. The strength had risen to 224,000; it was [...] in the limelight and although most new equipment was made for the ADGB, things were looking up, thanks to Mr Hore-Belisha.'[11]

THE 'WILD-GOOSE ENTERPRISE'

Not content with being at war with Germany, the British and French governments risked going to war as well with the Soviet Union, then in effect Germany's ally. Stalin wanted to push the Soviet frontier further away from Leningrad and attacked Finland on 30 November. The Allies were already concerned that Sweden was supplying nearly half of Germany's iron ore needs. An intervention to help the Finns, which could be justified, might also enable the Allies to secure the Swedish mines. But if that involved breaching that country's neutrality, it would be less justifiable; nor would it be wise. The Finns' initial success against an army over three times the size of their own encouraged the Allies. Churchill and Ironside were enthusiastic supporters of intervention. The Allies first tried to persuade Norway and Sweden to help the Finns, and to let them provide 'volunteers' to fight against the Red Army; the two neutrals rejected this early in January. The 'volunteers' would have included many Poles who had escaped to France late in 1939. The Allies then sought formal passage for Allied troops from Narvik to the Gulf of Bothnia, claiming a League of Nations resolution on Finland as justification. This would get men and supplies to the Finns and stop supplies of iron ore being shipped south within Norway's ice-free waters to Germany. Faced with a German threat of invasion if they agreed to the Allies' demand, the two Nordic states refused this also.

Brooke's view was clear. On 10 February he wrote that the Allies were making the same mistake as in the First World War by starting operations outside the Western Front (e.g. Gallipoli and Salonika). Six days later he told the new war minister, Oliver Stanley, of the dangers of reducing the strength of the BEF. 'I told him I considered this was the only front on which the war could be lost in 1940 if we were not careful, and might just win it if we were fortunate.' A German attack was 'a certainty', he added.[12]

Adam became involved when it was decided that, if a negotiated plan failed, part of III Corps would be earmarked for an invasion of Scandinavia. From Adam's 1961 account it was only towards the end of February that he was recalled to Britain and 'told of the extraordinary scheme being planned'. This must be a memory lapse, for already on 4 February the move of other III Corps units to

France was suspended and part of the corps HQ still in England had been formed into a Special Force HQ early in February.[13] Asking at the War Office about the plans, Adam was told that his corps HQ was to be built up to an Army HQ, although, 'whether I was to command it or not I never knew. Everything was in confusion, but thank goodness by the middle of March the whole thing was called off.' By this time the Finns had sought an armistice, but 'it was a near thing', for the III Corps HQ transport had already left for embarkation. Brooke's diary comment of 31 March on a 'wild-goose enterprise' was apt.

Apart from inherent dangers in the plan to invade two neutral countries and, in early April, to mine Norwegian waters, the Allies' plans gave Hitler his own excuse to invade Norway and Denmark on 9 April. (He also concluded from the Winter War that Stalin's 1937–38 purges of the Soviet officer corps had fatally wounded the Red Army; on this he was to be proved nearly but not quite right.) The Allies' operations in Norway after the German invasion were a complete failure and their forces finally withdrew on 1 June. Of the British contingent, two of the three brigades were Territorials, ill-trained and ill-equipped. An even more reckless proposal mooted was for a French and British air attack from Syria and Iraq on the Baku oilfields, which would certainly have meant war with the Soviet Union.

Calling off the Scandinavian adventure meant that III Corps would stay in France. Also on 9 April, as it happened, the corps took over the line between Giraud's Seventh Army on the left and Brooke's II Corps on the right. Lunching with Giraud at his HQ one day, Adam also met the commander of the corps immediately to his left, Lt-Gen. Robert Fagalde, whom he was to describe as 'an old friend' from his days as military attaché in London. Adam wrote in 1961 that Giraud had had six divisions of the best of the French troops, but that the two armoured divisions would better have been held in reserve.

The seeds of distrust between the two Allies were already sown, for the BEF corps commanders had doubts about the plan for a dash into Belgium. Adam recalled in 1961:

> Jack Gort, who had always preached the need for unified command and loyalty to commanders, was the last person to question the orders he received from above. Tiny Ironside had accepted completely the French plans, and he was the only person who had been in a position to have it examined in detail. To me it seemed that Giraud's adventure was absurd and that the French had too many divisions behind the Maginot Line and that their worst divisions were in the interval between the Maginot Line and the troops who were to advance into Belgium.

Adam himself then committed what turned out to be a tragic mistake in persuading Gort to allow the 51st Div., under Maj.-Gen. Victor Fortune, to occupy a 7-mile sector in the Saar area, in front of the Maginot Line, from 6 May. He considered it a good division and believed the duty would be an honour for the TA. The rest of the corps was busy training and constructing defences along the frontier. Adam considered the 51st a good division, although Lt-Col Lord Bridgeman (Gort's GSO1) differed: 'the reports on the 51st Highland Div. seemed to have been written by someone wearing rosy spectacles'.[14]

END OF THE *SITZKRIEG*

In London the failure of the Allied operation in Norway led to loss of parliamentary support for the prime minister. On 10 May he was replaced by Churchill – notwithstanding his own deep involvement in the Scandinavian venture. The Labour and Liberal parties, which had refused to serve under Chamberlain, joined the new government, which did, however, still include Chamberlain and Lord Halifax. Churchill's position remained uncertain *vis-à-vis* many Conservative MPs who were already regretting their abandonment of Chamberlain. Only late in 1940 was Churchill able to form a War Cabinet that excluded ex-appeasers.

On the day that Churchill took the lead, the *Sitzkrieg* gave way to *Blitzkrieg*. With *Einsatz Sichelschnitt* – 'Operation Sicklecut' – General von Bock's Army Group B thrust into the Low Countries. The Dutch fought their 'Four-Day War' until the threat of other cities suffering the same aerial devastation as Rotterdam forced them to give in. The Belgian eastern defences proved less substantial than hoped and the Germans advanced steadily. The French moved forward into Holland as far as Breda, with the BEF on their right flank up to the Dyle. Two divisions of I Corps (now under Lt-Gen. Michael Barker) were on the line, with the third held back, and one of Brooke's II Corps divisions was up, with another in reserve. Two other under-strength divisions were in general reserve, while the two divisions in III Corps were held 50 miles back on the Scheldt. These dispositions changed in the following days, and divisions were transferred from one corps to another as the battle developed.

By 13 May, Army Group B had reached a line stretching south from Antwerp to Namur and to Sedan, just within France, and then running eastwards. In the ensuing days it steadily pressed forward, with the British and French in Belgium withdrawing to the Scheldt even before the Germans launched their main attack on this front on 21 May. Also on the 13th – to the Allies' great surprise – General von Rundstedt's Army Group A crossed the Ardennes in force and rushed through the French lines near Sedan. The Germans, to their own surprise, in a few days reached the English Channel at the mouth of the Somme, cutting the Allied forces in two. To the north were the BEF, the French Seventh Army and the remains of the First Army; to the south were the bulk of the French forces, falling back to the Somme. The 51st Division, still on the Saar front when the Germans attacked, never rejoined the main BEF. With the three TA divisions on pioneer and lines of communications duties, it retreated with the French south of the Somme.

Overall, the Allies and the Germans were matched in the number of armoured fighting vehicles: each had some 3,000 tanks and 700 armoured cars. But the Allies' armour was spread from the North Sea to the Mediterranean, whereas the Germans' was concentrated.[15] And the Germans knew how to handle their armour, having thoroughly studied their potential (not least the battle doctrines promulgated by Percy Hobart, Giffard Martell, J.F.C. Fuller and Basil Liddell Hart) and learnt lessons in Poland. So while the Allies were swinging north-east into Belgium, the Germans exploited the situation further south. Not only were the weakest French divisions stationed west of the northern end of the Maginot Line, the French High Command vastly underestimated the penetrability of the Ardennes (as the Americans did four years later). Gen. Gamelin in October 1939 had mentioned to Gen. Ironside the possibility of an attack through the Ardennes, but then discarded the idea.[16] He constantly changed his mind about where and when the Germans were likely to attack. The outcome offered Liddell Hart a rather smug 'I told you so' in 1965, citing his own book, *Decisive Wars of History*, written in 1929 in which he had criticised the 'Ardennes fallacy' whereby Foch (the Supreme Allied Commander in 1918) considered the region an almost impenetrable massif; the Germans proved Foch wrong[17].

The Allies' reaction to the German offensive was to plan simultaneous attacks from north and south (the 'Weygand plan'), aiming to cut the Germans' thrust to the sea in two, before the infantry could catch up with the panzers. This appealed to the political and military leadership in London and Paris but ignored the realities on the ground.

Confusion was not confined to the Allies. On 17 May, Gort ordered the assembly of a scratch force of one tank brigade and two infantry battalions to attack the Germans at Arras. Rommel, who led the 7th Panzer Div., believed that the British were actually fielding five divisions; he hesitated enough to provide the British with a temporary but cheering success.[18] By midnight on 18/19 May, Gort saw three options: simultaneous Allied attacks from south and north to cut the enemy in two, the withdrawal of all the Allied forces in the north down to the Somme, or the withdrawal of the BEF across the Channel. The first would have meant the French 7th and the BEF trying a fighting withdrawal against Gen. von Bock in the north while attacking Gen. von Rundstedt to the south; the second required more time than was available and would have meant abandoning Belgium; the third appeared the most likely option.[19]

CONFUSION

On 21 May Marshall Weygand, who replaced Gamelin as Supreme Allied
Commander in mid-campaign, met Belgian King Leopold at Ypres. Gort
was not initially told of the meeting and arrived after Weygand had left but
was briefed by Gen. Billotte (who was killed after leaving the meeting). The
Belgians feared that a southward attack would leave them isolated and losing
even more of their national territory.[20] On his return from Ypres, Lt-Gen.
Henry Pownall, Gort's Chief of Staff, told Bridgeman to prepare an evacuation
plan, but the following morning (22nd) things looked better, and he was told
that it was not yet wanted. (It was not until late on the 26th that Gort definitely
put in hand the evacuation plan.)[21]

The confusion was exemplified by Operational Order No. 1 for the south–
north attack plan that Weygand later issued, which ignored all the information
given to him by Billotte.[22] Gort consulted his corps commanders, Brooke and
Barker, who, according to historian David Divine, were pessimistic. He wrote:

> Lieutenant-General Sir Ronald Adam, who commanded the new III Corps,
> was, according to a contemporary account of the conference, sound in his
> appreciation of the circumstances. All three generals agreed, however, that it
> was impossible to sustain the front on the Escaut [Scheldt] for more than
> twenty-four hours, and the question of a withdrawal to the old frontier
> positions to take advantage of the pill-boxes, trenches, and anti-tank works,
> which had been built during the winter, was examined. The meeting decided
> that no alternative existed.[23]

By 23 May the French and the BEF north of Lille were back along the Belgo-
French frontier, apart from a small triangle of Belgium from Ostend to Ypres,
where the Belgians were holding out (much the same area that had remained
unoccupied by the Germans in 1914–18). But the hope that the frontier defences
– reinforced so controversially during the winter – would provide cover, was
largely in vain. The 400 pillboxes built facing north were being turned to the
south. On the southern flank the Allies were confined to a long tongue of
territory stretching inland from the Pas de Calais. As a precautionary measure
the BEF was put on half rations. That evening Rundstedt, with Hitler's approval,
gave his famous 'halt' order to his panzers on the Aa Canal. The motivation for
this decision has been long debated. In any case, of immediate concern was that
the panzers had lost half their strength from battle or wear and tear, and the land
across the canal was broken by dykes and flooding. The order did not apply to
infantry, who made a number of crossings.

The following day, the 24th, Adam was given command of the 5th and 50th Divisions after the Arras battle, in order to plan the proposed southward thrust ordered by the supreme Allied command. He was to do this in conjunction with and under the orders of the French, and was to have a French division within his own command. Adam recalled that he was to have the last of the infantry tanks, but did not expect anything from 'vague talk' of fighter air support from England. On 25 May he went to the French First Army HQ, and 'did my duty by urging all to the attack. I found little of the offensive spirit there […] a number of vague promises were made.' He learnt that the French could not even spare a whole division. Adam reconnoitred the terrain as much as he could, and ordered bridging material as all the bridges to the south had already been blown. In 1961 he wrote:

> It seemed absurd to carry on the attack with the only reserves when it was clear that the French would not produce even a third of the troops needed. I rang up Jack Gort and explained the position and urged that the attack should be called off, because I must otherwise commit the two divisions to the move and I felt certain that the French were in no position to make an advance.
>
> Jack Gort did not take long to make up his mind and the attack was called off. It was the decisive act that enabled us to withdraw to Dunkirk and every credit should be given to him for taking it.

London and Paris now accepted that a north–south link up was impossible. On 26 May the war minister telegraphed Gort that he could 'be faced with a situation in which the safety of the B.E.F. will be predominate' [*sic*]. Gort replied: 'I must not conceal from you that a great part of the B.E.F. and its equipment will inevitably be lost even in best circumstances.'[24] At this time the enclave still stretched some 38 miles inland as far as the River Scarpe (8 miles south of Lille) and was between 10 and 20 miles across. The capture of vital high-level German documents, revealing a threat towards Ypres, confirmed the need to call off the southward push in order to close a gap on the northern front at Ypres and Mons.

Having lost the one opportunity Adam was to have of showing his ability to handle a major assault plan, he reverted to the role that was his strength: that of organiser. This meant that he had to bear the brunt of the growing British–French disharmony and differences of intent. On 26 May Gort ordered him to Dunkirk to organise the defences, even though Admiral Abrial was the overall commander responsible for the defence of the base. 'He [Adam] was to act in conformity with the orders of General Fagalde, provided that these did not imperil the safety and welfare of British troops'.[25] This offered a get-out if necessary.

THE DUNKIRK PERIMETER

The following morning Adam was sent to represent the C–in–C at a meeting with the French at Cassel to settle the disposition of forces within the planned perimeter. The officers met in an abandoned café under a glass ceiling. Adam arrived at about 7 a.m. and Bridgeman shortly afterwards. The latter recounted:

> Fortunately Fagalde [now commanding the French corps at Dunkirk] also came early, and armed with my precious map, I got them together on a side table, used by waiters in better times, and they had about ten minutes settling the occupation of the Dunkirk perimeter. It was done in a sensible and friendly way, and fortunately in English for though both spoke the other's language, Fagalde was the more bilingual of the two.[26]

Abrial and three other French generals then arrived. By Adam's 1961 account the senior of them, Gen. Koeltz:

> made a rousing appeal on behalf of Weygand that the time had come for us to stop our retreat and turn and attack the Germans everywhere. No one said anything for a bit and then General Fagalde rose and said he would return to his Headquarters at once and order an attack on Calais driving the Germans before him. We British looked at him with astonishment, but the French applauded him and the party dispersed, or rather we left as quickly as we could to get on with our job.

Historian Hugh Sebag-Montefiore, drawing on Bridgeman's papers and Fagalde's report of the meeting, wrote that, 'Behind the smiles and the handshakes Fagalde was seething'.[27] On the way to Cassel he had come across a British officer who told him that his orders had been to abandon all transport and to evacuate from Dunkirk. Until that time, the French were unaware of the British plans to evacuate. Sebag-Montefiore continued that Fagalde:

> was upset by Gort's decision to leave it to General Adam, 'a mere intermediary', to tell him and the other commanders what it [the perimeter allocation] was. Gort's instruction to Adam that he should say he would act in accordance with French orders not only failed to disarm Fagalde but had the opposite effect. Fagalde's suspicion that Adam's agreement to serve under French command was a piece of window-dressing was confirmed in his eyes after he had questioned Adam on how long the British would hold their perimeter sector, 'I only obtained vague replies, or no replies at all,' Fagalde reported. 'I then realized that it was all talk without substance, and I decided not to make any alterations to my plan to defend the entire perimeter with my troops.'[28]

This account does not agree in spirit with Adam's recollection. Later that day, at a meeting that included Abrial and Capt. Tennant RN, to discuss the defence of the perimeter, Fagalde said that he would have to draw in his troops from west of the town because of pressure from German armour. Adam continued that, 'I told him that after his morning's promise to General Koeltz, I expected to hear that he was on the way to Calais. "Oh," he said, "After General Koeltz's moving words, someone had to say something, and no one else appeared to be ready."' Adam's depiction of this gentle chiding of Fagalde is hardly compatible with the latter's account of their relations.

If the day of the Cassel meeting was indeed the first indirect indication to the French command that the British were planning an evacuation – codenamed 'Operation Dynamo' – eight days after Gort had first considered the possibility, then confidence between the Allies had clearly entirely collapsed. The French had still assumed the perimeter would provide a redoubt for further operations while the British saw it as a preliminary to a retreat to Britain. But at this time Gort was under orders not to tell the French that the British were planning an evacuation. This explains the 'vague replies' that Adam gave to Fagalde's questions about holding the perimeter, for Gort had decided the night before to give the evacuation order, and put Adam in charge of establishing the perimeter, with Bridgeman as his GSO1 and Maj.-Gen. Pakenham-Walsh as his chief engineer. Of his commander, Bridgeman wrote:

> I had known Sir Ronald Adam for some time but not well, though I liked what I knew. I was soon to find out how lucky I was. An old Etonian, he knew his profession thoroughly, he could make up his mind, was good at handling people, French and English, said what he wanted and what he meant, and then let his staff get on with what they had to do.[29]

On leaving Cassel, Adam's party was attacked by Belgian biplanes with German markings. Pakenham-Walsh was wounded and had to be admitted to hospital. Adam set up his HQ at La Panne, which had a direct telephone link to England (installed so that the previous Belgian King Albert could keep in touch with the London stock exchange). He sent an urgent appeal for air cover: 'Complete fighter protection essential if serious disaster is to be avoided'. But Churchill was determined to husband the RAF's dwindling fighter strength, refusing despairing appeals from the French government for the transfer of more fighters to France. The RAF was in action over Dunkirk, although few of the soldiers on the beaches were aware of it.

The position of the Belgian forces east of Nieuport had been 'too obscure' to take into account at Cassel; at midnight that day (27 May) they declared a ceasefire. The Belgians, in particular King Leopold, have been much maligned by the British and French. But Basil Liddell Hart argued that had the king left with his ministers for London on 25 May, the Belgian Army would have surrendered earlier still and so endangered even more the British and French position in the Dunkirk enclave.[30] The British had to blow the bridges on the Nieuport flank – hastily and with difficulty. 'Adamforce' initially comprised gunners, engineers and some infantry, with front-line troops coming in later.

On arriving at La Panne, Adam found that 'large masses of GHQ and other troops, mainly R.A.S.C., were in the vicinity, completely disorganised'. The following day, the 28th: 'the rabble of troops on the beachhead were useless for police or defence parties, and my idea was to clear them away as soon as possible'.[31] These comments, made three weeks after the evacuation, contrast with the conventional picture of British troops stoically queuing to be picked up. Bridgeman's proposal was that II Corps should defend the east, with I Corps between it and III Corps, which lay to the west, next to the French. In reality the situation was less neat, with leaderless groups of 'teeth' men drifting in, although these were generally well disciplined. The plan was for III Corps to embark first, followed by II Corps, with I Corps providing the rearguard. But the slow off-take of troops was worrying. Back in La Panne Adam phoned the War Office to complain of the small number of naval personnel and small boats. Unfair as his criticisms were, as he later acknowledged, they undoubtedly helped to speed up the evacuation. On 26–27 May only 3,373 men had been taken off; on 27–28 nearly 14,000, on 28–29 more than 38,000 (plus a few French). The take-off grew rapidly thereafter. When 'Operation Dynamo' was ordered, it was reckoned that about 45,000 men could be got away.

One consequence of the confusion concerned the heavy AA guns. On Bridgeman's account, the aide-de-camp to the commander of the 2nd AA Brigade, Maj.-Gen. Henry Martin, asked him for orders. Bridgeman replied that the guns were to stay in action until they ran out of ammunition. Then men who had rifles were to be organised as infantry and the others sent to the beaches.[32] This verbal order became garbled, but Martin did not question his understanding that all AA gunners were to leave. He reasoned that, in these circumstances, the heavy units should spike (sabotage) their guns. AA defence was thus left to Bofors and Bren guns. Some frustrated men on the beaches bravely but futilely fired their rifles at attacking aircraft. By Walter Lord's account:

> Sometime after midnight, May 27–28, Martin appeared at Adam's headquarters to report that the job had been done. With rather a sense of achievement, one observer felt, he saluted smartly and announced, 'All the anti-aircraft guns have been spiked.' There was a long pause while a near-incredulous Adam absorbed this thunderbolt. Finally he looked up and merely said, 'You … fool, go away.'[33]

Whether the ellipsis covers a deleted expletive or merely a horrified pause is unclear. Bridgeman concluded that the lesson was that, even under the greatest stress, orders should be in writing.

On 28 May Gort told Gen. Blanchard of his order to evacuate – the first official information the French had. The Frenchman at first refused to give his own forces a similar order, although later that day evacuation was authorised by Weygand. Sebag-Montefiore recorded that French troops, now permitted to embark, were being refused access to British boats:

> Fagalde was incensed, and warned General Adam in writing that if it continued he would be forced to order his French troops to defend themselves with their guns. Fagalde was mollified somewhat when Adam immediately visited the bastion, and promised to issue an order that the anti-French behaviour was to stop. But Fagalde was hopping mad again when he learned that, far from remaining in situ to ensure that his order was complied with, Adam shortly afterwards boarded a ship bound for England.[34]

Adam's 1961 recollection was that Gort:

> ... sent me off to see Abrial to make quite clear the orders from the British Government to withdraw for embarkation and that French troops would be taken off. Abrial was pretty sour and as he had received no orders that it was not to be a fight to the end. It was not a pleasant meeting.

ORDERED HOME

In Adam's documents there is a small sheet of paper, dated 30 May 1940 and inscribed 'by order of C-in-C', ordering him home 'by the first possible opportunity; in order that you may help with the reforming of the new Army'. A handwritten addition reads: 'You will report in person to the War Office.' The opportunity to head home arose that night, when he met Brig. Frederick Lawson and some other officers. The first boat they found proved unseaworthy, and with oars of different lengths. They then found a folding canvas boat in the dunes and made their way to a destroyer anchored in the distance: 'Fred and his staff officers at the oars and I coxed.' Despite his protests, Brooke too was ordered home by Gort and joined Adam on the destroyer to Dover. Here they briefed Admiral Ramsay, the 'Dynamo' commander, about the situation before driving to London to report to the CIGS. That done, Adam took a train to Camberley and was 'delighted to see Doff and the children'.[35] This typically laconic comment contrasts with the drama implicit in a letter to Dorothy a few days earlier, in which he expressed concern that he did not expect to get back from France.

Before her death in 1972 Lady Adam asked that all their letters be destroyed. One survives. Written from France on 27 January 1940 it opens, 'My own darling', and comments that there were no birds about except magpies and jays, and that in the hard weather a lot of geese inland and partridges. The French had stopped all shooting for the duration. He then asks her to send him more laces for his Norwegian boots – 'an enormous success'. He ends: 'Fondest love, sweetheart. Take care of yourself and don't worry. I love you ever so much. Your loving Ronald.'[36]

After the evacuation, Adam wrote in his official report:

> The whole problem of withdrawal was rendered very much more difficult by the lack of time for preparation, shortage of military police, and boats. French transport [which encumbered roads] and Belgian refugees added to the problem, and at one time it appeared that this disorganization would stop the withdrawal of the force. If suitable police arrangements could have been made on the 26th much subsequent trouble would have been avoided.[37]

In the circumstances, getting 340,000 Allied soldiers – three-fifths British, the remainder French with a few determined Belgians – away to safety was a remarkable achievement, one of courage, desperation and German errors. This was more than seven times the estimate when Dynamo began – and they would have been Adam's 'rabble' rather than the fighting troops who in large numbers got away later.

Lt-Gen. Harold Alexander was left in Dunkirk to command the British rearguard. On the night Adam left, and over the next four nights, another 90,000 British and 113,000 French troops were taken off the beaches. On the night of 3–4 June the last 27,000 French, including Abrial and Fagalde, embarked. Like most of the French servicemen, the admiral and the general almost immediately returned to France, to surrender three weeks later.[38] Fagalde's report, written at the end of 1940, displayed the humiliation, despair and bitterness felt by many if not most French men and women at that time. The search for scapegoats by many of both nationalities was not edifying. The accounts of the relations between Fagalde and Abrial on the one hand, and Adam and the other British on the other, have the air of traditional stereotypes: Gallic excitability compared with British phlegm; or viewed from the other side of the Channel, French honour and *la perfide Albion*.

The Dunkirk evacuation did not end the British presence in France. South of the Somme the 51st Div. and some pioneer units fought a valiant action at Saint-Valéry until overcome on 12 June. Bridgeman was proved wrong about the Highland Division. Fortune and the other survivors were to spend nearly five years in captivity. Adam recorded that he was very sad that, by posting them to the Saar area, he had 'ordered the fate of this excellent division'. On the same day as the 51st were overcome, Brooke arrived in western France to command the remaining British troops and the British and Canadian reinforcements being landed to try to bolster French resistance. They failed. Some 144,000 men (and some ATS) were withdrawn through 'Operation Ariel' by the end of June. British casualties in France and Belgium were 11,000 dead, 14,000 wounded and 41,000 taken prisoner.[39] Particularly remembered with the defenders at Saint-Valéry are the three battalions of riflemen sent to hold Calais and whose sacrifice alongside the French defenders helped ensure so many got away at Dunkirk.

7

GUARDING THE NORTH

Dunkirk may have been a deliverance; it was still a defeat. After France fell, Britain awaited invasion. The most obvious site of a German attempt to land appeared to be Kent and Sussex, barely 20 miles from France. But the whole of the south and east coasts provided many potential landing points. Overall, 500 miles of coastline were judged as offering access to armoured vehicles – a greater distance than along the French frontier from the North Sea to Switzerland, only two-thirds of which had been covered by the Maginot Line. Britain had no coastal Maginot Line, although the Channel provided a formidable moat. There were static guns defending some ports, and a limited amount of mobile artillery. In France, over 1,000 field and heavier guns, 850 anti-tank guns and about 500 AA guns had been lost, along with 59,000 vehicles, 20,000 motorcycles, over 100,000 rifles, large numbers of other small arms, and vast stocks of ammunition and supplies. Six hundred tanks were lost (two-thirds of them light tanks), leaving in Britain 213 infantry and cruiser tanks and 618 light tanks, plus another 132 obsolete tanks.[1] The army was down to one-sixth of its normal artillery strength. Lt-Gen. Andrew Thorne's XII Corps, which was responsible for defending Kent, Sussex and parts of Hampshire and Surrey, had at the end of June no anti-tank regiment or anti-tank guns – nor any tanks – in its whole area.[2] So weapons to fight an invader once ashore were few and poorly distributed.

The build-up of new equipment was slow: delivery of 25-pounder field guns was 35 a month. The establishment of a home defence division was 70 guns and, with 27 such divisions, 1,900 guns were needed. By August, monthly delivery numbers had reached 72, and there was also a steady if still slow rise in the supply of tanks, small arms and other needs into the autumn.[3] David Edgerton was more sanguine than most historians about the supply situation, noting that in August 1940 Britain sent 102 infantry and cruiser tanks and some light tanks to Egypt. But this move was because Britain dare not risk another disastrous defeat abroad. Certainly, over the ensuing months, production of heavy arms and aircraft increased at impressive rates. But that summer weapons were very short. Once convinced that the British would fight on, the United States provided 300 old 75mm field guns and 250,000 rifles (of a different calibre from the British).[4] Canada supplied large numbers of Ross rifles, already withdrawn from general service in 1916. Aircraft and other *matériel* ordered by the French from the United States were diverted to Britain, paid for by Britain's depleted currency holdings. Lend-lease supplies did not start until well into 1941.

Seventy years later we know the Germans had neither the means nor the stomach to attempt an amphibious landing against determined air and sea opposition. The Führer assumed the British would see sense and come to terms; he was already turning his mind to his real enemy, the Soviet Union. But the British did not know that, and it was as well that they did not. While it was the threat of invasion that led many of Britain's traditional elite privately to advocate a parley, the majority of the nation was inspired, if uneasily, by Churchill's rhetoric to face the possibility of battle in their own land.

As the evacuation from Dunkirk began, Gen. Ironside was on 27 May appointed C-in-C Home Forces. The plans he drew up, in the event of an invasion of Britain, were to delay the enemy at the beaches and then to 'corral' them at a 'GHQ Line' about 40 miles inland, where anti-tank and other defences could defend the main industrial areas. The basis of this line was such existing obstacles as canals and rivers, supplemented by many miles of dug anti-tank trenches and thousands of pillboxes. With the enemy held by these means the strategy was then to rush in reinforcements where needed. In addition, important communication centres (nodal points) were to be turned into anti-tank islands. All this aimed at preventing the panzers moving at will, as they had done in Poland, Belgium and northern France. Mines were laid and barbed wire and other beach defences erected, and potential aircraft landing sites obstructed. Less than two months later, Gen. Alan Brooke replaced Ironside. He favoured a more fluid defence, with less stress on the inland stop-lines and more on holding the coastal areas, with rapid reinforcement close to the landing places. The construction of pillboxes and stop-lines continued, but a greater emphasis was given to developing and strengthening mobile reserves as more equipment became available.[5]

On 8 June, a week after leaving France, Lt-Gen. Adam was appointed GOC, Northern Command, with headquarters in York. His command, one of five into which Great Britain was divided, bisected England south from the mid-point of the Scottish border as far as Nottingham and Northampton, from there sweeping north-east to the Wash. A less likely target for a major German invasion than Southern or Eastern Commands, Adam's region was nonetheless a possible target of feints or diversionary landings from Germany and Norway, or a major landing to drive towards the northern industrial towns. With the supply of heavy weapons shaky enough in the south and east, Adam's command came lower in priority. The fixed port defences in his area totalled four 9.2in guns, twenty-two 6in guns and sixteen smaller guns. Lacking substantial material means, and with a large proportion of untrained or partly trained men, it was ingenuity and improvisation that had initially to provide the main means of defence. The measures undertaken or planned in Northern Command included beach defences, minefields, explosive petroleum-based 'flame fougasses', the blocking of roads and rail, and the immobilisation of ports, canals, inland waterways, factories and mines.[6] Late in July, Brooke paid the first of six visits to Northern Command during Adam's time there. In his diary he briefly recorded: 'A lot of good work has been done here.'[7]

The reliance on obstructive and, if necessary destructive, measures served to emphasise the initial shortage of heavy weaponry. In September 1940 Northern Command comprised five infantry divisions and one tank brigade. By May 1941, when Adam left for London, there were four infantry divisions (each of three brigades) in coastal areas and, held back from the coast, three more infantry divisions, one armoured division and one armoured brigade. (By contrast, forces in the south and east at this time totalled eighteen infantry divisions, with another twelve infantry divisions, three armoured divisions and two anti-tank brigades in reserve.) The changes over the eight months look impressive, although the number of units does not necessarily reflect the amount and quality of weaponry in service or the forces' readiness for action. Northern Command's War Diary for January 1941 shows that although Adam had 287,000 men under him, over a quarter were still in training, and only 19,000 were in armoured or anti-tank battalions. Their formation into independent units for purposes of mobility is an indication of their weakness and paucity.[8] An important element of the action plan was co-ordination with the Home Guard, the coastguard, the navy and the air force. All ADGB came under the Air Ministry, with AA guns under Fighter Command. In the Northern Command area in July 1940 such defences comprised 277 heavy AA guns, 132 light AA guns and over 1,100 AA machine guns; in September there were rather fewer, following transfers to protect London and other cities.

MILITARY MISMATCH

Urgent defensive actions apart, Adam's experience during that year in Northern Command reinforced his conviction of the need to revolutionise the army's personnel policy. The fundamental problem was that, compared with the air force and the navy, many of the army's recruits were of lower intellectual, educational, psychological and physical calibre. The army was an unpopular service. Many of the survivors of the First World War, and their families, had little respect for the brass hats who they believed (with much justification) had sent so many tens of thousands of men casually to their deaths.[9] The fact that the French and German generals had followed the same methods of warfare from 1914 to 1918 was no consolation.

The senior officers in the Second World War had been junior officers in the First and knew well what had happened to many of their friends and contemporaries. This, and the growing shortage of manpower as the second war progressed, explains the caution and the economy with men with which most British generals conducted their operations in 1939–45, and for which they were criticised by some Americans. Furthermore, the increasing technological sophistication of weaponry as the war went on meant that proportionally more and more men were required to service and repair that weaponry, so fewer men – absolutely and relatively – were available for the 'teeth' arms of the army. Compared with the First World War, the air force and the navy held a larger proportion of Britain's armed men, and the demands of war production for skilled men was better recognised. Grappling for a balance between the competing claims on the nation's manpower – and increasingly its womanpower – was a constant problem for the authorities.

When war came again, many young men did not need their elders' advice to avoid wearing khaki. The National Service (Armed Forces) Act of 3 September 1939 permitted men registering for service to express a preference for joining one of the three services. Consequently, the number of men wanting to join the senior and junior services exceeded the needs of these services, which as a result could take their pick. Thus, at the first call-up proclamation in October 1939, 39,000 men expressed a preference for the navy and 68,000 for the air force, between them almost half the total registering for service. In later years, the proportion wishing to join the senior and junior services was sometimes greater still, at times well over half. Many fewer than this could be satisfied. Other than in the summer of 1940, the army attracted few volunteers. In that year the navy turned down four out of five men who wanted to join, and more men volunteered to join the RAF than waited to be called up. The service preference effect was magnified because men who volunteered ahead of the call-up date for their age group were also more likely to get into the service they wanted. Throughout the war the services maintained at least a nominal distinction between volunteers and pressed men. There are men (and women) still alive who are proud that they stepped forward ahead of time.

So the army was convinced that it had been left with many men who had not wanted to wear uniform, and khaki in particular, and others turned down by the other services. Many were of lower intelligence or skills, or of indifferent physique, or both. The army thus had a disproportionate number of the 'psychopathic tenth' of the male population, in the disdainful words of Robert Ahrenfeldt, the deputy assistant director of army psychiatry during the war.[10] Initially, men of poor physique and intelligence were rejected but, as the war continued, standards were lowered and such men were accepted. As Maj.-Gen. A.J.K. Piggott, who was responsible for recruiting, put it after the war: the army got 'all the unwilling, the least intelligent and the least desirable'.[11] Another observer, David Fraser (a Grenadier lieutenant on D-Day), was even more brutal:

> Universal service meant that all sorts were now conscripted. The small regular army had freely discharged volunteers if their conduct or attitudes were unsatisfactory. The Territorial Army had consisted of men willing to give their spare time – a moral elite. Now, in common with the general run of men quietly if reluctantly accepting the demands of the hour, there was conscripted every resentful or maladjusted misfit, provided he passed the medical test imposed. These took time to sort out. They were a tiny minority, but they heightened the disturbance felt by the majority at the sudden plunge into uniform.[12]

However, historian David French questioned this widely held wartime view, contending that the army 'attracted at least half its fair share, if not more, of the better-educated part of the population'.[13]

The army compounded its recruitment difficulties by lacking a coherent personnel policy to select suitable men for the required tasks. In a volunteer army, a potential recruit's right to choose his own corps was essential; the Army Act banned compulsory transfers between corps or regiments. Each controlled its own recruitment: part of the appeal to recruits was the glamour of one or other regiment's dress uniform, its colours and battle honours. A second Act passed on 3 September was needed to provide for compulsory transfers. Moreover, in peacetime there was time to ensure that slow learners could pick up the rudiments of military skills. In the wartime rush to expand, training was curtailed: some men were left baffled by their instruction, and were sometimes bundled into tasks beyond their capacity. Conversely, because there was no adequate schedule of army trades or a scientific selection policy, many other men were given duties below their abilities. Square pegs and round holes were innumerable. Disillusionment with the military authorities increased, and morale suffered.

When men registered for service, voluntarily or by call-up, the Ministry of Labour and National Service (MLNS) was responsible for allocating those with trade (i.e. skilled) experience to approximately equivalent trades within the army. But most men did not have a recognised trade. In some cases they had had one, but with so much unemployment during the 1930s, they had been obliged to take up any available work. Previous skills had become rusty or were unrecognised in the haste of recruiting a mass army. In theory, at the recruiting medical each man was seen by an interviewing officer, and on the basis of this was allocated to a corps or regiment. But interviews could not always be carried out. So the ministry allocated many men as 'indented' by the War Office for different arms – like so many blankets or steel helmets. So there was no guarantee at all that the numbers recruited met either the demand or the suitability of men to their postings. Indeed, when an interview did take place, and a man was earmarked for a particular arm, the MLNS sometimes had to overrule the recommendation in response to the needs for the numbers specified by the War Office. Men were posted on the basis of what little was known of them, which was sometimes only their medical grade. To find tradesmen as the war progressed, the ministry did what it could by continually combing out industry to find fitters, electricians, radio mechanics and other tradesmen for the army, indicating whether they were skilled, semi-skilled or suitable for further trade training. As many skilled men were taking up the service preference provision, the navy and the RAF were eagerly taking them on.

Army personnel procedures were thus in a mess. Adam later held himself partly responsible, for when militia conscription was introduced in 1939 he had as DCIGS asked for funds to set up a selection procedure. He was offered £5,000, which he considered quite inadequate:

> I blame myself for not having accepted it and tried at least a small-scale experiment, but our manpower problems were so great and we expected war in the Autumn, so nothing more was done about it.[14]

One positive step had been taken by the War Office. In anticipation of psychiatric problems arising from battle experience, early in 1940 it appointed a psychiatrist to each army command. But in the field of selection the initiative was left to individual commands: the first was in October 1939 when AA Command at the initiative of its commander, Lt-Gen. Pile, subjected certain specialists to ability tests devised by a Cambridge academic. More widely, from July 1940 new recruits undertook selection tests at the establishments and units to which they had already been posted. But, significantly, it was laid down that these tests were to assist COs and not to interfere with their judgement. Regimental officers carried out the verbal tests. When Adam took over Northern Command in June he found that the command's psychiatrist, Lt-Col G.R. Hargreaves (formerly with the Tavistock Clinic[15]) had already taken things further with more wide-ranging experiments for intelligence-testing many men. The results provided statistical confirmation of wild mismatches between men's abilities and the work to which they had been allocated. In October, Brig. J.R. Rees, the army's consulting psychiatrist and also a Tavistock veteran, arranged for low-scoring men to be referred to a psychiatrist.

On the basis of Hargeaves's experiments, in October Adam wrote to the War Office, urging them to take up the matter seriously. Further tests in Northern Command in January 1941 showed that 20 per cent of each infantry intake and 50 per cent of each Pioneer Corps intake were capable of more efficient service than in the corps to which they were posted. Conversely, 20 per cent of each infantry intake and 50 per cent of each RAC intake could not be fully efficient in those arms. Overall, Adam recorded, 4 per cent of all intakes were found to be 'useless' for training as soldiers, a rather less pessimistic assessment than Ahrenfeldt.[16]

During his year with Northern Command Adam also showed his interest in education as a means of improving morale and therefore fighting efficiency. In October 1940 he was appointed as colonel-commandant of the Army Educational Corps (AEC), an honorary position given to a member of the royal family or a senior officer. The duties are largely ceremonial, although a colonel-commandant could be a useful advocate in high places for a regiment or corps. A month earlier he took up the same position in his own regiment, the RA (and in 1945 the Army Dental Corps). More pertinently, at Northern Command on 18 October he issued a memorandum to all COs on education in a wartime army. Referring to an Army Council order issued the previous month, he stressed how education was:

> most important this winter and I want all Commanders to foster it as much as they can […] Our war-time Army, being a cross-section of the community, has within it, men who, prior to being called-up had entered on a course of study for a degree or some other professional, technical or commercial qualification. In many cases much can be done for these men.[17]

The use of educational facilities was arranged with local authorities, universities and colleges. But to cater for the educational needs of the army as a whole, Adam wrote that the solution was within the army. He wanted all commanding officers [COs] 'to appoint an officer who, in addition to his normal regimental duties, will be responsible for looking after the educational requirements of his unit in much the same way as officers are responsible for games and general welfare'. Putting education on a par with games was certainly a break with tradition and practice. Such officers should find out which 'officers and ORs [were] capable of imparting knowledge in various forms, e.g. Talks, lectures, control of discussion group and debates, and vocational training.' AEC officers, he stated, should be engaged only on educational duties. In Northern Command he had forty-five AEC personnel, headed by a lieutenant-colonel, with twenty-five other officers and nineteen warrant officers and sergeants. It is significant that, at this early stage in the development of army education, Adam understands that it is not only officers who have knowledge and experience to impart: education was not just a top-down activity. He had from the outset no anxieties about soldiers discussing and debating.

So, apart from putting the defence of the north-east coast in as good an order as the men and *matériel* permitted, Adam in those twelve months learnt a great deal that would inspire his subsequent actions. On 24 June 1941, Brooke recorded: 'lunched with Adam who was very full of what he was going to do as AG'.[18] He would have a full plate, with the AG's already ample responsibility for mobilisation and demobilisation, discipline, welfare, education, medical services and prisoners of war (POWs), to which was to be added the vague but crucial duty of maintaining morale. When Brooke became CIGS at the end of 1941, the periodic lunches (usually at the Carlton Grill), provided opportunities for the exchange of ideas and the discussion of problems between the two most senior men in the army. The friendship formed thirty years earlier in India between 'Brookie' and 'George' provided each with a sympathetic ear.

Adam's appointment as AG was straightforward. He needed no outside patron or reforming war minister to leapfrog him over more senior men. His quietly effective achievement as DCIGS, as corps commander with the BEF and as GOC Northern Command stood on his record. Sir John Dill, with whom he had served in France, was now CIGS, and his friend Brooke was C-in-C Home Forces. The permanent secretary at the War Office, P.J. Grigg, had worked with him for two years. They all knew him but probably all underestimated him. When he took up his duties as AG on 1 June 1941 he could extend the basis of the 'New Model Army' that he had begun under Hore-Belisha. Now, under the impetus of war, he introduced major – and to many, unsettling – reforms: first, improvements to the selection and training of recruits; second, better selection of officers; third, in parallel with the first two, measures to improve morale, especially through improved welfare and education. The problems in all three fields were already recognised by mid-1941. Adam's achievement was to implement reform, resist the powerful and widespread opposition, even at the highest levels, and to give strong support to those responsible, under his authority, for achieving the results required.

8

PEGS AND HOLES

Early in the war, the Scots comedian Will Fyffe told a joke how, on being called up and asked what his job was, he said that he was a plumber. To show his skill he was told to solder two pipes together. His report read: 'Joint perfectly done.' The army made him a cook.

This popular recognition of the army's chronic incapacity to allocate its human resources on a rational basis was not amusing to the War Office, and even less so to the many tens of thousands of men who were misallocated to jobs in the first two years and more of the war. Two weeks after taking up his post as AG in June 1941, Lt-Gen. Sir Ronald Adam wrote that the army was 'wasting its manpower in this war as badly as it did in the last'. A man was posted to a corps, 'almost entirely on the need of the moment and without any effort to determine his fitness for the corps in question'.[1] In military terms this was grossly inefficient. In personal terms, at best it meant poor morale; at worst it could lead to desertion or psychiatric breakdown. Encouraged by Brig. Rees and Lt-Col Hargreaves, Adam formed a Directorate for Selection of Personnel (DSP) that gathered 'a wealth of psychological talent from all over Britain': an inspector qualified in psychiatry, two deputy assistant adjutant-generals, two staff captains and an outside testing staff of 15 officers and 150 sergeant testers. By the autumn it had defined some 500 trades and other skilled employments.[2]

Initially, on registering for service, a man's assessment had usually been based on about five minutes with a regimental recruiting officer and a check on his educational level. But such officers had had no worthwhile training in personnel selection, nor had the regimental officers who administered the changes made in July 1940. Under Adam's new regime, a matrix test was devised to weed out what, in the terms of the day, were called 'mental defectives'. This was a non-verbal test, and so was independent of any educational standard the man had achieved. In civilian life such tests had indicated the ability to absorb knowledge. Concepts such as mental age and IQ (intelligence quotient) were rejected as mainly suitable for children. The pre-entry selection and medical procedures were then allocated forty minutes, including twenty on the matrix test. This was an improvement, although still not wholly satisfactory. These procedures were in turn phased out in favour of tests standardised to give the basis for an ability cross-section of the army.

The new tests put men into six Standard Grades: SG1, SG2, SG3 plus, SG3 minus, SG4 and SG5. SG1 comprised the top 10 per cent of the men, SG5 the bottom 10 per cent, with 20 per cent in each of the other SGs. An SG5 of doubtful physique would be rejected. As a result of these changes, the MLNS could allocate men to the different arms much more effectively and distribute men of intelligence to each arm, and so met their approximate needs. For certain corps, minimum intelligence levels were laid down.[3]

Sorting out army personnel had been made even more difficult by the hurried recruitment in June to August 1940 of over 300,000 men. This was a political decision at Churchill's insistence in order to impress on the British people the gravity of their situation and on the Dominions and the USA of British determination to fight on. But, like the doubling of the TA and the introduction of conscription in the spring of 1939, it is doubtful if Hitler was impressed. All three moves were grand political gestures that caused major administrative problems for the army in trying to find enough accommodation, clothing, supplies, weapons and, not least, capable instructors. Initially the men recruited in the summer of 1940 were formed into 120 infantry battalions, with a view to their being transferred to other arms as and when artillery, tanks and other equipment became available. Further army recruitment was suspended for some months until this mass could be digested, leaving the other two services with even better opportunities in the interim to scoop up the skilled men they wanted.

Moreover, in Adam's view, the establishment of a rational personnel policy was hampered by the practice of recruitment into and training by individual corps and regiments. This was a particular problem for the infantry, for whom the Cardwell system had assumed a sacred character. Ever since these reforms in the 1870s and 1880s, the line infantry regiments had been anchored in administration and (theoretically) in sentiment to a particular county, region or major city. The Cardwell principle was that each regiment comprised two battalions, one that provided training facilities at home while the second was overseas. In fact the home battalion was often an undermanned shadow formation. Second, the theory was that each regiment drew largely on local men; in practice there were always men from other parts of the British Isles in each regiment. As early as 1878 only three Highland regiments out of nineteen Scottish infantry regiments had more than 60 per cent of either officers or men from Scotland.[4] Up to 1900, only three out of the sixty-five territorially based British and Irish infantry regiments had 70 per cent of men of local origin, and only nineteen had 50 per cent; one had less than 10 per cent.[5] In time of war – even minor campaigns such as the Zulu and the Ashanti wars – cross-posting was necessary to make up numbers in a particular battalion or regiment. In the First World War transfers and cross-postings became dominant.

By 1917 the regimental system had effectively collapsed. Reliance on volunteers between the wars and the Army Act's block on compulsory transfers between corps meant that many corps and regiments were often under strength in the 1920s and 1930s. The regimental system only really worked well when it was least needed: in peacetime and during small wars.[6] In David French's words, the regiment was an 'imagined community'.[7]

For all its mythology, the Cardwell system was hollow from the start. Infantry officers' passionate intensity in its defence was a perverse proof of this.

A DISPASSIONATE EYE

With regard to the question of local postings, Adam viewed the problem pragmatically, although he recognised the desirability as much as possible. He stressed the advantage of posting men to units originating in home areas, and not just the infantry. This led to 'happier conditions in units', and it also would 'do away with a great deal of political criticism'.[8] However, infantry training was still taking place at too many regimental centres, a hangover from pre-war days when each regiment trained its own men in its own way. A month after he took up his post, the Executive Committee of the Army Council (ECAC) agreed to reduce the fifty-eight infantry and four machine-gun initial training centres to fourteen and one respectively, to be known as pool centres identified only by numbers. This saved some 14,000 trained men for other duties, and ensured more uniform methods and standards of training. But Adam was not satisfied. On 1 July Sir James Grigg, the permanent secretary at the War Office, warned David Margesson, the minister, that the AG had under consideration 'some rather more far-reaching proposals with regard to the formation of one Corps for the Infantry', which he may find necessary 'for urgent administrative reasons'. Grigg offered some reassurance to traditionalists: 'I may add that A.G.'s present proposals are addressed to the period of the war only, and are not intended to be perpetuated in peacetime.'[9]

The bombshell came on 19 July in a memorandum from Adam that the only way battle casualties could be replaced was by transfers from other regiments or from training centres: 'it is probable that the entire outputs of several pool centres will need to be drafted overseas in regiments other than their own'. He concluded: 'For these reasons, a project to form a Corps of Infantry is worth consideration', as the peacetime regimental system was now 'unworkable and almost a farce'. The formation of a Corps of Infantry, he stated, would make transfers from one regiment to another unnecessary as the filling of requirements would be 'a mere matter of posting'.[10]

This was highly provocative. Among the infantry and their partisans there was furious and widespread resistance. Adam recognised that the main argument against a Corps of Infantry was that of morale, but which he thought applied 'mainly to colonels and the more senior officers'. Would it be too cynical to suggest that the opposition to his proposal was partly because many such colonels would have risked being displaced or put in command of units of overtly disparate origin? Regimental identity was very important, although its intensity certainly increased the higher the rank. It was the officers and senior NCOs who were more conscious of what their forbears had done at Minden, Ramillies, Talavera or Waterloo, who revered the tattered colours that had been borne aloft at battles long ago and which now decorated the officers' mess or the regimental church, who dined off the regimental plate, who revelled in the quirks of each regiment's uniform, and who were grasped most warmly into the family of the regiment. The problem was to retain the inspirational element of the regiment but to eliminate the parochialism. Interwar, some COs had even considered officers who wanted to attend the Staff College as 'disloyal' to the regiment by seeking advancement elsewhere. Against David French's description of the 'almost metaphysical vision' of the regiment[11] soldiers often took a prosaic although passionate view of the military community of which they were a part. In all armies, the loyalty of the infantryman in particular is to his mates in his section, his platoon, and possibly his company. These were the men upon whom he relied in times of peril, and who relied on him in turn. As one First World War soldier put it:

> whatever its size a man's world was his section – at most his platoon; all that mattered to him was the one little boatload of castaways with whom he was marooned on a desert island making shift to keep off the weather and any sudden attack of wild beasts.[12]

For many men even the company, and probably the battalion was an abstraction. Yet, as the Salerno 'mutiny' (see chapter 11) showed, rank and file soldiers could identify not only with their regiments but with their divisions and with the Eighth Army as a whole, so long as such formations were winners and they were being treated fairly.[13]

NO CORPS OF INFANTRY

By mid-1941 over half the 120 infantry battalions hastily recruited a year earlier were being disbanded to form new units in other arms, so the AG's department had to juggle with large numbers of men. Adam argued that:

> there is little doubt that it [the regimental tradition] will continue if a Corps of Infantry is formed in the same way as units of the Royal Regiment of Artillery maintain their old traditions [...] It is not denied that 'tradition' is

most valuable for the morale of the British Infantryman but […] provided that identity of Regiments is maintained, and transfers and cross-postings especially in the senior ranks of officers and other ranks are restricted as far as possible, tradition and 'Esprit de Corps' remain, at any rate, in war. Officers and other ranks who have to be transferred soon assimilate the 'Esprit de Corps' of their new units.[14]

As for officers: 'Legally they can be ordered to serve in any unit in any arm.' But this mundane truth only served to emphasise the emotional basis of the reaction.

Perhaps Adam was misled by the fact that the cavalry regiments, along with the 'rude mechanicals' of the RTC, were now all within the compass of the Royal Armoured Corps (RAC). When the seventeen cavalry regiments had joined eight RTC battalions in the new corps, they retained in their names the historical distinctions between lancers, hussars, heavy and light dragoons, and dragoon guards (as well as the yeomanry, always uncomfortably linked in the TA). Their nominal identities were not impaired, even if their roles and equipment were often now less distinct. Within the RA, the RHA retained their role as mobile gunners, ending the Second World War with self-propelled guns. Indeed Adam's own regiment's tenacious insistence of its separate identity after the merger of the RFA and the RGA in 1920 (and its survival up to the present day) should have made him more sensitive to the infantry's wish to cling to their own identities.

His arguments were too rational. To compare the infantry with the artillery appears disingenuous, and suggests he did not fully grasp the psychology of infantry fighting. Or was he just deploying this argument to justify the changes he believed to be necessary? RA regiments were distinguished by numbers and after 1918 had only tenuous local links. Between 1914 and 1918 he had himself been transferred several times from one numbered unit to another. Although also nominally numbered, infantry regiments were better known by their names. Many were commonplace, based on a county or city name, but others were full of glamour – the Green Howards, the Sherwood Foresters, the South Wales Borderers, the King's Own, the Buffs, the Cameronians, the Black Watch – redolent of historic glories. Many regiments had nicknames: some were claimed with pride, others were dubbed by rival regiments and of a nature certain to provoke violence when openly used. For historical reasons, some regiments were known as light infantry or fusiliers, although the distinctions by the twentieth century were slight to non-existent. Different regiments had different traditions of behaviour, such as the extra-quick march of the rifle regiments, which did not slope arms; of uniform – even in the new battle dress – such as the hackles on the headgear of fusiliers, and the small duplicate badges worn by the Gloucesters on the back of their headgear; Scottish regiments who wore the kilt and those who wore trews; of music, such as the pipe and fife bands. These were the 'curious regimental customs' cited by RAMC Lt-Col Nichols in his 1937 Staff College lecture.

The rites and rituals of drill, battle anniversary parades, spit and polish ('bull'), clothing (appropriately called 'uniform', whether drab khaki or colourfully ceremonial), military bands, bugle calls and other procedures were all part of the process of persuading the members of a regiment or corps that it was, 'based upon a shared comradeship that transcended the inequalities of power and rewards that existed within it. It was something so fundamentally pure that it could call on its members to lay down their lives for it'.[15]

Regimental loyalty and devotion reflect that capacity of many − perhaps most − men and women to submerge at least a part of their individuality into a greater whole, formal or informal: a sports team or its supporters club, a social club, a religious body, an old school or college, a political party, a fraternity or sorority, a union, a freemasonry lodge, a trade guild, a class, a ship, a clan, a club, a tribe, a nation, a closely knit profession, or whatever it may be. Some religions and the military apart, few such groups demand that its members die for the greater good; hence the need for the military by strict discipline to reduce the individual to a part of its whole. Acting in unison can be seductively attractive. The individual is diminished, the collectivity enhanced.

As Lt-Col Nichols observed, the herd instinct is the basis of discipline but it can also override logical thinking. Getting the advantage of the former and counteracting the latter is the delicate balance needed. The need for disciplined conformity, on the face of it, is greater in the infantry than other corps. In the artillery the gun crew acts as a technical unit, each man with his own task, although capable of taking over others' tasks should they fall. Gunners stand in the second or third line of battle, although by no means beyond danger. In a tank or armoured car, the crew must act as a team (as on a ship or in an aircraft with several crew members). But the foot soldier, for all the parade ground and battle drill by section, platoon, company or battalion, is in the last resort alone on the battlefield, and in the leading rank. Like the pilot of a single-seat attack aircraft, or the battlefield mine-clearer, his success in beating his enemy – and his own life or death – depend ultimately on his own skill and his own actions, plus not least his own luck. Yet, ironically, after the technical and the armoured arms, and the parachute regiments, the commandos and the Reconnaissance Corps had their pick of CT1 men (of the highest combatant temperament; see below) and the best of the CT2s, the infantry included many men who were intellectually and psychologically the least suitable for that arm. So there is a paradox: disciplined conformity needs to be combined with individual initiative. In 1932 Basil Liddell Hart stressed that:

> To train infantry, which is essentially the tactical arm, is to exercise an art whereas to train the technical arms is to apply a science. The infantry soldier

is less of a technician, but he is a field-craftsman this is the title of honour to which he may aspire in the profession of arms.[16]

The following year Brig. Archibald Wavell called for a more imaginative training and education of infantrymen: 'fit, active, inquisitive and offensive – confident of making ground with their own weapons', and not just adjuncts to artillery and armour.[17] But this was not often achieved. Adam was disappointed that his reforms had not been able to raise the quality of the infantry as well as providing for more skilled men. Consequently, with the greater risk of being injured or killed, the infantry had a disproportionate number of psychiatric breakdowns and of desertions. The expression of fear, as recommended by Nichols, conflicted with the male identity inculcated in the army, or machismo as a later generation would call it.

General Horrocks wrote poignantly of the foot soldiers:

they must force themselves forward with a sickening feeling in the pit of their stomachs, fighting an almost uncontrollable urge to fling themselves down as close to the earth as they can. Even then they are alone amidst all the fury; carrying their loneliness with them.[18]

Poor Bloody Infantry, indeed.

Liddell Hart, Wavell and Horrocks, although infantrymen themselves, could view the issues rationally and were not unduly sentimental about the accumulation of infantry attitudes, traditions and actions that appeared to be under attack from Adam's proposals for a 'Corps of Infantry'. Margesson feared the political reaction, and the concept was rejected. It left among the infantry a dark suspicion of the AG. The appointment of Alan Brooke as CIGS at the end of 1941 did not help: the two most senior military members of the Army Council (AC) were now gunners, and old and close friends besides. Adam denied any bias, regretting the feeling in the army that the AG's department did not foster the regimental spirit in the infantry. He emphasised that from the deputy AG downwards the officers responsible for the plans at the War Office were infantrymen.[19]

Conservatism was not confined to the infantry. Recruits to cavalry regiments in 1939 may not have had horses but they still did foot drill with sabres hanging at their waists, as if those ghastly tanks had never been invented. Nor were gunners innocent. One anecdote had a training film on gun drill with a busy crew calculating the range, traversing and elevating, setting the fuse, loading, firing and unloading, all in a bustle of activity. Among the sound and fury, one man stood by apparently aimlessly. Enquiry revealed that in earlier days his duty had been to hold the officer's horse.

THE COMING OF THE GSC

The shortage of skilled men for all three services led to a committee being set up late in 1941 under Sir William Beveridge on the services' and industry's supply and use of skilled men. It reported in November that the army was particularly culpable of misuse. All recruiting of skilled men into the army was stopped pending the analysis of 9,800 alleged cases of misuse of skills, only 1,300 of which proved justified. But the effect on the army was salutary.[20] Having gone from virtually no job analysis at all in the beginning, the army had reacted by producing far too many categories. These were now rationalised down to nine trades: those on combatant duties, drivers (all vehicles), maintenance men (mainly mechanical engineers), signallers, layers of line operations (e.g. gunlayers, predictor operators), clerks and foremen, administrative and domestic duties, armed pioneers, unarmed pioneers.

After Beveridge's report appeared, many skilled men were left in civilian life in their reserved employment, with some called up later. The concept and interpretation of reserved occupations were also tightened up. One problem for the army was that it needed men to work with hand tools under any conditions, whereas the various skilled trades in civilian life had become narrowly specialised and accustomed to using specialised equipment. Industry's technicians were engaged mainly on production, whereas the forces' need was largely for technicians skilled in maintenance and repair, sometimes under battlefield conditions. Nor was the standard of men available as high as Adam would have liked, but the need was urgent. Unemployment in the 1930s, the demands of the munitions industry, the muddle of the TA mobilisation early in the war, and the continued reorganisation of the army made it difficult to find skilled manpower throughout the conflict.[21] Training centres were set up to train men – and increasingly women – for the services and industry. No system could be perfect and many men remained in the wrong job, as Adam recorded:

> When Antwerp was freed [in 1944], and divers required to clear mines in the harbour, the men were found within 24 hours by sorting their cards in the Hollerith machine. It made me feel rather guilty, as all who had been divers in civil life should have been in the Navy.[22]

In this instance, the system had failed at a very early stage. Other errors were corrected by chance. On one occasion Adam was telephoned by an army commander who had just been talking to men in a detention barracks. The commander had interviewed one young man who had been in trouble almost continually and found that his one wish was to be a cook. Adam promised to send him for training if the Army Council (AC) would suspend his sentence. This was done and the man proved a great success and ended the war as a sergeant-major instructor in the Army Catering Corps.

Brushing the infantry selection and training issue under the War Office carpet in 1941 did not solve the underlying problem. The infantry's victory over the corps concept proved of short duration and self-defeating, for it contributed to an even more drastic move that affected the whole of army recruiting. A year of reform was lost. The problem of mispostings and of the subsequent transfers – of square pegs obstinately jammed into round holes – remained. Defeated over the Corps of Infantry, Adam tried again: he was not easily deflected from a course he considered essential. Prompted from within the War Office, Beveridge had taken up the idea of a single training regime. With this backing, Adam persuaded the AC to tackle the problem again, and at source. In January 1942 it agreed to establish a General Service Corps (GSC) to which all recruits, irrespective of their potential as officers, NCOs or tradesmen, would be initially posted.

At a press conference on 28 May 1942 the AC stressed that the move was motivated 'solely in the interests of efficiency; its aim is to get men in the right place early in their Army career and to avoid unnecessary waste of time and instructors in training men, particularly specialists for an Arm for which they were unsuited'.[23] The degree of emphasis reveals the resistance encountered. Apart from learning basic military skills at their Initial Training Units, the recruits would undertake various aptitude tests under a staff of personnel selection officers (PSOs), assisted by sergeant testers and clerks. This was well before the availability of computers, but the classification of personnel was much helped by Hollerith's punched card records.

During the first six weeks of initial training in the GSC potential tradesmen were checked over, potential officers and NCOs noted, and men with psychological problems weeded out for service in a stress–reduced role (such as the Pioneer Corps) or for discharge. Importantly, each man's 'combatant temperament' could be assessed. Those judged to be CT1 – 'markedly suited by disposition and personality for combatant role' – amounted to 5 per cent of the men; those in CT3 (at the opposite extreme) were 3 per cent. Obviously many of the other 92 per cent took on combatant roles and acquitted themselves well. Not all stress problems could be detected at this stage, many were only revealed or created by battle experience. Of all wartime discharges, the highest percentage was for psychiatric reasons. During the war psychiatrists examined 225,000 men referred by unit medical officers (MOs), and recommended psychiatric treatment or medical downgrading for 80 per cent of them. In the second half of 1941 the army was every month discharging an average of 1,300 men who had broken down through psychoneurosis during training. The more stringent screening under the GSC reduced this figure markedly. Psychiatric interviews at an early stage could weed out psychopaths or other disturbed characters, and ensure that individuals of low mental capacity or emotional instability would not be placed in conditions beyond their capacity to cope. However, this was not the same as trying to make a precise prediction of how an individual might break down in combat.

By the end of the war, remedial psychiatry had made considerable advances but only after stiff resistance. Psychiatrists too had to learn a lot by moving from caring for individuals to caring for groups. They were also fighting on two fronts: on the one hand, against mental disease, and on the other, against resistance not only from some in leading military and political quarters but also from within the medical profession. The latter resistance delayed the provision of psychiatric treatment for troops sent to North Africa in November 1942, and its introduction later meant that few of those affected and not treated early on were able to return to battle. By September 1943 forward psychiatric centres in Italy saved many men from being sent to the rear.[24] Within six days of D-Day, 10–20 per cent of casualties were from battle exhaustion. However, the forward treatment by now available meant that in 1944–45 in north-west Europe one-third of psychiatric cases returned to duty.[25] Although women were normally subject to less stressful service conditions, 50 per cent of ATS discharges were for psychiatric reasons (compared with 30 per cent of men). Defence writer Georgina Natzio suggested that women were probably less able to cope with the demands of service life, and more likely to suffer from minor complaints, or were more willing to admit to them.[26]

Each man after his six weeks in the GSC would be passed on for further training with an appropriate arm or, in a few cases, an Officer Cadet Training Unit (OCTU), depending on his record during those six weeks.[27] However, selection testing did not provide a perfect fit between the aptitudes (and wishes) of the individual soldier and the needs of the army: practical demands of the moment ensured the latter took priority. Nor did any force go overseas with every man having gone through the new selection procedure. Nor could the system alter the fact that the army simply did not receive enough recruits of sufficient intelligence to fill all the skilled and exacting jobs.

Initially it had been planned that only the conscripts would go to the GSC, but the volunteers were of necessity soon included, although offered a better chance of serving in the arm of their choice. The GSC system was not applied to the Guards, 'who suffered no such unseemly interference in their well-tried ways'.[28] Almost all guardsmen were volunteers. At the other military extreme the Non-Combatant Corps, composed of conscientious objectors, avoided the full GSC system. They did foot-drill without arms and were allocated to passive air defence, baths and laundries, cooking, clerical duties, building and maintenance, and other duties not involving the handling of military material of an aggressive nature. Britain had the most liberal provision in the world for conscientious objectors. The United States, for example, recognised only members of such historically pacifist groups as the Quakers and Amish. Many other governments – and not just the totalitarian regimes – considered pacifism as treason and punished it with penalties ranging from hard labour to death.

SOOTHING THE COLONELS' FEARS

Renewed complaints by line infantry regiments that their independence and identity would be undermined by the GSC were once more rejected by the AC. But Adam was more emollient than in the previous year and wrote personally to all regimental COs underlining that the selection tests carried out at the time of a recruit's civilian medical gave 'only a small indication of a man's suitability, but they are valuable as a preliminary and will be retained'. But correct postings were only possible after 'thorough examination of each individual and the application of more comprehensive tests'. He accepted that the:

> breakaway from the traditional system of direct enlistment into a particular Regiment or Corps is probably causing a certain amount of disquiet [...] The present system of direct enlistment results in many men being bandied about from one Corps to another until the right niche can be found for them. Amongst these are a number who are quite unsuited for the Corps or regiment into which they have enlisted.
>
> I hope to be able to find out each recruit's capabilities early in his career [...] I hope and believe Corps and Regiments will not in the future be saddled with men who will never be anything but a handicap to their units.

Adam concluded emphatically:

> The regimental system is not to be abolished, and the fact that men will go early in their service into their correct Corps should help to foster the Regimental spirit and tradition [...] by getting the right man into the right Corps at the start I hope the disheartening effects on both units and individuals of continual transfers will be greatly reduced.[29]

It was hoped that the outcome would mean that the quality of the infantry was raised.[30] In principle all infantrymen were to be in medical grade A1, subject to minimum weight and height rules, under 34 in age, have good training records, and as much as possible have their local links and preferences respected. However, in the last resort the army's needs of the moment were paramount, but fewer men were disgruntled at their fate. Men earmarked as tradesmen did the same basic six weeks and, if approved for and then passing their subsequent trade training, had their grade and pay backdated to the date of enlistment. Under the GSC system there was a marked improvement in the pass rate for the trades. The overall failure rate for tradesmen fell from 16.7 per cent to 6.7 per cent, and for drivers from 16–20 per cent to 3 per cent.

When a similar selection system was applied in the ATS, radio trainee failures fell from 64 per cent to 8 per cent.[31] Originally the auxiliaries were confined to clerical, driving and such domestic duties as cooking. As the war progressed it was recognised that the women entering the ATS (who were mainly volunteers) were not only as capable as men in many fields but were often more intelligent and conscientious than the men available for some non-combatant roles. Not only did women take over many transport tasks, including maintenance, but they became adept as signallers, radio mechanics, electricians and radar operators, as well as acting as storekeepers, telephonists, cooks and officers' mess servants. By 1943 one-third of the 200,000 auxiliaries received trade pay, although the women's basic pay was only two-thirds of men's. This was justified on the grounds that all male soldiers had received weapons training, no matter what their later tasks. Lt-Gen. Sir Frederick Pile of AA Command argued in vain that his ATS should be paid the same as the gunners on the same gun-site.[32] That was a step too far for contemporary minds, and expensive besides.

The background to this was the changing structure of the army. At the beginning of the war the cavalry had only recently undergone mechanisation, which led to heavy demands for technicians, as did the general motorisation of all arms. The artillery needed men and women to operate AA predictors and radar, with the necessary engineers to maintain the equipment. Radio was replacing landline signals. Overall, the infantry (which increasingly needed its own tradesmen to maintain its more sophisticated weapons) was declining as an element in the army. Before Dunkirk it comprised half its strength, rising to 60 per cent in the aftermath, but falling to only 20 per cent by the middle of the war. It was outnumbered by all branches of artillery until the end of 1944, when a substantial AA force at home was no longer needed. At the peak, tradesmen made up one-quarter of the army's strength.[33]

Despite all the reassurance that the AG and other senior officers could give, opposition to Adam's reforms persisted. Gen. Bernard Paget, C-in-C Home Forces after Brooke, who ten years earlier had worked closely with Adam at the War Office and who succeeded him as commandant of the Staff College, was a firm opponent. He 'believed unreservedly in the vital part played in morale by the well-proven Regimental system, and by Regimental officers and NCOs'.[34] Paget's criticism of Adam was to reach explosive proportions later that year. The critics gained the ear of the prime minister about the War Office's alleged 'indifference to the regimental traditions'. But resistance was overcome.

Adam and his immediate colleagues had no doubt that the introduction of the GSC was a great advance and twelve of them celebrated it at a dinner on 27 July 1942. The menu was typed on a redundant army form, 'Posting Nominal Roll', and comprised smoked salmon, *consommé en tasse*, *poulet en casserole*, and Welsh rarebit. By the standards of rationing (let alone an army cookhouse or even an officers' mess) this was fine fare. But it was meagre compared with the dinner served in May 1941 to mark Adam's leaving Northern Command. On that occasion there had been twenty-seven present, including Lady Adam, and the menu was, again, smoked salmon, followed on this occasion by *petite* marmite, supreme of chicken doria, asparagus with *mousseline* sauce, ice pudding Cyrano with *petit fours*, mushrooms on toast and coffee.[35] In the 1940s smoked salmon was rare and expensive, and was certainly not farmed. In the fourteen months between the two events, the war had become much grimmer: 1942 was the peak year for shipping losses in the Atlantic and rations were at a low level. That the end of that year would mark the 'end of the beginning' could not be foretold. On neither occasion were wines or spirits mentioned. The fall of the Continent had abruptly cut off wine imports and the wine-drinkers of Britain (who were relatively few) had to survive the war on the stocks available in June 1940.

GAINS AND LOSSES

A detached judgement on the GSC came from Col Bernard Ungerson, the chief psychologist to the War Office in the war years. In 1953 he concluded that the system had five advantages:

- the number of men failing their training courses was reduced;
- the supply of tradesmen was improved;
- the supply of officers was improved as the PSOs could assess potential officer material (POM) immediately;
- the overall quality of men going to the different arms could be watched and controlled, so each arm got a fair share in terms of IQ, age, education and CT;
- the scheme recommended itself to recruits as each was personally interviewed and given the chance to express his own wishes.

Disadvantages he detected were:

- the system needed lots of high-grade manpower to operate (one PSO for every 120 recruits, plus sergeant testers and clerks);
- initially the selection process had taken place in isolation from corps, training and field units (although this was rectified when senior PSOs were attached to each arm);
- technical problems in assessing levels for tradesmen were encountered;
- recruits felt no firm allegiance to any corps and lacked a proper incentive to work hard at their basic training.[36]

Only the last gave any comfort to the critics.

During their basic training the GSC recruits – who numbered 710,000 between July 1942 and May 1945 – had cap badges with the Royal Coat of Arms but wore no shoulder strips. After that they went for their corps training, ranging from sixteen weeks for the infantry to thirty weeks for the Royal Signals. Despite Ungerson's reservation on this point, this was surely quite enough time for any colonel or regimental sergeant-major (RSM) to inculcate a sense of regimental or corps identity, and to justify Adam's confidence that an adequate *esprit de corps* could develop. Of course, transfers between regiments and other formations still could not be avoided when units had to be brought up to strength after combat. This was above all essential in the late summer of 1944 when the army's shortage of manpower reached a crisis. This was the result of overconfidence about the time needed to break out of the Normandy beach-head and about the expected level of casualties — they reached numbers comparable with the worst in the First World War.[37] When the V1 'buzzbomb' raids on southern England ended later that year, men were transferred from AA units to the infantry, often with inadequate training. Another 40,000 men were transferred from the navy and air force, or drafted in from these services as young reservists. The latter were of good quality but to provide the former both the senior and junior services took an opportunity to get rid of their least useful men.

In the early years immature men were particular victims of the army's lack of personnel policy. In 1939 there was an influx of young volunteers and, after 1941, more when registration at age 17 became the law. About half enlisted for patriotic reasons but immaturity in some cases led to early disillusion with the army. Many deserted. Others were of low intelligence or suffered from psychiatric disorders for which enlisting appeared to offer an escape. Poor literacy was common. The establishment of Young Soldiers' Battalions and special training units for older men was not a total success, as many of the officers and NCOs in charge were themselves rejects from other units. After training, the young soldiers were too often sent to small, isolated units, often guarding airfields, where they were at a disadvantage compared with, for instance, the RAF personnel. In September 1941 new special training units were set up to try to instil more enthusiasm and discipline and to handle more troublesome men, some of whom were immature even though aged up to 24. Overall some 4,000 men passed through these units.[38] Despite the difficulties, including a shortage of psychologists, Adam considered the procedure a success.[39]

More successful was the War Office's treatment of younger intelligent men. Some had no leadership potential but had to be found work that benefited the army. Those with leadership potential were sent on pre-OCTU courses. Some were graded NY ('not yet') and RTUed ('returned to unit'), where they were likely to be put on cookhouse duties. In 1943, on Adam's instructions, the Highland Fieldcraft Training Centre was set up, with 120 men undertaking ten-week courses to mature them and toughen them up, through fieldcraft, night marches, compass training, climbing, and living off the land (including eating raw meat). The school considered its first task to be to show these men how to look after themselves, so that later they would be able to look after their men. In all 1,286 candidates were trained at the centre, of whom 868 went on to OCTU, with another 51 sent for retraining or retesting; 367 were returned to their previous duties, with many soon promoted to NCO.[40]

Another group of stable and able young men went to university for a six-month course, mainly for arms demanding more technical skills: the RA, RAC, RE, Signals and RASC. After an entry week at an Officer Recruit Training Unit with the arm concerned, they then completed primary training and had some technical training during these university short courses.

In all three groups the number of young soldiers was small. Yet the measures taken show not only the army's increasing need to put to good use the manpower it had, but the increasing sophistication and care of its selection and training procedures.

CONSCRIPTING WOMEN

The ATS had been established just before the war – originally, as its name suggested, as auxiliaries to the TA. Few imagined at its outset the range of duties that its members would ultimately take on. But the ATS, compared with their air force and naval sisters, had major disadvantages. First, khaki is not a flattering colour, and the design of the women's uniform was no help in that regard either. By their association with the 'lewd, licentious soldiery', accusations of immorality were easily made. In vain did two parliamentary reports try to stem this slander. In December 1942 Adam wrote to all COs with a series of 'Do's and Don'ts' on manpower – and womanpower – policy. He urged:

> Do instruct the men on the importance of the Women's Services and impress on them the statistics show less immorality than among civilians. There is a widespread tendency among the men to discourage their womenfolk from joining the Services. This is having a very damaging effect on the national war effort.[41]

Anxiety about sexual laxity under wartime conditions was widespread, especially among the clergy and other guardians of public morals. Adam had several meetings with government ministers and senior clergy about the risks of venereal diseases and related matters.[42]

Adam was present at the Cabinet Committee late in 1941 that decided to conscript women, and was told by Ernest Bevin, the minister of labour and national service, that he had arranged for him to make a radio broadcast on the issue.

I thought that this was rather hard as he knew that I did not like the idea of conscription for women and I told him so. However, I gave the broadcast and got the letters I expected. As far as I can recollect many were annoyed at such an announcement being made at an important time when they expected something better. The others were angry at women being conscripted. I am afraid that I cannot have broadcast with conviction.[43]

Like the 1939 National Service Act, the 1941 Act was a spur to voluntary recruitment: far more women came forward for ATS service in the early months of 1942 than were conscripted. The moral advantage of being a volunteer rather than a pressed woman was strongly felt. But there were not enough volunteers: ten months later Adams was roped in to make a broadcast to mark the ATS's fourth anniversary, appealing to single women and married women without children to join one of the three women's services (conscription was only applied to women aged 20 to 22, although the law provided 30 as the age limit).[44]

As for a private life, like most people in Britain during the war years Adam had little. However, he and Lady Adam found a small flat in Roehampton, on the outskirts of London, with barely enough room for the twins, Bridget and Isobel, during their boarding school holidays. Their school had been evacuated from first North Foreland to Dorset, then on to a less exposed location in Gloucestershire. Their elder sister Barbara was in the Civil Service. Apart from an occasional walk in Richmond Park there was little leisure for their parents. Adam worked six and a half days a week, generally spending two of them outside London visiting Commands. His own office was in Hobart House, near Victoria Station, a mile from the WO, where he had two of his staff stationed. But much of the AG's department was 100 miles away in Cheltenham. He was also periodically away overseas for several weeks, in North Africa, the Middle East and India.

9

OFFICER-LIKE QUALITIES

Throughout the Second World War the British Army was handicapped by a shortage of able officers, which was attributed by senior officers to the service preference system that encouraged men of greater ability (or shrewdness) to opt for the other services. In 1938 the War Office had begun to compile the Army Officers Emergency Reserve (AOER) of men who would volunteer in the event of hostilities and who were considered as being able to offer suitable service. Many had been commissioned during the First World War. Others had a particular skill, experience or knowledge that a wartime army would require. When war broke out, many on the AOER were commissioned by the direct officer intake (DOI) method with the minimum of training. Some were in their forties or older. They included doctors, dentists, electrical and electronics experts, road and rail transport executives, port managers, construction engineers, architects, surveyors, lawyers, linguists and chaplains. These were mainly qualifications for 'tail' − rear-echelon − roles, such as transport, supply and administration, although some DOI men took on front-line duties.

It proved more difficult to find younger men suitable as officers in the 'teeth' arms. For all the inadequacies, in nature and number, of British weaponry and methods in 1939, both battle technology and doctrine had moved on since 1918. In the earlier war most soldiers had been recruited into infantry regiments to feed the insatiable Moloch of the Western Front. Bravery (or the ability to control fear) was a principle requirement of an officer. In the First World War the traditional sources of officers soon ran out, and as the war continued the social background of officers was widened to include more 'temporary gentlemen' − as they were sometimes condescendingly described − to lead the army in the front line. After the war, as traditional attitudes and social structures reasserted themselves, few war-gazetted officers remained in the army. Interwar, the WO devoted little time to the need to recruit a large army in the event of another war. Conscription was a subject of internal study in the early 1920s, but in the 1930s both the British public and their political leaders showed a determined refusal to contemplate raising another mass army. 'No conscription in peacetime' was pledged by successive prime ministers. This ended with the panic measures in the spring of 1939, which hampered the army's modernisation programme rather than facilitated it.

When war came again, officer selection methods had little advanced. In the early months university graduates with Certificate 'B' from the OTC were likely to be commissioned in the army immediately, while public schoolboys with Certificate 'A' did three months at an ORTU before being commissioned. Leslie Hore-Belisha, before his resignation in January 1940, decided that all entrants (except the DOI) should serve in the ranks before any selection process. His successors eased this rule, although there was some confusion for months as policy oscillated.[1] So the selection of potential officers from among the 1.7 million men who entered the army from September 1939 to mid-1942 was essentially based on the officers and NCOs at basic training units picking out those recruits they considered as POM – 'potential officer material' , or those who displayed 'officer-like qualities and powers of command'. These would be interviewed, perhaps for only twenty minutes, by the unit CO, who might or might not submit the men's names for OCTU. The weakness of this practice was that neither the regimental officers nor the NCOs had any training in personnel selection. So, as in the First World War, they tended to base their conclusions on personal hunch or preconceptions that there was an 'officer-producing class' from which officers should only (or at least principally) be drawn. Inevitably, regular officers tended to select men in their own image, from their own social class, men who had mainly been to public school, had been in those schools' OTCs, and were perhaps good at games. It was assumed that because parents had had the means to pay for a son's education, that son automatically had the qualities to be a leader of men. Selection for OCTU depended on education and employment records and 'a good interview'. As Adam recorded, 'a large number of "duds" succeeded in getting through the interview'.[2]

The system was summed up by one recruit in 1942: on their first day in an artillery unit his intake was told by their commanding officer 'that we all had potential to be commissioned. Then the BSM said: "Fall out the POs". Who? Those who had been in OTCs.'[3] In such circumstances many men with only elementary school education, or who had regional accents, were discouraged from applying for commissions. Having even mildly Left-wing views was often an automatic disqualification.

FIRST STEPS TO REFORM

In early 1941 the War Office was concerned not only that there was an appreciable shortage of officers but that many officers commissioned through the existing practice were unsuitable. A report by Capt. P.A. Studd, military assistant to the

Vice-CIGS, argued that the army would do better by taking in more men who had been temporary officers in the earlier war.[4] He dismissed doubts that men in their forties would be unable to learn modern military methods, by pointing out that the Home Guard, who were mainly men of that age group, had learnt a lot in six months; besides, he contended, those who had served in the BEF in 1939–40 had little to offer from their mere six weeks' of battle experience. Others took a less sanguine view of the current value of many former First World War officers: not a few suffered from latent psychiatric problems, which resurfaced under war conditions. The existing selection system was unpopular with regular officers – 'owing to the uncouth type of new subalterns', Studd noted – and also with ORs, because of its perceived unfairness. The behaviour of some TA officers also caused problems: some were noted not only for their inability to command but for a snobbishness that any good regular officer abhorred. The latter was fully aware of rank when on duty, but was usually confident enough to behave in a relaxed manner with his men when off duty. More generally, some privileges for officers, such as the use of army transport for private purposes, the reservation of local hotels and bars for officers only, and very wide differences in conditions on troopships contributed to poor morale. Officers on P & O ships converted to troopships lived as in pre-war days, with white-gloved stewards serving them pre-war meals at tables with white tablecloths, while the ORs were crammed down below and served standard army cookhouse fare. The widely different messing scales for officers and ORs on ships were narrowed, but the Army Council in 1943 refused to go so far as to abolish the whole concept of differences in catering scales, afloat or ashore.[5] There were limits.

The WO aggravated the officer recruitment problem by putting pressure on Command HQs to issue instructions, sometimes every six weeks, to all units, irrespective of their nature, to submit a stated number of men for commissions. Those COs who submitted 'nil' returns of recommendations were overruled and required to nominate men nonetheless. Furthermore, COs wanted to hold on to capable warrant officers and NCOs; so, rather than nominate such men for commissions, even more 'duds' were put forward.

'BLIMPISH'

In the same month as Capt. Studd wrote his report, a cadet who had recently passed through OCTU 168 was highly critical of the training, and was backed by other newly gazetted men and by cadets from other OCTUs. The training was, in the general view, of poor quality: they handled an inadequate range of weapons; their instructors had no recent battle experience and showed no appreciation of the changes that warfare was undergoing; there was no demonstration of new weapons; there were bullying NCOs; there was too much 'bull'. The cadets felt they were 'treated like peacetime recruits, assumed to be unwilling and stupid learners required to be driven to work'.[6] In Adam's words, the system aimed at 'training the cadet to be the perfect private soldier'.[7] Given the desperate need to have those with battle experience – and what modern weapons there were – in readiness to fight an invasion, some of the criticism was barely justified, but it showed how the enthusiasm of cadets could be undermined.

Also in the same month, the CO of the same OCTU 168, Lt-Col R.C. Bingham, let his frustrations get the better of him (or, perhaps aware of the adverse criticism, he was 'getting his retaliation in first'). On 25 January 1941 *The Times* published a letter from him:

> Our new armies are to be officered by classes of society who are new to the job. The middle, lower middle and working classes are now receiving the King's Commission. These classes, unlike the old aristocratic and feudal (almost) classes who led the old army have never had 'their people' to consider. They have never had anyone to think of but themselves. This aspect of life is completely new to them and they have largely fallen down on it in their capacity of army officers […] The new officers would be just as brave and technically efficient […] but they have been reared in an atmosphere in which the State spoon-feeds everyone from the cradle to the grave and no one feels any responsibility for his fellow men. This, Sir, is a sad reflection on our educational system.[8]

Justified or not, this 'Blimpish' letter – taken from cartoonist David Low's character 'Colonel Blimp' – cost Col Bingham his command. Apart from being politically incorrect decades before that concept was articulated, he had broken King's Regulations by writing to the press about army matters (*The Times* had refused to publish his letter anonymously). But one cadet at 168 OCTU thought that what he had written was in the main true, and recorded that all the officers and men at the OCTU sent Bingham a kind of round robin expressing confidence in him.[9]

The *Daily Mirror* columnist William Connor 'Cassandra' summed up his view of the overall situation in characteristic style:

> The process whereby a ranker becomes a commissioned officer is every bit as miraculous as the metamorphosis of a caterpillar into a butterfly, or a tadpole into a frog. The only difference is that the evolutions of nature are based on recognised principles, whereas the evolution from rough to smooth khaki is based on unpredictable quantities of prejudice, snobbery, friendship and sheer luck, mixed in about equal proportions.[10]

So there was a series of complaints, some contradicting others: uncouth new subalterns; too many ex-public-schoolboys; the exclusion of men with state education, regional accents, or Left-wing views; a lack of initiative and responsibility among the new entrants. The weakness of the system was evident. Rejection rates of OCTU candidates ranged from 20 to 50 per cent, and averaged about 30 per cent.[11] The return of failed candidates to their units reinforced resentment of and disillusionment with the selection system. Being marked 'RTU' after the rigours of OCTU was deeply dispiriting. By the time Adam became AG in June 1941 an attempt to remedy the problem had been made. In the summer of 1940 command selection boards were established, headed by a full colonel from the reserve and seconded by the COs of local units. From Studd's report it is clear that this had produced little improvement in the intervening six months. A candidate still stood or fell by the first impression he created.[12] So, if anything, the boards reinforced the impression of social bias in the selection process.

THE GERMAN MODEL

One of Adam's first acts as AG was to ask for 'the development of a test, preferably on the German model, for selecting officer candidates'.[13] At that time, the United States was not at war with Germany, and through the Americans the WO obtained a complete record of the German system. The subsequent capture of the records of officer cadets in a panzer battalion gave additional data. Some of the German tests were carried out on British candidates, but they were considered to be of questionable value: for example, a film of candidates' facial expressions during interviews was not considered a useful guide to character. As it happened, the Germans had already scaled down their use of such tests by 1939 and had abandoned them completely by 1941. For them, the problem was twofold: the remnants of the Prussian-style military caste found such tests too 'democratic' in that they denied the importance of inherited character; the Nazis found them too objective in that candidates' devotion to National Socialist ideology was not taken into account.[14] In the eyes of British experts, the German methods did not in any case have any scientific validation and were based on too many prior assumptions.

Given the pioneering role that the Craiglockhart hospital, in Edinburgh, had played in the First World War in treating shell shock (in the contemporary term), it was appropriate that Scottish Command should be a leading venue in studying new methods of selecting officers. Early in 1941 experiments had been undertaken by two psychiatrists, encouraged by the GOC, Lt-Gen. Sir Andrew Thorne, who before the war had been the military attaché in Berlin and had observed German methods. There was close liaison between him and Adam, then still GOC Northern Command. In these experiments, fifty officers attending company commanders' courses were given psychiatric interviews and intelligence tests, together with some German-style tests. The interviews and intelligence tests corresponded with the training school's own estimations of the officers' qualities, although the German tests did not.[15] As these officers were already experienced, had rather more self-confidence than the average cadet, and had been subject to reports from their superiors, the agreement level of 80 per cent between the psychiatric staff and the school staff was considered satisfactory. In the cases where the two sides disagreed, it was found that in nine out of ten cases the officers had underlying personality deviations that had escaped the course commander's attention. In some cases the psychological abnormality was severe.[16] A subsequent trial of another fifty officers produced 90 per cent agreement between the two sides. The results showed that the boards' assessment of the men after only forty-eight hours compared very closely with the COs' assessments after ten weeks of training.

In Northern Command the appointment of Lt-Col Ronald Hargreaves as Command psychiatrist in early 1940 had already proved a crucial step. The following year other staff still at the Tavistock Clinic prompted parliamentary questions about the army's selection methods. After Adam had set up the directorate for selection of personnel (DSP) he asked some of them to join it, including Eric Trist and Hugh Murray. They later wrote that the group:

> took a novel approach to the human resource problems facing the army. Rather than remain in base hospitals they went out into the field to find out from commanding officers what they saw as their most pressing problems. They would listen to their troubled military clients as an analyst would to a patient, believing that the 'real' problem would surface as trust became established, and that constructive ideas about dealing with them would emerge.[17]

With a psychiatrist with a roving commission attached to each Command in Home Forces, the problems could be quickly identified and remedial action taken.

DRAWING THE THREADS

Adam's achievement when AG was to draw these threads together. In December 1941 he, the director of personnel selection and the Scottish Command GOC held a conference in Edinburgh. The psychiatrists present pointed out that the only effective selection method combined intelligence tests with a psychiatric interview. The following month an experimental board was formed in Scottish Command. A regular officer presided, aided by a military testing officer, two psychiatrists and one psychologist, with two sergeant testers from the DSP staff. A medical specialist was also attached. Adam agreed that each candidate be interviewed by a psychiatrist and that the testing procedure should include an interview with the president, and the undertaking of some military and psychological tests. Various personality tests were tried, and some discarded.

By March 1942 a satisfactory technique had been developed and within a year almost all candidates for commissions went before a War Office Selection Board (WOSB). By the middle of 1943 'Wozbees' were established overseas to find suitable men who had failed or been overlooked by the old method for recruiting officers. In the UK batches of thirty to forty candidates were summoned twice a week to spend two to three days at a country house. They were put at their ease in close contact with the board members. The candidates undertook various aptitude and intelligence tests and had general interviews and, when possible or considered necessary, psychiatric interviews. They also took part in various practical tests giving them opportunities to display initiative and quick thinking. On the third day, the board met as a whole and placed candidates in their final gradings as potential officer material (POM) – or put them back as not developed enough, or failed them. In Adam's view, one of the most important tests was the 'leaderless group' procedure in which a group of ten to twelve candidates might be asked to build a bridge from material lying about and told to find a solution to the problem:

> Leaders arose within the group and might be discarded; if too successful they were made a casualty and another took charge. Discussion groups were carried out on subjects of general interest and the group was asked to take a movable object over the obstacle course as a team [...] The tests showed not only who were the leaders, but also those who fitted into a team.[18]

The classic test was when the group was taken to a stream (sometimes an imaginary one), given two or three planks, each shorter than the width of the stream, and several lengths of rope, and told to find a means of crossing to the other side without getting wet.

The proponents of the new system contended that it was clearly superior to replace the 'hit-and-miss interviews by a more objective technique based on psychodynamic theory', as the psychologist H.V. Dicks saw it.[19] Certainly the immediate effect during 1942 was a marked rise in the number of applicants for commissions. The new system was also felt to be fairer – both by candidates who passed and those who failed their entry tests. One study showed that the new methods resulted in one-third of candidates being rated above average, against one-fifth by the old method. Conversely, one-quarter were now rated below average, against over one-third previously. The average rating remained about 40 per cent of all candidates. In the House of Lords in 1948 Lord Piercy, who had been a pioneer in personnel selection in the 1930s, stated that 'the W.O.S.B.s did their work of selection with an impressive margin of superiority over the ordinary, traditional methods'.[20]

Not all agreed. Among the immediate critics were parents of public and grammar-school boys who were affronted that their sons had been rejected, even if the sons concerned considered the judgement fair (and in some cases welcome). Some parents contacted their MPs, who in turn raised the matter with ministers. So vociferous were these complaints that an expert committee was set up on Churchill's order; it produced a very favourable report on the new system. On this issue Adam had the firm support of Sir James Grigg (war minister) who wrote to him in May 1942:

> I am told that the President of the Royal College of Physicians [RCP] Sir Charles Wilson [later Lord Moran] is distrustful of some of our psychological tests. I suspect that he is thinking of those designed for O.C.T.U. candidates, but you had better get hold of him quickly and find out. You will remember that as the P.M.'s doctor he has free access to No. 10 Downing Street.

This memo is followed by a note written by Gen. Adam (promoted the previous month) in his precise hand, stating that the president of the RCP 'seemed eminently sensible to me, but he considers himself an authority on morale. I am taking him to an O.C.T.U. selection unit' and will send 'my consultant psychology [sic] to talk to him'.[21] There is no further reference to this matter. This was one of several occasions when Grigg and Adam evaded Churchill's grumbles.

THE 'TRICK CYCLISTS'

The new system ran into two problems, both arising from the employment of psychiatrists and psychologists. In the first place there were not enough psychiatrists available to provide even one for each WOSB on a continuing basis (and there were seventeen WOSBs formed by the end of 1942); there was a growing need of psychiatric treatment for battle casualties. Second, the very employment of psychiatrists met enormous resistance. The British Army never achieved the US level of having one psychiatrist attached to each division.[22]

In 1948 the editor of *Army Quarterly* wrote:

> During the Second World War few subjects caused more argument and engendered so much heat as the introduction of psychiatrists and psychologists into Army organization and procedure. The Army is innately a conservative body. The Infantry of the Line is perhaps the most die-hard of all the arms and viewed the Personnel Selection officers, their tests and their 'bags of tricks' with deep suspicion and mistrust. For years comment among regimental officers was caustic.[23]

This was in an age when most people were confused, worried or frightened by anything apparently to do with mental illness. The distinction between psychologists, psychotherapists, psychoanalysts and psychiatrists was little understood – and not helped by the opaque terminology, concepts and methods employed, and the controversies between and within these callings. The military members of a selection board might well have wondered, as the psychiatrist sat alongside them making notes about the candidates, that he might be making mental notes about them too.

Among those who administered army selection procedures, Philip Vernon and John Parry wrote in 1949 that: 'The layman is often frightened of people who are supposedly expert in reading character or in explaining human behaviour. He dislikes their inquisitiveness and their criticism of old-established ways of doing things, as well as their use of statistical evidence.'[24]

In an institution based on discipline, cohesion, tradition, hierarchy and authority such a detached approach to human behaviour was particularly unwelcome. To admit weakness was taboo: it undermined the masculine character of military life. The use of the term 'trick cyclist' was ostensibly disdainful; in fact it hid fear. Adam, however, unlike many of his contemporaries, military and political, did not shy from change.

According to Ahrenfeldt, 'For reasons that were primarily political, presidents of Selection Boards were instructed, in March 1943, that the duties of the psychiatrists should be confined to interviewing cases referred by the president, which must not comprise more than 50 per cent of the candidates'.[25] This gave the impression – to the lay members of boards, the candidates so interviewed, and their fellows – that the psychiatrists only interviewed 'the abnormals'. However, more plausibly than Ahrenfeldt's assertion of a political decision, Hugh Murray contends that the deciding factor was the inability of the limited number of psychiatrists to devote an hour to interview each candidate; some less problematical candidates were interviewed instead by psychologists.[26] Some tactless experts compounded the conflict by asking questions about sex and religion, which were much resented. Following exaggerated reports of their nature, such questions were banned. Inevitably, too, there were tensions between the experts and the military about the methods employed and the decisions reached. The former naturally believed that their conclusions should prevail; the latter tended to hold that 'bluff common sense' and their own experience over years of man-management were more important. Certainly it was a political decision that put a regular officer as president of each board, and in the end his opinion prevailed. Initially the role of unit COs in the selection task was not clearly worked out, and there was some resentment of this change imposed from above and when men whom COs considered to be POM were rejected. By and large, once COs were able to observe the procedures, opposition and scepticism declined.

A persistent difficulty was the reluctance of COs to nominate men for commissions, particularly when units were about to go overseas. Adam recorded how, in one artillery regiment six NCOs appealed against a refusal to nominate them, but the result of the delay was that two days before sailing the CO lost them to an OCTU (where all passed). In one armoured brigade that was being broken up there were found to be 128 POs, and in ten infantry battalions 178 POs who had been disregarded by the earlier method.[27] In December 1942 Adam wrote that COs continued to have, and had always had, two great failings, in putting forward the 'clerical types' and the 'warrant officer types': the first were not usually fighters and the second were often better as WOs.[28]

'ALMOST BOLSHEVIK'

One attempt that sought to overcome this problem – with Adam's strong advocacy – was 'Regimental Nomination', whereby it was hoped that it would become a matter of pride for a unit to produce a good array of candidates. Under an experimental project in Scottish Command, four battalions or equivalent units 'of good reputation' were asked to select candidates whose names could be put forward in the name of the regiment. These units nominated groups of company size (100–200 men), each then split into platoon size groups (20–30 men). In the presence of the army commander and a WOSB team the men were addressed by their COs on lines that Murray described:

> to get our regimental candidates we are all going to vote: yourselves, the NCOs and your officers. We want to know if you can put up people so good that they can do better than people who are put up in any other way. Choose good ones. You may have to fight under them.

Each man was asked to write down secretly the names of other men, first from his own platoon, then from his company, whom he considered to be POM; he need not nominate anyone at all. The aim of the exercise was to see how four groups – privates, junior NCOs, senior NCOs and officers – envisaged potential officers. Men who received a considerable number of nominations from three of the four groups were discussed at a unit conference where the CO then gave his opinion and his own grading of each man's potential. Men chosen were invited to apply for a commission. The proportion of the 114 regimental nomination candidates who subsequently passed WOSB was 56 per cent, not significantly higher than the 54 per cent who had been selected by other methods. But the great advantage of the method was that the supply of candidates of nearly 7 per cent of unit strength compared very favourably with the usual 0.1 per cent that had been put forward each month by unit commanders. Murray concluded that the factor limiting the normal number of applicants was the 'in-group' mentality of field force units, particularly when about to go overseas.[29] Men who lived and trained together, and who might well depend on each other for their survival, tended to develop a close-knit sense of identity.

Adam's paper before the Army Council (AC) argued that the quality of candidates thrown up by the experiment was superior to that forthcoming in the orthodox way, and he wanted to extend the experiment with a view, if again successful, to general application. The arguments against a general application of the scheme, as recorded in the minutes, were that:

- It might become regarded as a right of other ranks to select their officers;
- However secret the ballot, questions would be raised why this or that candidate was not successful;
- 'Even in today's army' only a minority of men had the quality to appraise the requirements of an officer's character;
- Once started, the system would be difficult to stop;
- It was not certain that equal results could not be obtained by the orthodox way, especially if units were ordered to produce a fixed quota.

This last point went against all experience; its deployment stressed the emotional power in the resistance to the proposal. The C-in-C Home Forces, Lt-Gen. Sir Bernard Paget, who was in attendance at this meeting, said that he and the majority of army commanders were against it.

The AC agreed not to proceed with a further trial as there was, as the record shows, 'a strong body of opinion in the Council against it'. But COs were to be addressed on the urgency of the matter of finding good POM and the AC asked Paget to lend his personal influence to this end. Both the three civil and the five military members were divided. Present were Grigg, who presided, both parliamentary under-secretaries, Lord Croft (Conservative) and Arthur Henderson (Labour). The latter 'saw nothing dangerous in the scheme as presented, which had the hallmark of success'. The military representation was led by Brooke. Adam obviously favoured the proposal, but whoever else favoured it – if anyone – among the military is not recorded.[30] To suppose that the 'Blimps' were all in khaki is mistaken.

On many occasions during the war both Brooke and Grigg supported Adam, and certainly protected him from Churchill, who more than once tried to oust him. On this occasion these two did not back him. Brooke's attitude appears ambivalent, for support from him and Grigg would certainly have got the measure through. The event contributed to Adam's reputation as a dangerous radical. It further harmed his relationship with Paget, who was on close terms with Grigg. The following day, the C-in-C wrote by hand to Grigg stating that the AG was 'a serious menace both to morale and discipline'. Regimental Nomination was not the only matter that provoked Paget's reaction at that meeting (see chapter 12).

In 1960 Adam wrote of the Regimental Nomination experiment:

> This small experiment shewed that the men chose the right candidates in
> their company, as the WOSB passed most of those selected. Outside their own
> companies the men usually selected someone who was a good footballer or
> prominent in a concert party. In fact the test showed that the men in the subunit
> were the best selectors and the senior NCOs were the worst. I wanted to do the
> experiment on a larger scale, but the experiment was regarded with the greatest
> suspicion and as almost Bolshevik, so it was abandoned.[31]

The irony was that Stalin, at this time in a desperate struggle with the Germans,
was re-establishing the privileges of his own officer class in the Red Army and
relying less on those of proven revolutionary and proletarian origin (many of
whom he had already had shot).

A HALFWAY SUCCESS

So the AC fell back on a system that had shown its failings already, by insisting
that COs submit a quota of candidates irrespective of the nature of the unit.
Although intellect and educational qualifications were by no means the sole
requirements of an officer, it was questionable to demand that, say, the Pioneer
Corps submit the same proportion of names from among its traditional ranks
as, say, the Intelligence Corps or the RE. However, at that time, apart from what
Ahrenfeldt called 'dullards', the Pioneer Corps included many highly intelligent
'friendly enemy aliens' – mainly German and Austrian refugees. (One British
pioneer, Alexander Bernstein, refused a commission because of his Left-wing
views, was to write an outstanding war novel under the name of Baron.)[32]

Adam's search for ability in the army included drawing on these refugees. Shortly
after becoming AG, as he recorded in 1960, he visited one pioneer company in
which distinguished professors, doctors, lawyers and scientists were engaged in
digging trenches. Some were clearly of fighting material and there were a number
of potential leaders; he was horrified by the waste of talent. It was difficult to
get a change in policy, but later in 1941 the government was persuaded to allow
men to transfer to various corps, including the Intelligence Corps. Here, their
linguistic abilities were to prove valuable in interrogating prisoners and pursuing
war criminals. About 12,000 were transferred from the pioneers but it was not
until 1943 that Adam could get permission for them to serve in fighting units or
to be commissioned.

More generally, on the War Office Selection Board (WOSB) system Adam
believed that:

In wartime mental stability is essential for the leaders as men's lives depended on it. The psychiatrists could assess the tests results and could form a good estimate of personality, and interview all the doubtful candidates [...] The results were remarkable.[33]

On the other hand, an appealing (if romantic) form of scepticism about the WOSB system that was more than mere anti-intellectual prejudice was to ask, as popular historian E.S. Turner has done, whether the system could have coped with the eccentrics – say, T.E. Lawrence or Generals Wolfe, Gordon and Wingate?[34] This issue was recognised. A WO report on the early experiments commented: 'If we were to take out all the unstable we might lose many geniuses and potential VCs'.[35] (A notable figure in Second World War fiction is the wildly eccentric Brig. Ben Ritchie-Hook in Evelyn's Waugh's *Sword of Honour* trilogy. Devoted to 'biffing' the enemy, he is supposed to have been based on Lt-Gen. Sir Adrian Carton de Wiart.)

Turner argued that: 'It is impossible to show, statistically, how effective the boards really were, since the rejected candidates [...] might have made good officers, for all one knows to the contrary'.[36] Overall, Murray agreed that evaluation of the WOSB system was difficult.[37] But that did not invalidate the method. Apart from anything else it led to a general improvement in morale by helping to dispel the – at the time justified – belief in 1939–42 that social class was the main determinant in whether or not a man got a commission. Towards the end of the war, a large-scale follow-up study overseas of some 5,000 officers was undertaken, and of another 2,000 in France, to compare the ratings currently given by COs and previously by the OCTUs. There was a fair correlation between the two, but Adam concluded that the COs' views differed so much that, scientifically, the follow-up was not of great value.[38] Nor did the WOSB system solve the problem of officer supply: just before D-Day, 200 Canadian officers were seconded to the British Army, and in the Far East some Australian officers served with the British Army.

How effective was the WOSB system from the point of view of the potential officer? Those who got through were presumably, in general, satisfied. One exception was George MacDonald Fraser, later to achieve fame as the author of the *Flashman* novels: 'The general view throughout the army was that [the boards] weren't fit to select bus conductors, let alone officers.'[39] Dudley Anderson explained why he turned down the opportunity for a commission:

I refused, for the second time in my army career. Every officer I had respected as a leader had, with the exception of Lieutenant Weeks, been killed or wounded. The fatality risk was too high. On the other hand, as an officer [...] I would like to inspire my men and lead them into action. Then I would probably be killed, and I did not want this. So I declined.[40]

This may not have accorded with the demands of heroism, but it was wholly rational; he did survive the war in the front line as an infantryman. Alex Bowlby, an ex-public schoolboy who persistently refused to take a commission – or to take the procedure seriously – put an unusual twist on the problems of communications between the ranks and between the classes: 'Not many officers felt at ease with a rifleman from the same background as themselves. They seemed afraid of not being able to maintain the proper distance between ranks.'[41]

THE CLASS ELEMENT

Bowlby's comment cited above reflected the British class structure in the 1940s, which in the WOSB context raised a major concern related to the educational background of successful candidates. Analysis of the results in a six-week period late in 1942 showed that 60 per cent of Home Command cadets successfully completed their courses. (So in these intakes at least, when the WOSB system was still shaking down, the failure rate was about as high as or higher than under the old system.) Those from public, secondary or grammar schools exceeded this level of success at 70 per cent, against 40 per cent of those who had had elementary education only. In most cases, the successful elementary school candidates had undergone adult education in some form.[42] This result reflected the tripling of the number of candidates in the months after the new system was introduced. The proportions varied somewhat later, with the public school element rising and elementary element falling back. Overall, during the war 34 per cent of officers came from public schools and 21 per cent had elementary education only, with the secondary/grammar sector providing slightly under half the total.[43] Of the men undertaking WOSB tests, under half got through: from mid-1942 to mid-1945 48 per cent of the 125,000 men assessed for WOSB in Britain went on to OCTU; in the Middle East 44 per cent of 12,700 candidates were successful.[44] So something like one-quarter of men considered as POM at one stage or another were finally commissioned.

So although education and social class were still significant elements in the selection of officers there was some leavening of the officer corps during the war years. Not all agreed. *The Economist* contended in 1943 that 'the Army at home remains, in some respects, as hidebound, as unsympathetic and as favourite-ridden as ever'.[45] But then, Donald Tyerman, the acting editor, had experienced a run-in with the more conservative elements in the War Office when he wrote part of a pamphlet – *British Way and Purpose (BWP)* – that aroused criticism (see chapter 10). On the other hand, David French thought it debatable as to whether WOSB cadets became better officers, and stressed that the crucial issue was whether officers, irrespective of origin, were effectively trained. Commanding officers in both the Mediterranean and 21st Army Group (the force preparing for the invasion of the Continent in 1943–4) found little to choose between the products of the WOSBs and the earlier systems of granting commissions.[46] The real issue was that psychological testing at an early stage provided a quicker means of assessing leadership capacity.

From direct experience, William Shebbeare – writing anonymously in 1944 as 'Captain X' – considered that the tests and WOSBs were still subject to personal prejudice and asserted that the social origins of officer candidates were still somewhat restricted. But he found that the younger majors and colonels, whether regular or wartime appointments, were less aloof, especially those who shared front-line dangers with their men in the 'teeth arms'.[47] By October 1942 the average age of COs in the Royal Regiment of Artillery was 42, in the Royal Engineers, Signals, Guards and line infantry age 41, and in the Royal Armoured Corps (RAC) age 38. In the first two years of the war, the inadequacy of many officers led to 133 regular lieutenant-colonels and 265 TA lieutenant-colonels being removed from their commands.[48] It required a war to judge their inadequacy.

Of the men recruited into the General Service Corps after July 1942 only 6 per cent were considered to be POM (with the same proportion as potential NCOs). Under this system men were considered POM on the basis of tests and an interview with the personnel selection officer at an initial training unit, and were graded OR1. Together with men also considered suitable by their CO they were sent to WOSB and perhaps to OCTU. If they passed their course there, they went on for further training for the arm to which they were destined. Newly commissioned officers for infantry and RAC postings could put forward the names of three regiments that they hoped to join.

THE SERVICE PREFERENCE ISSUE

The background to the whole officer-quality problem for the army was the service preference system[49], as a result of which:

> the Army had to be content to take, along with much excellent material, a great deal represented by the leavings of the other services […] The OCTU, as one not unfriendly critic put it, was a large-scale undertaking in the industry of making silk purses out of sows' ears.

So wrote Lt-Col J.H.A. Sparrow in his report *Morale* written for the WO in 1949, one of several monographs on wartime issues that Adam had commissioned before his retirement. During the war, Sparrow was responsible for the quarterly reports on the state of army morale; after the war he became a leading Oxford academic.

The WOSB system was adopted, and adapted where necessary, by the ATS, the other services, and by Dominion and some Allied armed forces. In the RAF the effects of scientific selection were dramatic: flying training failures fell from 48 per cent to 25 per cent.

Overall, Murray concluded:

> The choice of officers in any army is a conservative process. It was a very considerable event for an army in the middle of a war to take such radical steps as to introduce psychiatrists and psychological tests into a procedure for choosing its officers and to allow a novel type of military institution to be created for that purpose.[50]

This 'considerable event' was due to Adam.

The conservatism of the army (and most of its political masters) was shown above all by the rejection of Regimental Nomination. The anger, and the anxiety, that the experiment aroused was because it struck at fundamental elements of military society, hierarchy and authority. It showed that the rank and file soldiery was as perceptive in assaying the qualities required of an officer as was the elaborate and carefully constructed WOSB system, and certainly superior to traditional choosing the 'good type' methods. It also undermined a crucial element common to both the pre-WOSB and the WOSB systems: reliance (at least in part) on the views of those old stalwarts of army tradition, the senior NCOs. In the Regimental Nomination experiment they proved to be the weakest element. That episode demonstrates Adam's willingness to consider a pragmatic approach to a pressing problem, even at the risk of affronting traditional military and political attitudes. If a change appeared to him to be rational, and likely to achieve the end desired, he would argue his case firmly. In contrast to his contemporaries' conservatism, Adam's radicalism on this occasion lay in accepting 'the wisdom of the crowd' as an element in officer selection. He lost that particular battle, but the intellectual and moral victory was his. Despite the rejection of Regimental Nomination, the 'Wozbee' in itself was, despite some certain weaknesses, a major advance on the 'hunch and preconception' method of selecting officers.

A further measure of Adam's success was the WOSB's retention after the war, albeit in attenuated form, and its adoption (with appropriate changes) by the civil service (the CSSB, or 'Cizbee') and by major companies such as Unilever, Imperial Chemical Industries and Philips Electrical, when seeking potential executives. However, after Adam's retirement the army itself backtracked to some extent from both this and other of his reforms.

10

DYNAMITE

The first major reforms put through by Gen. Adam as AG were specific changes to the army's procedures: the scientific selection of men during their six weeks' basic training for their further employment, and more discerning officer selection. Putting into place the necessary structures – the GSC and the WOSB – required administrative changes, in principle simple to introduce, although facing difficulties and delay in practice.

His third reform had the much less easily definable objective of raising morale. This was an acute problem when the war was going badly for the army, and which would continue to do so until towards the end of 1942. Until then, the army's successes had been limited to the underrated East African campaign and securing the Levant and Iraq from Nazi takeover. The rest had been retreats and defeats: Norway, Dunkirk, western France, Greece, Crete, Tobruk, Hong Kong, Malaya, Singapore and Burma. In North Africa, Britain and the Axis were playing ping pong along the Libyan coast. In such circumstances, maintaining morale among 2½ million UK soldiers and nearly as many Dominion and Empire troops scattered over three continents was not easily tackled by administrative action. No member of the AC was specifically responsible for morale until 1941, when it was given to the AG. Adam was aware of Napoleon's dictum that 'morale is to the physical as three to one'; in this war, Adam concluded, it was six to one.[1] Before the war, little thought had been given to the problem of morale in a conscript army. In 1960 Adam admitted:

> I was as much to blame as anyone, for I was chief instructor at the Staff College for more than three years and commandant for a few months. I can only recall one lecture dealing with morale in a conscript Army.[2]

Adam appointed Lt-Col John Sparrow to report each quarter on the army's state of morale. Sparrow did this partly by taking off his badges of rank and, like Henry V before Agincourt, mixing anonymously with soldiers. 'What was morale?' he asked, and could find no more precise definition than the 'attitude of the soldier towards his employment'.[3] So his task covered a wide scope, and was subject to much debate, confusion and controversy.

Some improvement in morale could be directly achieved by changing the army's character and practices to recognise that it was now a mass army in a democratic society. Among such morale-boosting moves were: improved food and accommodation; better training of all kinds and at all levels; informing men of the purpose of their training and postings; training officers to be more responsive to and approachable by their men; reducing officers' privileges; more open, fairer and effective selection methods; more leave, including compassionate leave; improved health facilities, especially abroad; reducing excessive drills and 'bull'; smarter uniforms. Also, as the war's end approached, setting up a fair demobilisation system. The establishment of the Army Catering Corps, Adam wrote in 1961, revolutionised cooking in the army under the advice of Sir Isadore Salmon of the Lyons catering chain. (Many a wartime and post-war soldier must have wondered what army food had been like previously.) But many problems affecting morale were largely beyond the immediate scope of administrative change: regular mail for troops overseas; long tours of duty overseas (shipping was short); better and ample arms and equipment; better generals; victory itself. Slowly the WO grasped that success in war was not just a matter of hardware and battlefield planning.

Such issues apart, the army also sought to improve morale by increasing the men's understanding of why the war was being fought. When Alan Wood (who had to write under the pseudonym 'Boomerang') was recruited in 1940 there were no pep talks for the soldiers: 'Not a word about why we are in the army. It is taken for granted that the morale of the army needs no uplift'.[4] 'Captain X' described his early experience and his experience of the army's leadership: 'We are a leaderless legion. The Army, which aims at giving the private soldier all the mental attitudes of a sheep, also deprives him of a good shepherd'.[5] These writers were among the articulate. Others understood even less: when GOC Scottish Command Lt-Gen. Thorne one day in 1940 gave a lift to a hitchhiking soldier he was shocked by how little the man knew of Britain's war aims. The cocoon in which Britain's political and military elite dwelt meant that it took some time to sink in that in this war it was necessary to take the people along with national policy. The British sheep would not be led to the slaughter as naively as they had in 1914–18 (well, in 1914–16). One great contrast with the earlier war was that a better-educated and a much more sceptical generation had to be persuaded and inspired, not simply ordered, into battle. Adam, Thorne and some other senior officers understood this; not all did.

Historically the British Army had comprised an officer corps mainly drawn from the aristocracy and the upper middle class who commanded ORs mainly drawn from the lowest levels of society (Wellington's 'scum of the earth'). It exemplified Disraeli's 'Two Nations' (deeply divided between those of great privilege and those of great material and psychological deprivation). The Liberal war minister

Cardwell's hopes that his reforms in 1868–71 would attract men from the upper levels of the working class and from the lower middle class were almost entirely disappointed. 'Going for a soldier' was still a poor ambition in both classes. Britain did not have the compulsory military service normal in continental Europe, which at least in principle put all sections of society through the same basic experience.[6] In the British Army there was an unparalleled gulf between officers and other ranks. In the First World War the great revolution in the British Army had been that for the first time in its history it consisted of a complete cross section of the male population of Great Britain. Only slowly after 1914–15 did even its more perceptive leaders recognise that to fight a war of such severity, lasting so long, meant that it was necessary to explain Britain's war aims beyond simply the call to serve king and country. Although the YMCA had a comprehensive educational scheme for the army, it was only gradually accepted by the military authorities that an understanding of the conflict could provide men with better motivation and also offer an outlet for grievances. F.-M. Haig came to see the value of this, but too late: educating officers at battalion level was only introduced in September 1918.[7]

EDUCATION AND MORALE

Although H.A.L. Fisher, historian and author of the 1918 Education Act, had described army education as 'the greatest invention since gunpowder', in the lean post-war years it was sharply cut back.[8] The Corps of Army Schoolmasters became the Army Educational Corps (AEC) in 1920. It taught the children of ORs in army schools, boy entrants, and adult ORs the 'three Rs' and map-reading. The AEC's wartime role was laid down as to assist in the maintenance of a high spirit of devotion and well-being – recognition of a morale-building role. However, in 1935 it was decided that in wartime the corps should take over cipher work from the Royal Signals. On the outbreak of war most of its officers and NCOs were dispersed to this end, only to be reassembled later.

Recognition that the situation was different from 1914–18 first came in the summer of 1939, when there was a 'vociferous demand' by the YMCA, the Workers' Educational Association (WEA) and the Universities Extra-Mural Consultative Committee for a scheme for education for the militia.[9] On the initiative of Ian Hay Beith, a popular playwright (under the name Ian Hay) and appointed by Leslie Hore-Belisha as WO publicity director, camp libraries were set up in the few brief weeks of the militia's existence in the summer of 1939. On the outbreak of war more ambitious plans were pigeonholed. Undeterred, in December these bodies, plus Toc H (a soldiers' welfare body set up under Church auspices in 1914–18) came together to form a Central Advisory Council (CAC) to lobby the WO about educational facilities for the services. The CAC's vice-chairman was A.D. Lindsay, Master of Balliol College, Oxford.

It had twenty-three regional committees based on universities around the country. Also prominent was W.E. Williams, the secretary of the WEA and editor of its bulletin *The Highway*, who also had experience in publishing with Penguin Books, the great cultural success of the 1930s. Another active figure was George Wigg, who doubted that senior officers understood the ideological nature of the war then beginning: 'democracy vs. fascism'. Wigg was later commissioned in the AEC and after the war was elected as a Labour MP. The CAC operated on a non-party basis, although the WEA and many lecturers in the University Extension System did have a Left-wing slant. However, the National Council of Labour Colleges, a Marxist body, was excluded from participation, although some of its lecturers were individually engaged in CAC activities.[10] Members of the Peace Pledge Union and initially 'friendly enemy aliens' – refugees from Axis countries – were banned from involvement.

The harsh winter of 1939–40, which curtailed much military training, the chaotic nature of the call-up, the long nights spent in cold huts and barracks, the blackout and the boredom of the 'phoney war' were factors that convinced the WO that the state of morale demanded action on both the educational and the recreational fronts. Hore-Belisha and his successor, Oliver Stanley, were sympathetic. In March 1940 a grant of £3,000 was made to the CAC. A committee appointed the following month under the Vice-CIGS Lt-Gen. Haining, reported in the autumn on the need to extend educational facilities, covering 'the Humanities' (history, geography, international affairs); 'the Utilities' (vocational subjects); and 'Arts and Crafts' (hobbies).[11] The methods recommended included lectures, the use of local authority and technical college facilities, and correspondence courses – all aiming at counteracting the effects of another bleak winter during which army morale, following a boost after Dunkirk, slumped. Waiting for the expected invasion with inadequate arms and training did not encourage cheerfulness among the soldiers, whereas the RAF basked in the glory of 'the Few' and the navy was busily countering U-boats and surface raiders.

Haining's report had two aims: 'to keep the soldier mentally alert with a view to increasing his military efficiency' and 'to maintain his morale'.[12] Lord Croft later claimed the initiative for proposing in August 1940 that lectures on 'current affairs' should be introduced to keep the troops aware of the moving picture of the war and to 'stimulate martial ardour in the breasts of our fighting men'.[13] Croft saw the solution to fragile morale in physical training and games, recreation and entertainment, mental stimulation through lectures on ethical issues ('Why are we fighting?'; 'Why were our allies defeated?'), military history, the role of the Dominions, and general educational activities.[14] He was exceptionally influential and active as parliamentary under-secretary. After thirty years in the Commons, Croft had been ennobled by Churchill and held his post throughout the coalition years (longer than Grigg).

Thus organisation of the army's morale campaign was split between a now reactivated AEC and an external, civilian body, under the general title of 'army education'. In December 1940 the WO appointed Maj.-Gen. Harry Willans as director-general of army welfare and education. Under him, as director of army education, Croft got F.W.D. Bendall, a Board of Education official, appointed in preference to Williams, whom he considered too Left-wing. The Army Council assured Croft that the educational work would be on a non-political basis. At that stage he said that he was 'well content with this safeguard'.[15] In this respect, as in the other two fields of reform that Adam tackled as AG, the problems were recognised before he took over and initial steps had been taken to counter them. Nevertheless, his drive pushed them much further.

ROOTS OF CONTROVERSY

Croft's concern about Williams was an early signal of the controversy that would dog the army's educational effort throughout the war. He, other Conservative ministers and many senior officers saw the morale problem as a functional one of maintaining the will to fight. S.P. Mackenzie records one divisional commander greeting his educational officer with: 'I don't care what you do to keep the chaps quiet, but don't educate them'.[16] The attitude of COs was important: opposition was mainly from older men whose influence diminished as the war progressed.[17] One AEC sergeant was given a severe reprimand for stating that intelligence tests had shown 'a very imperfect correlation between the distribution of ability and educational opportunity'. This was considered to be 'sheer socialism'.[18]

Some involved, and not only on the civilian side, saw the matter in a wider perspective as educating a nation in arms. Yet it would be a mistake to see that issue as clear-cut between a crusty old guard and young war-recruited radicals. Apart from Adam and Haining, other senior officers such as Nye and Paget saw the wider picture. The devil was in the detail of what comprised 'education'. Paget for one preferred to consider the issue to be one of citizenship rather than education. As a fervent Christian he also believed that army education should have a religious bias.

Adam was at one with the civilian educationists in seeing an opportunity to widen the horizons of men and women whose formal education had for the most part ended at age 14, whose pre-war lives had involved little mental stimulus in their leisure hours and who now had a great deal of empty time on their hands. Paradoxically, in view of later events, in the early stages it was regular AEC officers (many of whom had been NCOs before the war) who accepted education as a normal part of army life and wartime officers who considered it a distraction from the primary task of fighting the war.[19] Over the next two years these positions were broadly reversed. Two civilians involved, Hawkins and Brimble, were scorching about the regulars: 'It would be dishonest to pretend that they were anything but obstructions to the forward march of army education.'[20] Yet it all depended on what was meant by 'education'.

During Adam's time at Northern Command, he recalled in 1961 that he was, 'horrified at the utter lack of knowledge of the average man as to the war, what we were fighting for, and what we were fighting against'. Told by the director of Military Intelligence that it was impossible to prepare information leaflets about war aims, he issued a training instruction that officers should make notes from the newspapers and, in duty hours, discuss current affairs with their men.[21] This was the first step towards compulsory education. On Adam's prompting Maj.-Gen. Williams in May 1941 submitted to the Executive Committee of the Army Council (ECAC) a memorandum on making such discussions compulsory throughout the army. Given the shortage of AEC officers he suggested that platoon commanders lead discussion groups on the basis of written material supplied to them. However, the new minister, David Margesson, was worried that this would lead to political agitation and that young subalterns would be outclassed in rhetoric by 'the barrack-room lawyer and political axe-grinder'. Willans's response was that political argument was going on anyway and that it was far better to have it out in the open, for 'far from producing anything in the way of subversive opinions, it would go a long way to strengthen morale and combat boredom, which is the agitator's and the German's best friend'.[22]

The AEC establishment of 350 officers and NCOs was more than doubled by volunteers from within the army, who were not exclusively former teachers or lecturers. In September 1940 more than 800 lectures, and in January 1941 some 4,800 lectures, were given by both full-time and part-time lecturers, military and civilian. Local authorities opened their technical schools and other facilities to service personnel. This activity grew substantially: in the six months to March 1943 more than 51,000 lectures were given; in the same period a year later, nearly 69,000. That was the record inside the army. Outside, the CAC's activity rose from under 22,000 lectures in the six months to September 1941, to 88,000 two years later, and peaked in the six months to September 1944 at 112,000. Intensive schools rose from 15 in the first period to 348, but made their greatest contribution in the demobilisation period with 724 courses in March–September 1945, catering for more than 20,000 students.[23]

Attendance was voluntary and in the men's free time; to make them compulsory in free time would have been resented. But the voluntary method produced only a 20 per cent take-up, and that by men already interested in current affairs and other activities. It was the other 80 per cent who needed to be motivated. By the time Adam took over as AG a more radical system was required to ensure that, as much as possible, the lectures should be in training time. The appointment of the permanent secretary at the WO, Sir James Grigg, as war minister early in

1942 brought a more supportive approach. But some senior commanders, such as Paget and Montgomery, disliked too rigid a timetable being imposed, from fear that it would hamper the overriding need for combat training. The latter initially suggested that education be included in the padre's hour.

TWO-WAY PROPAGANDA

While conservative-minded ministers and officers required reassurance about the political content of the lectures and discussions, the captive audience for the lectures and discussions needed reassurance of another kind: that it was not just propaganda thrust at them from on high. In the early stages apathy and cynicism were widespread, the result in many cases of the men's experiences before the war. Army education historian S.P. Mackenzie described how 'Us *v.* Them' attitudes towards the army authorities were widespread, understandable in an institution based on hierarchy and authority. If the concept of independent thought and discussion in even a minimally academic setting was novel to many men, it was just as much to regular officers and NCOs deeply imbued with obeying orders. In the army, debate was a threatening concept. Many senior and junior officers were displeased: the former mainly from principle or prejudice, the latter more often from the onus of another duty, which made demands that some found irksome or worse. Backed by their sergeants, 20-year-old subalterns could exert their authority in normal military duties. Open discussion of current affairs with hard-bitten and cynical men ten or twenty years their senior was not so easy. Nonetheless, the growth and diversification of the various types of educational activity gradually convinced the army at all levels of their value, although there remained a large number of sceptics.[24]

Lectures could be boring or enthralling. 'Boomerang', a trenchant critic of the army, at the receiving end found ABCA (Army Bureau of Current Affairs) lectures the most boring way of imparting information.[25] Ingenuity – sometimes even just a title change – was often needed to engage audience interest. For instance, 'Hitler's rise to power' was more of a draw than 'The growth of Nazi Germany'. The ATS were generally less aware of or interested in current affairs than the men, but some issues could be successfully personalised: 'The prospect for Poland' fell flat; presented on another occasion as, 'Would you marry a Pole?' the subject brought ready and animated participation.[26] ATS education officers were appointed from the autumn of 1941 onwards. Only 5 per cent of the women had General School Certificate (taken at age 15 or 16) and under 1 per cent Higher School Certificate (at age 17 or 18). One survey found that 70 per cent of them did not know they could vote at age 21.

A letter in the WEA journal *The Highway* raised an issue about the auxiliaries that applied equally to the men: how could they be taught about democracy 'when in fact the girls are being conditioned by a (comparatively) beneficial dictatorship'?[27] This summed up the problem of open discussion in the army. Would not discussion of current affairs and the way the war was going risk the discussion of military matters, possibly the discussion of – and then the questioning of – orders? And from there to questioning both the military and civil social order?

The men in AA Command apart (who were summoned to bursts of activity), troops stationed on routine duties in the UK and in rear areas overseas were often more prone to boredom and low morale than front-line men, although they had greater opportunity to exploit the educational facilities offered. But the activities of the AEC were not limited to the 'tail'. It was considered essential to keep 'teeth' troops aware of events in other parts of the front and in other theatres. In 1944–45 the 21st Army Group in north-west Europe produced twenty-nine separate news-sheets for different formations, many on a daily basis. Divisional information officers went forward: one AEC officer jumped at Arnhem and was never heard of again.[28]

TEXTS FOR DISCUSSION

Lectures were only one instrument of army education. As well as films, displays and radio services, four regular printed media were also introduced. The first periodical was *War*, produced fortnightly by the Directorate of Army Education, within the Directorate-General of Welfare and Education (DGWE), under the AG. The first issue in September 1941 included articles on the battles in the Western Desert, tank fighting on the Eastern Front, and an article by an escaped POW from France. This series was under direct military control and politically unexceptional. Published in alternate weeks, *Current Affairs* dealt with wider issues, and from time to time ran into criticism. The first issue was distributed to COs to explain the project. In a foreword, the CIGS (then Gen. Sir John Dill) stated: 'Interest in current affairs, including the events of the war, induces confidence; confidence is one of the ingredients of unshakable morale.'[29] Both pamphlets provided officers with the basis for their discussions with their men. A September 1942 issue of *Current Affairs* was entitled 'Here are the Americans'; the following July 'Balkan Background'. In the summer of 1942 appeared the first issue of a third series entitled *British Way and Purpose* (*BWP*) which, as its name implies, was more openly propagandist in nature. It was produced by a new body, the Army Bureau of Current Affairs (ABCA), which came under the DGWE but was separate from the Directorate of Army Education (DAE). Willans appointed Burgon Bickersteth (who had previously advised the Canadian contingent in Britain on educational matters) as director of army education, while Williams took over ABCA (and became

Self, Shorncliffe, summer 1907.
('Firepower' – the Royal Artillery Museum)

Delhi Durbar 1911, gallop past by RHA: 'the horses *ventre-à-terre*'.
(National Army Museum)

The officers of N ('Eagle') Troop, RHA, India, *c.* 1912. Left front: Adam; right front: Brooke. (Liddell Hart Collection for Military Archives)

The British other ranks of N Troop, India, *c.* 1912. (National Army Museum)

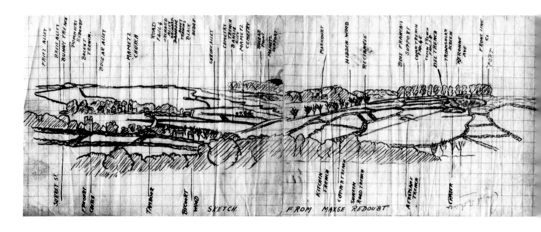

Sketch by Adam of enemy lines, the Somme, 18 May 1916.
(Liddell Hart Centre for Military Archives)

'Hankelow Court in the County of Chester'. (Richard Bailey)

Allies 1940, before the deluge: from left, Admiral Abrial, Lt-Gen. Dill, Lt-Gen. Brooke,
Lt-Gen. Adam, French President Albert Lebrun, Gen. Pagezy, Gen. Lord Gort, General Voruz.
(Liddell Hart Centre for Military Archives)

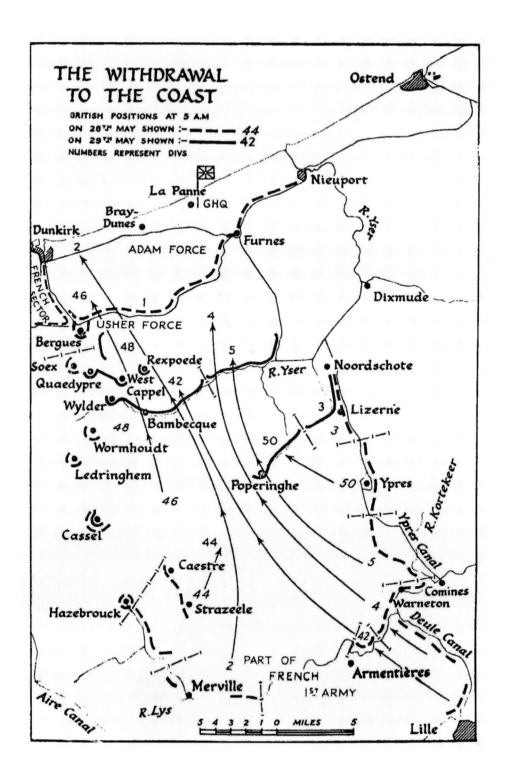

The retreat to Dunkirk. (Liddell Hart Centre for Military Archives)

Troops on the beach at Dunkirk waiting for evacuation.
(Imperial War Museums NYP 68675)

The French destroyer *Bourrasque* sinking, loaded with soldiers.
(Imperial War Museums HU 2280)

Insignia of III Corps, BEF: woven in green on white ground. (Imperial War Museums INS 5287)

Insignia of Northern Command, 1940-41: green felt on blue ground. (Imperial War Museums INS 5038)

Adam with his senior staff, Northern Command.
(Isobel Forbes Adam)

Adam, GOC Northern Command, and Brooke, GOC Home Forces,
inspect coastal defences in 1940. (Imperial War Museums H 9486)

A recruit taking a mechanical ability test.
(Imperial War Museums H 17185)

WOSB leaderless group initiative test in a London suburb.
(Imperial War Museums H 33534)

ABCA information display.
(Imperial War Museums H 34965)

ABCA discussion in the Middle East on post-war medical services.
(Imperial War Museums E 23887)

Opposite: Moravia 1948: The chairman of the British Council
'hoist aloft in a chair as a guest of honour by the young bloods
brandishing the while in time honoured fashion a decanter of
wine, which, conforming to local custom, he subsequently did his
best to drain in this elevated position'. (The National Archives;
text by A.C. Hawkins, Deputy British Council Representative in
Czechoslovakia, 1948)

General Sir Ronald Forbes Adam, GCB, DSO, OBE, 1947.
(Isobel Forbes Adam)

known as 'ABCA Bill'). Croft recalled them as 'both ardent Left Wingers […]
I was frankly alarmed when he [Williams] was made Director of ABCA which
leaves him so largely a free hand.' He thought Bickersteth to be 'woolly, verbose
and up in the clouds'.[30] But Bickersteth was sufficiently down to earth to have
won an MC in the First World War.

Croft had reason to be alarmed. H.A.L. Fisher had once likened army education
to gunpowder – and, to Williams, ABCA was 'dynamite':

> It ordains that, at least once a week, in the middle of the working day platoons
> shall sit down and discuss Current Affairs. Once a week a soldier shall not
> only be entitled to ask, but encouraged to ask 'Why Black Markets Are
> Allowed' […] or 'Why Women Are Being Called Up'. No one pretends that
> they always get an answer or that they will get a proper answer. The significant
> thing is that they can ask. They can talk. They can unbosom themselves of
> doubt, ignorance and anger. It is a very long way from Balaclava to A.B.C.A. –
> but the jump has been made.[31]

Relations between Bickersteth and Paget were aided by their common religious
beliefs, and the former was gratified by the GOC's finding the first two *BWP*
pamphlets 'first rate':

> Had Adam […] expressed a similar view I should have been less taken off my
> guard but to hear the Commander-in-Chief, under whom all field forces in
> this country, say it, was a different matter. I did try to play the devil's advocate a
> bit, pointing out difficulties, not from my point if view but from his, but he still
> insisted that the British Way and Purpose booklets were what the men should
> have wherever they are.[32]

The historically minded such as Williams and Lindsay (the CAC's vice-
chairman) saw a parallel between the discussion groups and the Putney
Debates in the Cromwellian army in the 1640s, and welcomed this. Others,
more concerned for the breakdown of discipline that those earlier debates had
shown, were less sanguine.

Williams identified three groups of critics of ABCA: 'the clamorous Left-
wing' wanted more radical changes, including political commissars; 'the
garden-city idealists' feared the army would pump its own propaganda into
the troops; 'Brigadier Blueface and his myrmidons [are] convinced to the last
ditch that the soldier is a good-natured clod who is best left in his ignorance'.
Reassuring these groups – and the last was by far the most vocal and most
highly placed – called on Adam to display those diplomatic abilities that he
had shown in 1938–39 when maintaining a precarious peace between Hore-
Belisha and Gort.

Williams detected gains to army discipline with young platoon officers getting closer to their men through their two-way discussions. The officer he saw as a group-leader not a lecturer: 'His role is to take the chair, not the floor.' This process gave officers their own opportunity for self-education in citizenship, he concluded. More senior regimental officers may not have articulated it in those terms, but many came round to the conclusion that the overall effect of ABCA discussions was positive, or at least less negative than early reactions assumed. Although at all levels some maintained their scepticism, indeed opposition, in time it declined. Subaltern Tony Bickersteth, despite his uncle's association with ABCA, was scathing. In his unit, current affairs were handled in informal discussion huddles until:

> A.B.C.A. inflicted its pamphlets upon us. This amazing body issues a lurid red pamphlet called 'War' every second week and every other week a slightly less lurid but equally cheap and nasty one which, on the outside, looks like a cheap propaganda leaflet. I daren't produce it in front of the men while I am talking on the subject it deals with, because the immediate reaction would be, 'He's had this propaganda shoved down his throat, and now he's trying to shove it down ours', and they will not play.[33]

POLITICAL TENSIONS

Discussions about the Soviet Union and post-war domestic policy were two fields of political contention. Britain's relationship with the Soviet Union in the Second World War was on the basis of 'my enemy's enemy is my friend'. There was little confidence between the Western Allies and the Soviet Union, and little exchange of confidences either. Churchill had no difficulty with this, despite, only eighteen months prior to 'Operation Barbarossa', having advocated British intervention on the Finnish side in the Winter War. British communists and fellow travellers had to stand on their heads much more outrageously. The difficulty about presenting the new ally to the British public, civilian and military alike, was that those most knowledgeable about the Soviet Union were mainly communists and fellow travellers. One such was D.N. Pritt. Elected as a Labour MP in 1935, he was expelled from the party early in 1940 for justifying the Soviet attack on Finland, and sat on as Independent Labour. Not officially accepted for the CAC panel, he undertook some lectures at regional level arranged by sympathisers George Wigg and Gilbert Hall of the AEC. In his lectures, in his own words, Pritt 'put over a good deal of carefully disguised propaganda'.[34] In mid-1941 he was banned from lecturing to the forces and carried on a year-long campaign of protest with letters to Grigg, the prime minister, the air minister and officials, before he finally accepted defeat. Other Left-wingers felt to have overstepped the mark were also dropped. However, Grigg wrote to Churchill in March 1943 saying that anti-Soviet lectures would not be tolerated any more than pro-communist ones. 'Indeed I have banned lectures from Miss Rosita Forbes [a novelist] on this very ground', he added, with evident satisfaction that even-handedness had been demonstrated. Another lecturer, 'who spoke disrespectfully of Premier Stalin', was dropped.[35] Given that there were some 9,000 part-time and full-time speakers giving tens of thousands of lectures each year, the level of serious complaint was limited.

EDUCATION AS A PARADE

In the summer of 1943 it was agreed that compulsory education for the troops would continue the following winter, notwithstanding the higher tempo of preparation for the forthcoming landing on the Continent; indeed it was thought that the continuation might lull German expectations. Through private interviews at WOSBs, convalescent centres and transit camps, it appeared that ABCA was reasonably well carried out in some 60 per cent of units, and that in another 10 per cent the men had got something out of it. Given the demands of campaigning, troop movements and other priorities, this was a creditable record. But Adam was well aware that such success as ABCA had in considerable measure was due to the fact that it was a parade.[36] It was done in 'the King's time'.

As far as the printed material was concerned, things also went politically smoothly in the main: 118 issues of *Current Affairs* appeared over four years and only a few caused controversy. Williams wrote in the first issue that political neutrality would be observed. Croft himself accepted that the first few issues were quite free of political bias. But issue No. 12, which criticised British press barons, was never distributed. No. 25, on the Soviet Union, initially met with Croft's *nihil obstat*, but when others criticised it he changed his view. Overall, Adam was quite confident:

> The pamphlets were prepared by the best authorities available and we had a great triumph when our pamphlet on Russia was produced. We received letters of protest from a Right-wing MP and the Russian ambassador; we knew therefore that we were in the middle of the road.[37]

Croft was ever vigilant. In December 1943 he wrote to Grigg: 'The Russian bias crops up again'. This time it was in a pamphlet that compared Soviet agriculture with pre-enclosure English farming. The pamphlet 'is propaganda from first to last and not very subtle at that'. Its writer, Sir John Maynard, Croft noted, was a member of the Fabian Society, as if that moderately Left-wing association was some gang of Bolsheviks.[38] Lower down the scale, Henry Longhurst was still furious forty years later, writing of 'the insidious rubbish fed compulsorily to the soldiers by ABCA, the Left-wing Army Bureau of Current Affairs'.[39] In mid-war he had resigned his commission to stand for Parliament but lost his seat in 1945. So he had a personal grudge.

The *BWP* booklets had a rockier ride as they dealt with matters of domestic and foreign policy that were in essence political. The first issue, on what Britain was fighting to preserve – freedom, democratic institutions, religious and political liberty, the legal system – was on reasonably common ground, although the author did stray into the politically sensitive question of policy in post-war Britain. The second issue was more provocative. It had four authors, including the *Economist*'s acting editor Donald Tyerman, whose article considered what post-war economic policy might be. He wrote:

> In wartime there is no unemployment. There is full employment on war-work. The lesson that full employment should also be possible in peacetime is being learned. The lesson of equality is equally pointed. In wartime, the stock of goods and services is strictly limited. It has, therefore, to be shared out with the greatest possible equality.

This was more than an implicit attack on the pre-war government. Another article criticised the public school system. The texts were passed by the censor, an AEC major.[40] Too late, Croft objected that as to what domestic or foreign policies might be followed after the war was a question that should wait: winning the war should come first. A copy of the pamphlet in the National Archives still bears his indignant handwritten margin comments.[41] He and those of generally conservative mind, including Grigg, had difficulty in keeping the lid on this simmering pot. On the other hand, *BWP* 3, on citizenship and the empire, gained Croft's seal of approval.

'STRONG BEVERIDGES'

The biggest row was over an issue of *Current Affairs* late in 1942. That autumn, Sir William Beveridge's report to the government on 'Social Insurance and Allied Services' was published, providing a blueprint for social security after the war. It stressed the need to avoid the five evils that had blighted the country in the 1930s – want, disease, squalor, ignorance and idleness. It had an extraordinary success for an official document with the driest of mandarin's titles: a record 635,000 copies were sold. Williams asked Beveridge to prepare a text for the December issue. Adam read the text, found it a 'factual summary of the plan' and, before leaving London on a duty tour, told Williams to show it to Grigg.[42]

This was not done. The pamphlet's appearance in print provoked questions in the Commons. The minister withdrew 60,000 copies of the pamphlet, a decision approved by the War Cabinet on the grounds that the report was Beveridge's personal conclusions, not government policy. Croft, who said that he had known nothing of the planned publication, described how Grigg, 'with his usual courage, tackled wrong-doing with complete disregard for his personal fortunes [...] took the whole responsibility on his shoulders'.[43] Bickersteth had another perspective: that Croft 'succeeded in getting the Conservative backbenchers behind him, and Grigg rather tamely capitulated'.[44] He also feared that the minister thought the episode could lead to Churchill digging in his heels and forbidding ABCA altogether.[45]

An intervention came from the political gossip tract *The Week*, which before the war had proved a constant irritant to the Chamberlain government by publishing leaks from inside the governmental machine. Its editor, Claud Cockburn, blamed the public brouhaha on Croft: 'the same man who once described General Franco as a "great Christian gentleman" [...] started the game. For some time, it is understood, Lord Croft has disapproved of the "tendency" of *Current Affairs*.' According to Cockburn, Williams:

> ignored the threat of Croft to 'go to Conservative Central Office about it'. Lady Grigg rang Williams about something else and mentioned it would [be] better to hold everything, as 'They have gone to the Prime Minister'. Apparently Croft had led a delegation to the PM to protest against the 'dispensation of strong Beveridges to the innocent troops'.[46]

Grigg, a former Whitehall mandarin never at ease in the Commons, tried to defend his position: 'Neither A.B.C.A. nor the rest of the Army education scheme [...] are intended to be Left Book Clubs, nor are they intended to be branches of the Primrose League [a Conservative Party organisation]'.[47] The minister's objection was not that ABCA should not discuss Beveridge but that the publication appeared to give the proposals official approval when they had not yet been debated in Parliament. Six months later, a replacement pamphlet on social security appeared with a closely supervised text. It included a summary of Beveridge's report by another hand, extracts from parliamentary debates held in the meanwhile, and from Churchill's recent broadcast on post-war reconstruction and the heavy costs that would be involved.

Other contentious issues arose. Early in 1944 Bickersteth recorded having a 'tussle' with the war minister over *BWP* 16 on India: the men were asking about illiteracy, poverty and the refusal by Britain to grant home rule, whereas Grigg – a former civil servant in India knighted for his services there – wanted 'a panegyric on our rule'. He vetoed a retired Indian civil servant in favour of his own nominee, who wrote a text more to his choice, with no reference to the contemporary political situation in India.[48] When Williams wrote *Current Affairs* 48, with its 'When the Lights Go On' article about post-war opportunities, Croft was furious. Williams, he wrote in a memorandum, was attempting to forward socialist propaganda. Why, he asked, was there no mention of the positive aspects of Britain in the 1930s? Unemployment had never been at German or US levels, and had fallen well before 1939. Health and housing had improved. This was true, but did not reflect a common perception. The Jarrow march of unemployed from that distressed northern town to London in 1936 was a more potent memory. Croft believed that most generals were political innocents and that 'someone with no political prejudice but with a real knowledge of affairs' should be appointed to oversee both ABCA and the DAE. However, Williams had submitted the text of *Current Affairs* 48 to Grigg, who had consulted both the Deputy Prime Minister Clement Attlee and the Lord President Sir John Anderson, and got their blessing. Croft lost.[49]

FORCES' NEWSPAPERS

The fourth periodical publication was a series of posters with their own problems. A series with the slogan 'Your Britain – fight for it now', included views of idyllic countryside but also trod on more sensitive ground. One issue in 1942, under the same slogan, showed a bomb-damaged terrace of houses merging into a modern block of flats – an implicit promise of a better Britain to come. Another with the slogan, 'Look Ahead – In War prepare for Peace', so annoyed Paget that he ordered its withdrawal from Home Forces. He thought it 'undesirable at the present time to direct men's minds away from the immediate urgency of the war effort'.[50] This was a recurrent and by no means unjustified theme among some military and political leaders. The anxiety was that paying too much attention to the longer term would undermine men's willingness to risk sacrifice in the immediate future. In the spring of 1942 the poster was certainly premature: the war was going badly in North Africa, Russia and the Far East. It was six months before 'the end of the beginning' that Churchill discerned after Alamein. It was not the time to divert attention from immediate needs. In the spring of 1943 it would have been a little more justifiable to consider the post-war world; in the spring of 1944 even more so.

Fortnightly map reviews showing the progress of the war in different theatres were pinned up in camps and barracks. They provided easy access for soldiers, only half of whom, even in Home Commands, ever saw a newspaper or listened to the radio.[51] Overseas, the forces published twenty-four newspapers by serving journalists, some of whom, such as Hugh and Reg Cudlipp, became notable Fleet Street names after the war. But again there was a problem in controlling them to the satisfaction of all: if the various publications were to be locally relevant and topical it was impossible to exercise central editorial control. Some articles from *8th Army News* were republished in London newspapers. One such article criticised treating post-Mussolini Italy as a co-belligerent, which reflected many soldiers' attitudes. Churchill demanded to know who had authorised the article and was told 'General Montgomery'. Another article criticised a well-known star then on tour in the Middle East for not having done her bit earlier in the war. Churchill asked the same question and got the same answer, Adam recorded in 1960.[52] Adam was made specifically responsible for army newspapers. *Daily Mirror* columnist William Connor ('Cassandra') was called up – according to rumour because he had caused offence to officialdom– and edited *Union Jack* in North Africa. In Adam's view, 'He was a very good editor and we never had any difficulty'. Adam thought the correspondence columns an excellent safety valve for the troops' grouses, and of assistance to the morale committee in preparing its quarterly reports to the Army Council.

These activities required personnel and finance. In September 1943 the head official for finance in the WO raised a query about a request for an additional fifty-seven officers and NCOs for the AEC. Adam pointed out that at barely 1,000-strong the corps was only three times its pre-war size (the army itself eventually expanded fourteenfold from its regular strength), although backed up by the more than 9,000 civilian lecturers and many others within the army. He contrasted this with the Pay Corps, up from 624 to 16,400, excluding ATS and civilian employees. The army, he also stressed, spent three times as much on welfare as on education, which cost £500,000 a year – equal to the cost of thirty-five tanks or twenty bombers, a number that might be lost in one night's operations. At the same ECAC meeting, the Vice-CIGS Lt-Gen. Haining put the case for education strongly:

> the Army Council could not escape the obligation, issuing from statute and the circumstances of war, that there had been committed to their charge and care millions of men and women, many of whom were at a crucial stage of their educational lives, and many of whom were ill-educated in any case. His military experience had led him to believe that education in proper proportion and suitably imparted, sharpened the mind and wits of the student, stimulated his self-confidence and morale and therefore make him a better soldier. It should be the constant aim of the Army Council to return troops to civil life better equipped, than when they left it, to engage in the struggle for a livelihood.[53]

Adam could not have had a better ally than Haining. Croft, who chaired the meeting, said that the individual should 'be called upon' to undergo any instruction to make him an efficient and better soldier, and 'encouraged' to attend any other form of education. He added that his military colleagues might have a different view but he wanted to record his views. The soldiers present favoured Haining's view: the aim was to make a man 'a more enlightened individual, a more intelligent citizen, and, therefore, a better soldier. These three aims are inextricably interwoven.'[54] Croft's fury at being outflanked is understandable.

OFF THE POLITICAL RADAR

Because of political squabbles, notorious at the time and since, the run-of-the-mill activities in army education during the Second World War risk being overlooked. The army had to deal with 10,000 illiterates, a minute proportion out of an army of 3 million. Six-week intensive courses led to two-thirds being able to read and understand a newspaper and almost all could write a letter home unaided. The impact on their morale and self-respect was considerable. Many more read or wrote with difficulty. At the other end of the literacy scale, by August 1943 more than 43,000 men (some in German prison camps) and women were undertaking 585 correspondence courses. Also politically low-key were the music circles, play readings, educational visits to historic and industrial sites, choral societies, art groups and brains trusts held in Britain and abroad. At its peak, the army book centre sent out 1 million books and ½ million periodicals a month, plus many Sunday newspapers. At Coleg Harlech in Wales, more than 4,600 British and Allied officers undertook courses in group discussion techniques. Selected groups of British, Canadian and American personnel spent a week at Balliol College, Oxford, to study their own countries' current situation and post-war hopes.

One activity that risked political displeasure was the London District ABCA play unit, which provided a means of raising issues when discussion groups could not interest the troops. J.B. Priestley wrote two plays for it, including one on anti-Semitism. A play by another writer, *Where Do We Go From Here*, was about a Tyneside family between the wars. In the absence of the war minister, Lady Grigg ('a thorn in Orwell's flesh', when broadcasting for the BBC Eastern Service[55]) attended the dress rehearsal and approved it. Adam recalled: 'I waited with some trepidation for the press notices but Lady G had been quite right and they were all favourable'. From London it went on tour.

A different (and unusual) aspect of Adam's attitudes appears in James Marshall-Cornwall's memoirs. A contemporary of Adam at 'the Shop' and his successor in 1940 as commander of BEF's III Corps, he described him as an 'old friend'. As GOC Western Command in 1942 he decided to form a 'Western Command Symphony Orchestra' from some eminent Austrian musicians and singers in the Pioneer Corps:

Although welcomed, locally, my initiative found less favour at the War Office. I soon received an irate letter from the Adjutant-General, upbraiding me for the misuse of military manpower and ordering me to return my tenors to their picks and shovels. Questions were even asked in Parliament […] about my misdemeanour.[56]

Adam makes no mention of this incident. Possibly Marshall-Cornwall was ahead of his time in giving a high profile to 'friendly enemy aliens' when they were still excluded from commissions and combat roles.

In contrast with the claims − positive and negative − about army education Mackenzie provided a deflating assessment:

Current-affairs and citizenship education in the Army did not on the whole produce the dramatic results forecast either by its more enthusiastic proponents or its more ardent foes. It did not generally help create a more advanced conception in the soldier's mind of his role in society, nor did it, on the whole, lead him to think and act as if he knew better than those in authority. The achievements of this form of education tend to be more prosaic.[57]

Yet the more prosaic achievements provided many men and women with broader horizons and the opportunity to overcome the handicap of the deadening commonplace education – though 'instruction' might be a more accurate word – doled out in so many of Britain's elementary (and other) schools in earlier years. Army education in general, and the pre-release education and training programmes and the post-release support for further and higher education gave a generation of Britons chances that they would not otherwise have had.

In 1993 the *RUSI Journal* had two articles on Adam: one was by a Capt. J.D. Goode that excoriated Adam;[58] the other, by Georgina Natzio, gave a different assessment of him. She lacked direct experience of Adam and of his time but added a perspective that Goode lacked:

He was the man the Army's wartime servicemen and women needed. Many sent to overseas theatres, and indeed those serving at home, felt the benefits of his influence: it is not an exaggeration to say that his involvement in these matters not only eased tedium and provided relief from the blacker side of war, but enhanced many lives permanently.[59]

In 1946, still smarting from his experience Croft wrote:

it was never my intention that this army [education] machinery should be used to turn the Army into thousands of debating groups on vexed questions of home policy, which I realized must lead to Party political arguments, which have always proved harmful to any Army, whether at war or peace.[60]

He had warned some 'high officers' of the dangers, but 'in their innocence and simplicity they were hard to convince and took no steps to stop a trend which was to say the least unfortunate'.

Adam managed to float above this *melée* unscathed, despite his warm espousal of army education in general, his sponsorship of ABCA in particular, and not least his ease at having Bickersteth and Williams – Croft's 'ardent Left Wingers' – in influential positions with ready access to him. His instructions to Williams that the Beveridge text be cleared politically were disregarded. So he escaped free of charge in that fracas. After Williams' death in an air crash in February 1943 Adam took a more direct oversight, with a deputy AG put in charge of three departments: Welfare, Education and ABCA. But he still avoided censure by the seriously critical elements. Even Croft, so suspicious of Left-wing influences, exonerates him. Could Croft have considered Adam 'innocent and simple'?

THE HUMANE TOUCH

As war minister Leslie Hore-Belisha was determined to improve soldiers' welfare. But the army's budget in 1938–39 was concentrated on rearming, and the WO had initially to rely on private benevolence. Motor manufacturer Lord Nuffield gave £1½ million to create a trust fund. As in the earlier war, a spontaneous movement grew up around the country. County welfare committees were set up and unpaid welfare officers appointed, with finance from public subscription. The YMCA, Church Army, Salvation Army and other voluntary organisations joined in. The Women's Voluntary Service was started from scratch. Local authorities also played a part. The effort began by providing woollen comforts and other gifts for the servicemen and women. By 1945 14 million gifts of various kinds, 41 million cigarettes and large numbers of books had been distributed.

Only after Sir Ronald Adam became AG did the WO set up, late in 1941, the Directorate-General of Welfare and Education (DGWE), working in co-operation with the voluntary movement. As the war went on, the scope of official action widened, one objective being to maintain morale and, amongst other aims, to relieve anxiety among men and women away on duty about what was happening at home, and vice versa. As with education, this widening and deepening aspect of army life demanded extended concern by regimental officers for their men's wellbeing, especially those overseas. Later in the war, service personnel abroad could record airmail gramophone records for families, which proved very popular, and lightweight airmail letters in theory provided rapid contact, but were often delayed: in December 1943 Adam was shocked to learn that they took two to three weeks to reach North Africa, and sometimes longer. He was also concerned at the poor acclimatisation training given before men were sent into battle, the lack of air ambulances, other medical inadequacies, the poor administration in 15th Army Group, and that razor blades were not an army issue.[1]

An early welfare move by the government was to empower the Ministry of Pensions to give war service grants to needy families that underwent a sharp fall in income when the breadwinner enlisted. Nonetheless, many families suffered from the effects of the 30 per cent inflation by 1944, some experiencing malnutrition until the government tardily increased allowances. Other morale-boosting measures included getting urgent news of air raids on towns from which serving men and women came, and the granting of more generous compassionate leave so that UK-based men and women could visit families in blitzed towns. For men long posted overseas there were particular problems: by 1943 some regulars had been abroad for nine years, some war-enlisted men for four. The shorter RAF and navy tours abroad were resented by soldiers. In 1943 the 'Python' scheme was introduced to rotate such men. Though good for morale, the scheme created a permanent wastage of personnel from overseas commands because of the numbers in transit.

Long absences created marital stress. Sparrow recorded, 'The number of wives and fiancées who were unfaithful to soldiers serving overseas almost defies belief.'[2] In July 1941, just after Adam's appointment as AG, his department created a free legal service to deal with such problems and generally to handle insurance, mortgage payments and hire-purchase difficulties. Each Command formed a small legal service; in London Command a larger one dealt also with overseas cases. Ranks up to sergeant could receive legal aid certificates without revealing their pay and allowances. Service welfare officers and civil organisations tried their best to effect reconciliation in marital disputes. If this failed, the Services Divorce Department, set up a year later, stepped in. Overseas sections were formed later. By the end of 1945, 175,000 legal cases had been dealt with: 94,000 concerned divorce, with 50,000 already granted. Many civilian probation officers volunteered their help, and nearly 5,000 lawyers gave pro bono services.

Just after D-Day, the now Maj.-Gen. Lord Bridgeman (Adam's GSO during the Dunkirk evacuation) was appointed deputy AG to oversee welfare. Unlike his predecessor he did not have education and ABCA in his remit. His comment in his memoirs on the evident reluctance to put ABCA under a Tory peer illustrates the febrile mood on the issue.[3] On the other hand, Left-wing influence was reduced when a few weeks later Burgon Bickersteth – one of Croft's 'ardent Left-wingers' – was succeeded as head of army education by a politically neutral academic.

Other aspects of welfare included the entertainment programmes provided by the ENSA[4] with talent drawn both from professionals and from within the forces. Radio stations were set up in different theatres and, as we have seen, newspapers. Both feature and documentary films were made or sponsored (notably *The Way Ahead*, *Next of Kin* and *Desert Victory*). Adam, while on a visit to North Africa, noted the good facilities at the American Red Cross Clubs and suggested to the NAAFI that similar establishments should be set up for British men and women on local leave:

I had a theory that if you provided men and women with furniture, linen, glass and cutlery that they could be proud of, you would find that there were far fewer damages. These clubs were well furnished and the restaurants were delightful with small tables, good linen and excellent glass and cutlery. Men coming back from the front could get a bath, shave and haircut, clean underclothing, a suit pressed and a manicure. The last became very popular as it gave the feeling that you were really out of the battle.[5]

The scope and nature of the army's welfare role evolved piecemeal and reached its full effectiveness only in 1944–45, with 21st Army Group the first force to leave the UK with a fully organised welfare service. After the liberation of Brussels, the best hotels were taken over as leave centres, and were respected by the men, as Adam expected. Welfare services were not confined to ORs. Traditionally officers had been expected to provide for their own welfare, and when most had private means this could be assumed. But a growing number of officers commissioned from the ranks began to ask for facilities for themselves, especially for leave accommodation at reasonable prices. The Nuffield Fund and the YMCA set up officers' clubs (for all the services) in London and elsewhere.

So, under Adam's stewardship, the army recognised its need to provide substantial pastoral care beyond the services of the traditional padre and the wet canteen. Of course, the purpose of morale-boosting was to make for happier and therefore more effective soldiers. In 1944 the *Daily Telegraph* was expansive:

A tall, burly man with a chubby face, a charming smile and a genuinely accessible pleased-to-meet-you manner, a tunic moulded to him and leatherwork with the liquid polish of Aldershot in peacetime [...] Adam's real distinction, indeed, lies chiefly in his clear grasp of the meaning of a vastly expanded Army and of the difference between that and the small professional Army to which, by training, he himself belongs. So far as it can be achieved, things must seem to be 'fair' in such an Army, and it is one of the achievements of the A.G. and the War Office that 'wangles' and 'soft options' and the disreputable social pulls that marked the last war are so much less in evidence this time.

ROLL ON DEMOB

The gradual build-up of military manpower meant that plans had to be made for demobilisation when the time came. Michael Howard, a Coldstream Guard and later a military historian, described his experience. Towards the end of the war he was appointed as his battalion's education officer, 'which meant nothing when we were in the line and little out of it'. He gave the occasional lecture on current affairs and regarded the ABCA offerings as 'bumf'. But once the war was over, he found that education became a serious business:

> The War Office, under the guidance of an extraordinarily enlightened Adjutant-General, Sir Ronald Adam, realized that, however skilfully it was managed, the demobilization of the troops would take a long time, and meanwhile something must be done to occupy them. Resettlement courses should be provided to train them in new skills; and, as responsible citizens, they should be prepared to think seriously about the political, social and international problems that would confront them as voters.[6]

It had taken nearly six years to expand the British Army from under 1 million – including regulars, regular reservists, Territorials and militiamen – when mobilised in late 1939 to just under 3 million at the end of the war. This figure excludes the 146,000 deaths from battle and much the same number from other causes, as well as the 470,000 men and women invalided out or otherwise discharged during the war years. The ATS was up from 24,000 in 1939 to 191,000 in 1945, already down 20,000 from its mid-1943 peak. So some four million men and women were in its ranks at one time or other. The slow build-up of strength had been determined by overall needs, plus the time taken to equip and train the troops. At the war's end, the run down in numbers could be a great deal faster. Curiously, plans for demobilisation began as early as October 1940.[7] This suggests that the bureaucratic machine was just trundling on, or that at the time of Britain's greatest peril the WO was supremely confident of ultimate victory (or of early defeat?). A committee set up early in 1941 under Sir William Jowitt reported the following year when – with the USSR and the USA in the war – ultimate victory was more discernible. Early plans were essential, for the WO was only too aware that in 1918–19 demobilisation had been a disaster. The 'very scientific and logical scheme' at that time – in P.J. Grigg's words – was geared to getting the economy back to normal as soon as possible. Employers were able to ask for individual men and they tended to choose those who had most recently been in their employ and whose skills had not atrophied by four years in the trenches. So men who had volunteered in 1914 were passed over for later enlistees. Grigg described how the system 'broke down helplessly because nobody could be sure that it was just and proof against wrangling'.[8] The upshot was mutiny at home and abroad. The 1918 electoral slogan 'a land fit for heroes' proved a swindle, with many ex-soldiers reduced to selling matches in the gutter as a cover for begging. During the Second World War this bitter memory informed much public sentiment and a fear of a similar situation occurring when peace returned.

Adam found that all records of the demobilisation procedure in 1919 had been destroyed and the only information available was in newspaper files, questions and debates in *Hansard*, an article in a service journal, and a chapter in Winston

Churchill's history of the First World War. To avoid a repeat of the 1918 situation he believed it essential to have a system that was fair and easily understood. It was agreed that this time demob would be based on the 'first in, first out' principle. However, its straightforward implementation would produce its own anomalies and injustices. It would be unfair to retain older men who had volunteered early on but who had been initially held back in industry. On the other hand, releasing men just on the basis of greater age would be unfair to men aged 25 or 26 who had served throughout the war. Adam considered a points system, such as the US was planning on the basis of length of service, age, time served overseas, marital status, number of children, wounds received and decorations awarded. He opposed taking into account whether a man was married or not, because that had not been a factor when men had been called up, and it also disregarded the fact that men serving at home had had more opportunities to marry than men overseas. He was sympathetic to taking account of overseas service, but the only record uniformly available to COs, a man's pay book, did not state when he had been posted overseas. Finally, only length of service and age were taken into account, and an easily understood graph established.[9] For example, a man of 22 with four years' service would be in the same release bracket as a man of 40 with one year's service; a man aged 24 with four years' service would have equal status to a man of 30 with three years' service. This class 'A' covered some 90 per cent of servicemen. Men with skills valuable in reconstructing the economy – in industry, transport and housing, for example – could agree to be placed in a special class 'B' offering early release, subject to their agreeing to work for a period anywhere in Britain as required. This condition proved quite a deterrent to men potentially in this class. A third class 'C' covered cases deserving early compassionate release.

GERMANY TO BE DEFEATED FIRST

When the release scheme was being modelled it was clear that Germany would be defeated before Japan, so that although some men could be released when victory in Europe was achieved, many more would have to be retained for the war in Asia, either in that theatre or for training forces for it. So, as Howard noted, the process of reducing the army would take some time. Meanwhile, there was a lot the army could do to implement the principle enunciated in the Haining report that the army should 'return troops to civil life better equipped than when they left it, to engage in the struggle for a livelihood'.[10] Troops on occupation duties in Europe and elsewhere had to remain in service, but now had more time on their hands. The education and resettlement programmes aimed at ensuring that those hands were not too idle. The armed forces, labour and education ministries prepared extensive and detailed plans for education and training for men and women approaching demobilisation.

For army personnel, a committee drawn from the CAC and the WO had been appointed under Lord Croft's chairmanship in August 1942. It proposed programmes in six fields: technical (building, engineering, mechanics, radio, etc.); the sciences; commercial subjects, including law and accountancy; the humanities; the arts; and 'health and home' for the women's services. The programmes envisaged four hours' resettlement training a week, plus an hour each for ABCA. On this basis, 130 different detailed six-month courses were drawn up, with handbooks prepared, instructors earmarked, with some appointed by the end of the war. The programmes would be rolled out on the basis, depending on circumstances, in each theatre of military operations, with students moving from unit to brigade, division and corps centres of study as required. A major handicap was the shortage of books, for the Blitz had destroyed 4 million books in publishers' warehouses, many of them suitable for the army's needs. Under the resettlement programme it was decided that each unit of 500 or more men and women should have 500 books, mainly on vocational matters, and each Command 5,000 books: some 3 million in all. By the end of the war 1.2 million had been delivered. Adam was eager for their use, recounting how at one unit he found the books all packed up as the storeman believed the books would be damaged if issued. 'He was quite surprised when I told him that I wanted to see them destroyed by constant use.'[11] By mid-1946 1.7 million books were distributed, although few of the technical books required were in fact produced.[12] To help personnel already released, 380 resettlement offices were set up around the country to give general advice and help find employment. Thirty industries established training schemes for both able and disabled persons, but employers were not asked to give priority to ex-servicemen and women because during the war many civilians had faced quite as great dangers as had many in uniform.

Late in 1944 the government produced a white paper entitled 'Reallocation of Man-Power between the Armed Forces and Civilian Employment during the Interim between the Defeat of Germany and the Defeat of Japan'. This cautious wording was adopted to try to calm impatience that the war would end soon, for in the late summer, with Paris and Brussels liberated, spirits had been jubilant. On 22 August 1944 Bickersteth recorded Adam as expecting the war to end by 15 October at the latest, with Gen. 'Pug' Ismay, the prime minister's chief of staff, even more optimistic. 'It will be interesting to see if these cheerful prognostications prove correct'.[13] They did not, confounded by the failure of 'Operation Market Garden' at Arnhem and confirmed by the Ardennes offensive in December. There was a very cold winter to fight through. Moreover, at this time there was no reason to suppose that the war against Japan would not last throughout 1945 and into 1946 or even beyond, with bloody battles through Burma, Malaya, the Dutch East Indies, the Philippines and every Japanese home island.

The government considered that, once victory in Europe had been achieved, it was paramount to maintain public interest in pursuing that remote war. For the British people, the Germans were the enemy that had devastated their cities and killed 60,000 civilians, 30,000 merchant seamen as well as most of the 230,000 British servicemen and women, with a comparable number of Commonwealth and Empire servicemen. (In 1914–18, 1,570 civilians in Britain were killed by air raids and coastal bombardment.) Gen. Slim's troops fighting stubbornly in appalling conditions far away in the Burmese jungle understandably considered themselves 'the forgotten army'. Of the 2.9 million men in the army in June 1945 only 315,000 were in the Far East. As early as April 1943 Adam, on a gruelling visit to the Middle East and India, found that a recent broadcast by the prime minister on the war against Japan was being interpreted as meaning that troops out East would be demobilised later than those nearer home.[14] This belief had to be dispelled urgently.

RESISTING CHURCHILL

In February 1945 the WO issued regulations for release from the army. Yet politically all was still far from clear. Adam wrote in 1961:

> I was determined to fight any attempt to modify the scheme we had sold to the Army and which was fair and simple. Several attempts were made, but all were warded off. One reason was that Ernest Bevin was convinced of the fairness and resisted all political attempts at change.

Some years later Bevin, the wartime minister of labour, told Adam that just before the 1945 general election Lord Beaverbrook, a close ally of Churchill, had said to the prime minister that he must let out all the men that industry required if the economy was to get on its legs again – totally disregarding the political lessons of the First World War. Churchill sent for R.A. Butler, Bevin's successor in the caretaker Conservative government in the spring of 1945, and told him that he would announce the change in the release scheme in the election broadcast that he was about to make. Butler replied that in that case he had better look for a new minister of labour. Churchill 'pleaded with him as only he could, but Butler remained firm. Finally Winston said, "Well, I shall have to do the alternative broadcast, I will attack Laski."'[15]

Churchill's wartime broadcasts had inspired the nation. However, when it came to election broadcasting all his persuasive and inspirational skills evaporated, especially in his attack on Harold Laski, the chairman of the Labour Party, and his foretelling 'a socialist Gestapo', if Labour won. The great war leader suddenly found himself the subject of scepticism, if not ridicule.

RESETTLEMENT

So, after the defeat of Germany, demobilisation began as planned on 18 June 1945, with 750,000 men of all three services scheduled for release by the end of the year, with other young men called up to replace many of them. The women's services were rapidly run down and further recruitment suspended. Men and women not due for immediate release began, according to circumstances, their pre-release programmes. In the event, much of the planned resettlement training was upset by the welcome if unforeseen surrender of Japan in mid-August, only three months after that of Germany. So existing plans were to a large extent thrown aside and, in the urge to get home for Christmas, the number released was nearly doubled.

Attempts were made to make the procedure as humane as possible: a group of young convalescing officers was appointed to answer on a personal basis all queries from wives anxious to see their menfolk again, ending the letters with, 'Yours sincerely' instead of the usual formal style. One further change (a lesson learnt from 1918) was that at each release depot an officer thanked each man and said goodbye: 'It had been one of the grouses of soldiers demobilised in 1918 that they left without a word of thanks from anyone', Adam wrote in 1961. *The Times* was enthusiastic about the first day's release proceedings, which were certainly exceptional for the 1,400 men and women concerned. There was 'almost a garden party atmosphere' at Guildford, with a band from the RA, a cinema, and Adam among the guests to explain how the demob system would work.

However, even the accelerated rate of demobilisation was criticised by impatient men and their families in the latter part of 1945. Churchill, now in opposition, joined in to urge faster release, which provoked one commentator to note the 'piquant spectacle of a Tory urging disarmament on a Socialist Government'.[16] In India, RAF men went on strike about their slow release, and in Britain men chafed at delay so that men overseas in the same release group could get home for their simultaneous release. Some waiting their turn were riled by being put to work alongside German POWs bringing in the 1945 harvest. Despite the grumbles, Adam attributed the relative ease of the army release scheme to the circulation of an ABCA pamphlet and the resulting discussion groups.[17]

Adam found Grigg's successor as war minister in the new Labour government, James Lawson, valuable in easing the strains of demobilisation. Prior to an official visit to 'the Shop' at Woolwich, Adam began to describe the protocol involved but found that Lawson already knew all about it, having been there at the end of the First World War as an RA driver with the duty of polishing the academy's plate. Adam is generous in his appreciation of Lawson:

> He was always thinking of ways to help the serving man. His popularity enabled him to talk to men and women in the Army in a way that got their attention.

He made a trip to India and the Far East at the very difficult moment, when demob was starting and the war against Japan had to go on. His talks to the troops gained their confidence and got over the difficult situation.[18]

As in 1919, but in a different and certainly more positive way, psychology and politics took some priority over economic needs in speeding up the demobilisation process. Nonetheless, a significant degree of pre-release training was achieved. After release, many men and women were assisted with refresher courses and further education and training for intermediate qualifications, and others for education at university level and for the professions. The few universities at that time had to adapt from dealing with callow youths straight from school to accepting undergraduates who had been squadron, ship and battalion commanders with serious experience in the arts of war. In war service some students outranked their tutors. The government made payments for fees, books and a general grant of up to £160 a year, except for those at technical college and university in different towns, for whom grants were adjusted to living costs. A married applicant might receive an additional £110 grant for his wife and £40 for each child. These provisions were much less extensive and generous than the 'GI Bill of Rights' available in the US, but they were a significant development in war-impoverished Britain. This was the first time that there had been extensive national educational grants, and this set a pattern for the expanded higher education in the coming years.

POWS

One of the responsibilities of the AG's department was for both British prisoners in enemy hands and captured enemy soldiers. For both it dealt with the International Red Cross regarding, amongst other matters, the repatriation of seriously injured men and of 'protected POWs' (mainly RAMC). Such transfers went in both directions after April 1943. Other returned prisoners were escapees, those who had achieved 'a home run'. Adam made it a rule to interview them all, 'partly to hear their stories, but chiefly to congratulate them and to find out what posting they wanted after their leave'. It was essential to ensure that their exact escape routes were kept secret and that no information about those who assisted them should leak out. 'In nearly every case it was the peasants in the occupied countries or the men in the underground movement, which at great risk to themselves, helped the escaped men to get away', Adam recorded. The Poles in particular took extraordinary risks.[19]

Adam recorded one difficult incident, one of several brushes with the prime minister, when commandos captured during a raid on Guernsey were ordered by Hitler to be handcuffed. In retaliation, Churchill ordered that all German prisoners in Britain be treated in the same way. When Adam received this order he protested to Grigg and was told to go directly to the prime minister. He found him:

> in bed with a cold and reduced to smoking cigarettes. If I had known this before, I do not think I would have braved him. However, I delivered my protest; my reception was not cordial and I left hurriedly. We carried out a token handcuffing with such handcuffs as we could lay hands on and the exercise was treated in a lighthearted manner by guards and prisoners. Within a day or two the handcuffing was countermanded.[20]

Unlike their treatment of Soviet prisoners the Germans generally observed the Geneva Convention with regard to Western Allied prisoners. Red Cross parcels were essential to the POWs for sustenance and morale and – despite some pilferage en route – they were usually delivered, and camp visits by neutral Swiss and Swedish representatives took place. Despite difficulties, books were also delivered and over 100 examining authorities allowed candidates to take examinations by correspondence. By the end of 1944 some 14,000 candidates had applied to sit examinations; 5,700 had already submitted their final papers, and 4,500 had passed.

In 1918–19 no help had been given to returned British prisoners, who at nearly 200,000 were about as numerous as in the Second World War. In the second war a more humane and imaginative atmosphere prevailed and plans was drawn up to handle their liberation. However, there was ambivalence in officialdom towards POWs, 'a simultaneous idealizing and scapegoating'. For historical reasons, prisoners were regarded both as 'casualties' and as men awaiting trial by court of enquiry to re-establish their military rights.[21] This attitude was evident within the ECAC, as Adam wrote in 1960 of the proposed treatment: 'There was considerable resistance from some, who quite naturally perhaps, regarded the prisoner of war as an offender and not deserving of special treatment, and some who regarded it as unnecessary.'

Such an attitude might apply to some soldiers who individually or in groups had not resisted as hard as they might, but when large numbers had surrendered under orders (at Tobruk and Singapore, the most obvious cases) the men could not be blamed for the tactical errors of their superiors or the strategic errors of the government. To charge such men would have proved embarrassing.

Such sentiments did not reflect Adam's own feelings and he took a positive plan to Grigg, who got Cabinet approval the next day. Thirty Civil Resettlement Units (CRUs) were set up in different parts of the country, each with accommodation for 240 ex-POWs.[22] Attendance was voluntary, with weekend leave, military discipline at a minimum, staff carefully selected and trained, and the amenities good, with both staff and ex-POWs sharing them. The staff included vocational officers and personnel selection units, MLNS officers, medical officers (with visits from the CRU group psychiatrist), technical officers in charge of workshops, civilian liaison officers, and women social welfare officers to deal with welfare problems and links to families. Most of the OR staff were ATS, providing an aid to readjustment to a mixed-sex society. The help of earlier repatriates was enlisted. Men on average spent one month at the CRU although up to three months was possible. Psychological difficulties in adjustment to freedom tended to emerge in two to three months. In some cases psychopathic and depressive behaviour emerged, sometimes requiring hospitalisation.

Adam considered the CRUs a great success and was sorry that more ex-POWs did not seize the opportunity. About a quarter did so – 40,000 to 50,000 – while almost as many were in contact with the programme on a day basis. But for many men who spent up to five years as prisoners, anything smacking of the army, however relaxed, was unwelcome and they sought release as soon as possible. After all, the army had been the agent of their incarceration and suffering and many were reluctant to prolong the association. Recognition of the effects of their experience both by the men themselves and by their families was often difficult: reactions to release varied from utter passivity to the unconscious adoption of the captors' brutality and authoritarianism. Refusal of a CRU place was often to a man's disadvantage. A follow-up study found that of men who had been to a CRU 70 per cent were still in the same job a year later, whereas of ex-POWs who rejected the CRU opportunity only 30 per cent showed such stability of employment.

As the war approached its end, the situation of Western Allied prisoners in Europe sharply deteriorated. The Germans started to transfer tens of thousands of Allied prisoners westward from eastern Germany and Poland. Like the first winter of the war, the last was exceptionally harsh. Temperatures early in 1945 were well below freezing and many POWs suffered from hunger and dysentery. When railway facilities proved inadequate the men were force-marched west. Many died from cold, hunger and disease; others who tried to escape or fell out from exhaustion were shot by their guards. Some trains and columns of marchers were attacked by Allied aircraft. Some 2,500 to 3,500 died en route.[23] Those freed by the Red Army complained of hardships, but in Adam's view were well treated by Soviet standards, being given Soviet rations and allowed to hitchhike to rear areas.

Whatever the privations of Allied POWs in Germany, the Japanese treatment of prisoners was far worse. There was no regard for the Geneva Convention by Hirohito's soldiers. Only the strongest physically and psychologically survived: one in four of the 50,000 UK prisoners in Japanese hands died in captivity, compared with one in twenty of the 142,000 taken by the Germans and Italians. The one positive element that might be discerned in the Japanese treatment of Western military prisoners was that officers and other ranks were not separated, and so could support each other. After immediate treatment on their release from captivity for malnutrition, disease and psychological problems the ex-prisoners could recuperate to some extent on the long voyage home.

Georgina Natzio summed up Adam's contribution:

> There is little doubt that he was the prime source of support for the creation of conditions within the Army which ultimately assisted in an easier readjustment for troops returning home in 1945, some after long absence. Their needs, it was recognised by the medical services, were akin in some respects to returning homecoming prisoners of war.[24]

CONDEMNED TO DEATH

Apart from the imagination shown in the educational, welfare and demobilisation policies that Adam oversaw as AG, his humanity in personnel matters showed elsewhere. He was responsible for the army's discipline, including detention barracks at home and abroad. During the war 179,000 men (and a few women) were court-martialled. Holding convicted men in prison was costly in money and manpower, depriving the army for other duties of even their possibly limited services as well as those of their custodians. The WO was reluctant to release from the army all but the most recalcitrant, for that implied rewarding bad behaviour. In many cases men could be released from detention back to their units under probation.

Adam's view on the death penalty was clear, writing in 1960:

> The figures for the first world war did not show that there was a deterrent effect in the death penalty; 3080 officers and men were sentenced to the death penalty in 1914–18 by court martial and in only 346 cases was the capital penalty enforced. 266 of them were for desertion, of which 91 were already under suspended sentence and 40 had already been sentenced to death.[25]

After the First World War, increasing opposition to the death penalty led to the AC agreeing in 1928 to limit it to cowardice, desertion, treachery and mutiny. Two years later, the House of Commons reduced this to treachery and mutiny. During the Second World War the desertion rate was in fact low. In late 1939 in all theatres it was 31 per 10,000 men (i.e. 1 man in 322); in 1941 it peaked at 88 per 10,000 (1 in 113) and was down to 54 (1 in 185) in the closing months of the war.[26] Nonetheless, some Middle East commanders were concerned enough about discipline that they called for the reintroduction of the death penalty for cowardice and desertion. This would have required a change in the law. On 5 June 1942 Grigg wrote to Churchill: 'If legislation is necessary, the facts and figures must be very serious. But if they are serious, we can't afford to tell them either to our friends or to our enemies.'[27] The law remained as it was. The typescript of Adam's 1960 document reads: 'I was glad' the penalty was not reintroduced, but – with typical caution and self-effacement – he altered this in his neat hand to read, 'it was fortunate'. Adam had an almost pathological aversion to expressing a personal opinion.

Battle stress was much more widely recognised in the Second World War than in the First, when initially 'shell shock' had been widely dismissed as being a psychiatric condition. Adam's view was that:

> All human beings suffer from the emotion of fear. A brave man is one who can control his fears, the coward is one who cannot do so [...] For to all human beings there is a limit to endurance and in war it is sometimes impossible to ensure that this is not reached.[28]

Such stress was felt particularly strongly by men in 'teeth' units such as the infantry, and these arms suffered the most from desertion after battle. Much depended on the morale within units. Serious cases of desertion led to sentences of three to five years' penal servitude, although senior officers reviewed sentences after a short time and often suspended the term if the men could be returned to normal duties, subject to three-monthly reviews. In 1942 the Directorate of Military Training took over all detention barracks, and the men were put through hard training and came out of detention fit to take their place in battle again. Psychiatric examination led to some men being discharged. Moreover, half of all men in detention were of low intelligence, and a quarter of all offences were committed by the same men. Efforts were made to raise their educational level or stabilise their behaviour as much as possible. This more imaginative approach led to better results in 1943 and onwards.

Deserters in the UK were often rounded up fairly easily or gave themselves up. Family problems were often the cause. Adam's easing of the rules on compassionate leave helped, and such measures as a 'request hour' each week at which a man could talk to an officer about personal matters without an NCO being present. In one command, this reduced absenteeism by 25 per cent. Regarding writing letters to MPs, Adam believed that his soldiers were 'free citizens in a democratic country', and if a man did take this course it would be because he had failed to obtain redress or advice in the orthodox way: 'again it was a matter of man management'.[29]

THE SALERNO 'MUTINY'

Late in 1943 Adam had to face the issue of mutiny in a major way, and he handled it with humanity and decisiveness. Shortly after the Allied landing on the Italian mainland at Salerno in September 1943, a crisis led Mediterranean headquarters to demand the rapid despatch to the bridgehead of a further 2,000 infantry. Those available were mainly in holding camps in Libya, mostly having 'got their knees brown' in fighting across the desert with the Eighth Army. Some had barely recovered from wounds or illness. They did not relish being transferred to the US-led Fifth Army; perhaps even more they resented being transferred to other British regiments. As Second World War army historian John Ellis commented, 'If an army preaches the virtues of battalion, division and army loyalty, it might reasonably be expected not to flout such a concept just to scrape together an amorphous draft of replacements.'[30]

On this occasion the men were certainly misled by officers at the holding camp. Some 500 of the men selected were from the 50th (Tyne-Tees) Div. and the 51st (Highland) Div. The news filtered out that they would be transferred to the 46th and the 56th Divs with the Fifth Army. Whether rumours that the 51st was to be sent back to 'Blighty' had reached the men is disputed, but it was mainly officers' clumsy, indeed deceitful, handling of the men that was the spark. However, a sure factor was that the 51st had been imbued with an exceptional degree of group identity. Rebuilt by Maj.-Gen. D.N. Wimberley after the fall of Saint-Valéry in 1940, he insisted to his men that, 'if wounded and separated from your own units, do not allow yourselves to be drafted into other battalions, but see that you come back to us'.[31] The men, good soldiers that they were, found themselves caught between two incompatible demands. The transfer of Eighth Army men to the Fifth Army was an added insult.

Once ashore in Italy, 192 men from both divisions dug in their heels, although several times as many other battle veterans did accept their lot. Returned to North Africa under guard, the 192 (later reduced to 182) were court-martialled for mutiny. Their defence officers had six days to prepare their case – as against several weeks for the prosecution. There were other aspects that displayed the unfairness of the trial, as historian Saul David has demonstrated. Some evidence was presented quite mendaciously to the court, such as the assertion that the men arrived at Salerno while the battle was at its most critical stage. It was in fact over, and the men could have been returned to 'their own specific units' without impairing the campaign. Moreover, it is doubtful if the men were guilty of more than refusing to obey orders – not mutiny, which implies a conspiracy. Persuaded by the army's Deputy Judge Advocate General, Lt-Col Lord Russell of Liverpool, the court found all but five of the men guilty of mutiny.[32] Three sergeants were sentenced to death, corporals to ten years' penal servitude, lance corporals and privates to seven, except for one private who got five years.[33]

By pure chance the sergeants were saved from death and the others from the years in prison. In November 1943 Adam was on a visit of inspection in North Africa, Italy, the Middle East and India. In the first theatre his itinerary report records only that on 11 November he met Russell (who presumably did not mention the trial) and that on 18 November (two days after the men had been informed of the sentences) he was visiting No. 1 Military Prison where the sergeants and corporals were held.[34] On hearing of the matter, he immediately suspended the sentences. Yet in his official report to the ECAC on his return to London, Adam made no mention of his action; nor did he make any mention at all of this tour in his 1961 manuscript; he described the main features of all his tours of inspection abroad as AG, except this late 1943 visit to North Africa and beyond. It is from two letters exchanged with Gen. Montgomery in April 1944 that his role emerges. 'The men's refusal to go into battle was inexcusable and cannot be condoned', Montgomery wrote. But neither he nor Alexander, the 15th Army Group commander, had been consulted. 'I think that it is one of the worst things that we have ever done', Adam wrote in his reply. He blamed Alexander's poor administration in general, while Montgomery was more specific about the inadequacy of the Maj.–Gen. Charles Miller, the administrative head.[35]

The officers who told the men of Adam's decision did not explain that 'suspension' meant more than just 'postponement'. The men were sent back to duty, resentful of their treatment and labelled as mutineers and cowards. Some deserted and had their sentences reactivated when recaptured. Later, Adam appointed Lt-Col Thomas Main, an RAMC psychiatrist, to look into their individual circumstances, including the men's psychiatric state. He reported in January 1945 on the basis of interviews with the men still in detention. Main's report made clear the unfairness of the treatment the men had received, their deep and justifiable sense of resentment, and the vengeful spirit that animated the intermediate army authorities. Main concluded mildly: 'The plans for rehabilitation of the men after the first sentence was suspended were not wholly successful; the opportunity to restore and stimulate morale was not taken, and this led to a rapid failure of discipline.'[36] This convinced Adam that the men still in custody should be released, but the army thought it inopportune while the war was still on.

The severity of the sentences, the deviousness of officers at several levels, the contemptuous treatment of the men in the units to which they were sent on release, the refusal to grant them the campaign medals that they had earlier earned, added up to a serious miscarriage of justice. Misleading reports to Parliament by ministers, culminating in the refusal to review the cases in 1947 and as late as 1982, when the surviving men were in their seventies at least, did no credit to the British Army. It was as if the military machine, frustrated over its inability to shoot deserters, consciously or unconsciously wished to echo the fate of Admiral Byng in another part of the Mediterranean nearly two centuries earlier. He had been shot, according to Voltaire, '*pour encourager les autres*'.

Going on to India and Burma, Adam became deeply aware of the feeling among the troops that they were forgotten – he was the first administrative staff officer above the rank of lieutenant-colonel even to have visited some commands – and he urged that the prime minister or other minister should refer in a broadcast to the troops' role out there. He found a similar sentiment among soldiers in Italy early in 1945 when north-west Europe was the centre of attention. They were certainly not 'D-Day dodgers' as one foolish MP dubbed them. The campaign 'in sunny Italy' was difficult and bloody.

Adam's humanitarian feelings were not limited to British and Allied troops. In his report to the ECAC he noted the effects of the Bengal famine then raging, the result of poor harvests, a cyclone and a tidal wave, the loss of Burmese rice supplies, and governmental incompetence in bringing in supplies from elsewhere. The starving were driven out of Calcutta to die in the countryside; the number of famine deaths were unknown but, Adam reported, cholera was killing 10,000 a week. He did not spare one acid comment from the official report: 'Racing was still going on, however, on just as big a scale as peace-time, and the Bengal Club is serving the usual large meals.' [37]

On another tour early in 1945 Adam found commanders in Italy still concerned about desertion, especially during that very cold winter. In the previous year more than 3,000 men had been court-martialled for various offences, including desertion. But he concluded, 'I do not think that there is much that we can do'. [38] He was aware of unit morale problems, for another small mutiny had arisen among drafts ordered to the Queen's Brigade, of the 56th Div., which had 'a long run of ill success and this was well known throughout the army'. [39]

Another overseas morale problem could be solved more easily. Travelling on to India he found that incoming drafts of men were stationed for up to two months at the transit camp at Deolali. Long periods in transit camps were not new: this camp was the origin of the army slang 'going doolally', or mad. Adam found that old sweats in transit homewards were telling the newcomers of 'the horrors of life in India and Burma'. Adam simply got the theatre commander to set up two separate camps. Transport shortages were a problem, even when the Mediterranean was reopened, as he found for the sick men whom he encountered in Egypt waiting for two months for hospital ships to bring them home. [40]

12

FRICTIONS

In an article in the *RUSI Journal* published in 1993, F.D. Goode described how, as a 23-year-old regular infantry subaltern, he was posted in mid-1940 to the WO. His article is of interest in showing that even when the national peril was at its greatest, departmental and personal infighting in Whitehall was still carried on at full pitch. Writing of Gen. Adam, Goode wrote that, 'Sir Ronald combined inefficiency with vanity, ambition and strong Socialist principles. He did incalculable harm to the Army and the country'.[1]

There are no traceable suggestions in any other comment, official or unofficial, that Adam was inefficient, nor did Goode provide any evidence to sustain this wild assertion. On the contrary, Adam's record as DCIGS in keeping the balance between Gort and Hore-Belisha in the WO in 1938–39 was a considerable diplomatic achievement; this at a time when the demands on him during the reorganisation and expansion of the army were heavy. His organisational abilities were outstanding also in his supervision of the perimeter around Dunkirk, the prelude to saving nearly 340,000 Allied soldiers from death or capture. The charge of 'inefficiency' conflicts with all other evidence. Vanity: well perhaps, but again there is no objective evidence, for, unlike many contemporary senior officers, Adam published no self-justifying memoirs. His accounts of the war years are remarkably self-effacing (frustratingly so for the biographer). Ambition may be a grievous fault, but there is no evidence that Adam had any greater or more distorting ambition than any of his contemporaries. In fact, on the contrary. The tenor of Goode's article suggests that it reflects his immediate superiors' own frustrated ambitions. Adam had, after all, leapfrogged over others more senior when he was picked out by Leslie Hore-Belisha to be DCIGS. Adam too picked men for their ability not their place in the hierarchy. This consideration is suggested by Goode's assertion that the AG, 'chose many retired officers and promoted to staff officers many of his soldier clerks. We suffered throughout the war from the poor quality of the "A" [administrative] staff work'. More authoritatively – in a letter signed 'Jorrocks' – Lt-Gen. Sir Brian Horrocks, who amongst other commands led XXX Corps in 21st Army Group in 1944–45, wrote to Adam on his retirement in that he had always 'felt that the "A" side had been handled with vision – a quality only too rare in the army today'.[2]

As for Adam being a socialist, there is that comment by him, recorded by Liddell Hart in 1935, that a socialist government would be less fettered by vested interests if introducing a co-ordinated defence scheme. On the same occasion he suggested the nationalisation of transport was necessary for the effective defence of London. He certainly supported Labour in 1945 and possibly later. His promotion of adult education after the war may well be considered a 'Left-wing' cause, and he had a sceptical eye for the effects of private education on British society.

Of army education Goode wrote:

The GS [General Staff] became increasingly concerned at the spread of socialist political propaganda in the Army by the AEC and later by the Army Bureau of Current Affairs. We made many protests and indeed some COs refused to use the pamphlets. But the PM was too busy to deal with such matters. And the AG continued to spread his politics.

However, Croft – who could sniff out Left-wing tendencies at a hundred paces – exonerates Adam: he was 'far too busy to watch continuously political tendencies'.[3] So either Adam was fairly impartial in politics or he covered his back from his political masters with considerable skill. His obituary in *The Times* described him as 'tenacious and adroit' in fostering progressive policies in army education.

Goode initially came under Maj.-Gen. Archibald Nye as director of staff duties, under the CIGS. This passage suggests the antagonism towards Adam was departmental as well as personal:

One day the DSD sent for me and said 'The Adjutant General wants to take over MS [military secretariat, responsible for appointing officers]. Go over there and find out why he must not'. I spent two very useful days investigating the MS branches […] I reported that if MS was not independent it would have a disastrous effect on the Officer Corps.[4]

He continued:

Next I was told to prepare a paper to stop the AG's proposal to form a Corps of Infantry and break up the Regimental Tradition. Of course Ronald Adam was a gunner. The General Staff successfully quashed the idea.

The formation a year later of the General Service Corps was a more far-reaching form of the Corps of Infantry concept, in fact if not in name. When Alan Brooke became CIGS, late in 1941, Nye was appointed Vice-CIGS. Whatever his views on the regimental tradition Nye (who had risen from the infantry ranks) proved to be a keen supporter of Adam's fostering of army education.[5]

After field service in 1944–45 Goode was appointed a deputy assistant AG in April 1946, so that a few weeks before Adam left the WO their paths may have crossed again. His article is a minor historical oddity, although useful in revealing the rivalries within the WO. What is noteworthy is that rancorous animosity towards Adam by a junior officer should have remained unalloyed half a century later. Although commonly described as genial, Adam was not a man to brook incompetence. He had, one contemporary remarked, 'a brow like thunder and a tongue like whiplash'.[6] It sounds as if the young Goode had suffered a tongue-lashing and never forgot or forgave it.

SUGGESTIONS PLEASE

Burgon Bickersteth, a valuable if excitable contemporary observer, asserted that many of Adam's 'ideas are anathema to the Secretary of State and to the C-in-C [Paget], who look upon him as a dangerous person'. Bickersteth continued:

> Adam, anxious to get constructive ideas from young officers, proposed there should be suggestion boxes in each unit – not obviously for complaints, that would be highly improper – but for sound, constructive suggestions. This was looked upon as most dangerous and a short step to Soldiers' Committees, Commissars, and all the rest of the Russian system. I think it is most sensible.[7]

Bickersteth was too cynical, for in fact the Army Council (AC) in March 1943 also agreed it was sensible. As Adam described the procedure, NCOs and ORs (but not officers) could in their own names put suggestions about equipment, training or administration into the boxes, which were dealt with at unit, divisional, Command or, if affecting the whole army, the War Office. He stressed the importance of men receiving an answer within a reasonable time and an explanation if the suggestion could not be met. 'The idea was welcome and seldom abused.'[8] But Adam did not win every time. Resistance to abolishing compulsory church parades was strong during wartime and he could only achieve this just before he retired.[9] While some saw compulsory parades as an aid to discipline, others – including some believers – concluded that it damaged real religious belief.

Besides the dispute over Regimental Nomination there were further brushes with Paget about discipline. The first concerned saluting. Both the RAF and the growing number of US forces in Britain in 1942 had more relaxed rules than the British Army's practice. The variety of Allied uniforms and badges of rank also caused confusion. At the same meeting of the AC in September 1942 that rejected Regimental Nomination, the reformers won two skirmishes. It was agreed that although the general rules on saluting should be retained, saluting when 'under cover' – except on service premises and when addressing an officer – in railway stations, restaurants, hotels, etc., would no longer be required. Paget was a stickler for saluting, seeing it as 'a gesture not of subservience but of mutual respect'.[10] A month earlier he noted: 'Saluting has noticeably improved in the Field Army, but elsewhere it is getting worse [...] any new rules that relax the standard are to be deplored.' He always spoke of discipline and morale together, as being mutually supporting and associated. In the same report he complained that, 'The spirit of discipline and self-sacrifice has been discouraged for many years by both political leaders in Parliament and in the Press; but in spite of this adverse criticism we can be confident that we still retain those tough fighting qualities for which our troops have been famous in the past'.[11] A related issue was the rule that when an OR saluted more than one officer, only the senior officer present should return the salute. Sometimes officers of the same rank did not know their respective seniority in that rank, and there was confusion here too. After a long correspondence within the army and consultations with the other services (the WO found the RAF shamefully lax in this matter) it was agreed that all officers present should salute. 'Hence, you may see in Whitehall half-a-dozen generals and brigadiers all saluting a private', one newspaper reported.[12]

A further contentious issue before the AC was whether officers and ORs should be allowed to eat and drink together in public places. It was decided that they could, although officers should 'exercise proper judgment in consorting with other ranks'. Again, this was following the lead of the RAF, which did not object to men who flew together from socialising together. (If on operations a sergeant-pilot was in command of the aircraft, commissioned officers in the crew, such as navigators, were subordinate.)

On a third issue the AC recorded a draw. A 1940 instruction had forbidden the polishing of equipment, a practice pleasing to parade ground enthusiasts but making men dangerously conspicuous in action.[13] General Pile of AA Command wanted a ruling on which parts of guns should be cleaned and polished and which should be cleaned and oiled. Arthur Henderson, Croft's parallel parliamentary secretary in the Commons, questioned whether, in a period of inactivity, 'trouble would ensue' if men were put to tasks that 'appeared to them out of keeping with the requirements and realities of war'. This reflected the dispute over whether the morale of men fresh from action was best maintained by the return to the 'bulling' of equipment and other steps to reassert parade-ground-style discipline. The Council agreed not to rescind the Army Council Instruction (ACI) but to exhort an 'improvement in personal smartness'. Paget said that he was sure that exhortation would not be abused and that in any case the 'best units were disobeying the ACI'.[14] This was a curious position for someone with strict views on discipline.

It was this rather fractious meeting of the AC that led Paget to write to Grigg:

My Dear Secretary of State

I much admired your handling of the rather difficult meeting yesterday. It struck me as <u>sinister</u> that at this stage of the war we should be discussing three items designed to lower the morale and discipline of the Army: I ask myself how and why they should be. My conclusion is that the A.G. is a serious menace both to morale and discipline. I spent today with the 46th Division and wish that this could have been with him. It was a great 'morale-matter' to see all ranks so keen and so full of fighting efficiency. I asked all the C.O.s and R.S.M.s about candidates for commissions and am quite satisfied that they are honestly doing their best to pick them. Two units have been asked what they would like to do for a visit and both voted (all ranks) for a command parade and a talk. One guard had polished brasses and when I complained, the C.O. said it was contrary to his orders and to the usual custom but the men had done it on their own for my visit: this is difficult to compete with.

I hope you will soon come down with him on another visit to the Field Army.

Yours ever
B. Paget [15]

One can question a senior officer's ability to judge whether 'all ranks' did indeed welcome a parade, even with a limited degree of 'bull'. Ears closer to the ground suggested that parades to impress visiting brass hats and dignitaries were deeply unpopular.

Two months later, Paget again clashed with Adam. His diary records that on 26 December 1942 he wrote, 'a strong letter to AG about his exuberance of paper, interference in my command and nagging of COs; sent a copy to the S of S.' A week later he recorded: 'Saw CIGS who, as I expected, tackled me on my recent letter to AG. He was very kind and concerned about possible effect on my career of reputation for being "difficult" [...] My only regret is if I add to the worries of the CIGS.' [16]

This accusation of interference by Adam echoes Hobart's description of Adam in 1938 as being 'a great centraliser' and 'wanting to do everything himself'. On the other hand, Paget's relations with Grigg were close, as the letter shows. In the former war minister's memoirs published after the war, Paget gets seven mentions, Adam none. In 1946 Grigg wrote six newspaper articles on the greatest contemporary British generals, among whom he included Paget for his role in preparing the army for D-Day. Nonetheless, there was ample evidence to accept John Colville's view that Grigg 'respected men for their competence and not at all for their position'.[17] Colville, as assistant private secretary to three prime ministers – Chamberlain, Churchill and Attlee – had unequalled opportunity to assess men and matters. If the war minister had not had a high opinion of Adam he would hardly have tolerated and supported policies about which he had doubts and, more positively, defended him against Churchill's whim.

CHURCHILL AND ABCA

Adam and Paget had in common Churchill's suspicion. Brooke recorded on 17 May 1943 that 'Winston was in a bad mood, mainly owing to his dislike for Paget.'[18] Adam recalled an approach to the prime minister from some MPs about the setting up of the ABCA. In a letter to Grigg, the prime minister noted the 'dangers to discipline of discussions by regimental officers', and ended: 'Pray consider the matter and let me hear your personal views. Meanwhile please suspend action.' Grigg's response did not satisfy the prime minister who replied that, 'there could not be controversy without prejudice to discipline', and that the war minister should set 'the persons concerned in it to useful work'. Adam recounted in 1960 how Grigg:

> showed me the note. I was very keen on the project and knew that Sir James was in favour of it and I said 'What can we do?' Sir James opened his desk and put the note at the back of the drawer and closed it and said 'I wonder if he remembers his notes'. Very few ministers would have had the courage to have taken this line and it was successful and we did not get another note until April 1943. This was about an ABCA poster and by that time ABCA was fully established.[19]

Despite the occasional controversies Grigg was a firm supporter of army education as a booster to morale and as a builder of a sense of citizenship. At an AEC course in Beirut in July 1944 he told his hearers that:

> education remained until quite recently, limited except for the privileged few, to the three Rs, and little beyond that. There was no realization of the conception of education as a means of enabling ordinary men and women to give to life and to get out of life its fullest value.
>
> But that is the purpose underlying our scheme for education in the Middle East; and that also is the purpose of the White Paper [the basis of the Butler Act of 1944] [...] to create a better way of life for which we are now fighting. If democracy is to be made to work effectively under modern conditions, the people must be educated to realize their individual and collective responsibility, as citizens, for the good of the country.[20]

As a former civil servant Grigg was unlikely to have read a scripted speech without subjecting it to close scrutiny. The son of a carpenter, he had won scholarships to a grammar school and to Cambridge. His translation from mandarin to minister was unusual, unexpected and, with some, unpopular. He described how, in February 1942, he had been asked to see the prime minister, assuming that he would be asked to succeed Sir Horace Wilson at the Treasury and as head of the Civil Service. A few minutes before he left for Chequers the war minister, David Margesson, phoned to say that he was being replaced. Churchill received Grigg in his bedroom. 'In ten words he asked me to be Secretary of State for War. In less than ten words I agreed.'[21] The adaptation to being a minister and having to speak in Parliament was difficult for Grigg. He knew it was galling for MPs to see a civil servant suddenly on the front bench: 'Civil Servants in general are the secular enemies of the House of Commons.'[22] With Churchill and the Chiefs of Staff deciding major policy, Grigg's responsibility as war minister was mainly for organisation and administration, for which he was well suited. He may have quietly circumvented the prime minister at times but he did not overtly oppose him.

THE CAIRO PARLIAMENT

The Middle East was the scene of conflict over the intrusion of political issues in an acute and public form. Paget was sent out as C-in-C early in 1944 when it was decided that command of 21st Army Group should go to Gen. Montgomery because of his greater battlefield experience. Paget's own recent experience in the field had been as a divisional commander in the miserable Norwegian campaign in April–May 1940. Once North Africa and southern Italy had been cleared of the enemy, the Middle East was rather a backwater. So not only was Paget rather brutally snubbed, but many of the men in his new command had been themselves passed over from more stringent duties. On arriving he found a wide range of official and unofficial educational activities going on. What had started as a music club had turned into a debating society, which evolved into the 'Cairo Forces Parliament' in which Left-wing views were dominant. A clumsy attempt to limit the scope of debate resulted in the humiliation for the army authorities; trying to promote an official, controlled forum failed. German propaganda stirred the pot, claiming that the British Army in the Middle East was in revolt and had set up a parliament. Clumsy censorship did not prevent the news reaching Britain and questions were asked in the real Parliament. Those such as W.E. Williams and A.D. Lindsay who saw a parallel between the ABCA discussions and the Putney Debates during the seventeenth century civil wars were no doubt gratified, but this parallel was threatening to those who looked to Oliver Cromwell for more military reasons.

CHURCHILL AND THE 'TAIL'

The Middle East was also the scene of a brush between Adam and Churchill over the size of the army's 'tail', which the prime minister was 'always attacking'. This came up on Adam's first overseas trip as AG in August 1942. The army's 'tail' in the theatre totalled 130,000 men, of whom 30,000 were unfit. Adam recalled in 1961:

> Gen. Smuts [South African prime minister] was present and said: 'Prime Minister, I do not think you understand the situation in this command. It contains not only fighting fronts but lines of communication, a base and factories behind the lines. If it did not manufacture so much, you would have to ship it from England.
>
> Some said that because the prime minister had been a cavalry soldier – at which time when a horse was wounded, it was destroyed and another brought up to take its place – he did not realise that tanks and mechanised transport could not be replaced unless they were totally destroyed. They must be repaired if possible in the field, in field workshops or at the base, and this required numbers of engineers. In fact, this criticism had its value for it made the staff very careful to make the best use of the men available. The prime minister, however, twice concluded a conversation with me: 'At any rate you are better than the Royal Air Force. They require 60 men to keep one fighter pilot in the air and some 90 men to keep an eight man bomber crew in the air.'[23]

Churchill's worry about the size of the 'tail' was a constant, which was evident before Adam became AG. In February 1942 he held down the overall size of the army to 2 million, only reluctantly agreeing to later increases (it reached almost 3 million by June 1945). He urged 'wise economies, by thrifty and ingenious use of manpower, by altering establishments to fit resources'.[24] Military bureaucracies are as liable as any other to inflation and, as Adam noted, Churchill's pressure did lead to economies in manpower. Adam, too, on his overseas tours, saw graphic illustrations of rear-echelon sloth, incompetence and indifference to the needs of front-line forces. But in 1944 the limit on army numbers had serious consequences as it underestimated both the high level of post-D-Day casualties and the length of the war.

The prime minister's animus against Adam was evident on other occasions. Who knows how the handcuffs episode rankled? ABCA was certainly an element, both in respect of the (small) number of men engaged in it and, much more likely, from the views communicated to him about its political tendencies. In his history of the Second World War the only reference to ABCA is in an appendix, recounting how, in July 1943, he had asked Sir John Anderson, the ex-civil servant and the non-party Lord President, for a report on ABCA. Anderson reported:

My general impression of ABCA is that it has proved a most successful experiment, that the Army Council is to be congratulated on having decided to launch it in spite of the possible dangers, and that those responsible have shown both initiative and restraint.[25]

The prime minister had to accept this but in his reply wrote:

Every effort should be used to prevent extra time, money, and military personnel being absorbed in these activities, which, although admirable in themselves, must not be allowed to unduly cumber the military machine and increase the heavy disproportion of non-combatant services. Above all, no man fit to fight should be drawn into this organisation, and the utmost vigilance must be used to correct the tendencies of all such bodies to magnify themselves and their numbers.[26]

Apart from this, ABCA does not get a mention in his war history; Adam gets no mention at all.

Brooke vigorously championed Adam against the prime minister, recording on 17 January 1944 that Churchill wanted, 'again to get Adam out of the AG job, and wishes to send him to Gibraltar. Luckily S of S [secretary of state] is prepared to fight alongside of me.' In October 1944 Brooke recorded about Adam: 'In spite of all the criticisms I have heard during the past year, and there have been many, I could not imagine anybody in the Army more capable than him to carry out the duties of AG.' In December he had one of his periodic lunches with Adam, who 'told me of his various troubles'.[27] Their thirty-year friendship provided them both with a reassuring sounding board for the pressures of war.

There were times of more congenial relations with the prime minister. On the same occasion in Cairo as the argument about the 'tail', Adam recalled in 1961 that Churchill asked Smuts at lunch why, when he had had Gandhi in his power in South Africa, he had not done anything about him, as he was 'a great nuisance' to Churchill. Smuts replied that he had put Gandhi in prison, but that the only result was that Gandhi had made him a pair of carpet slippers. He went on to say that Gandhi was not only a great politician but also a great religious leader. 'You are a great politician, but nobody could call you a great religious figure.' To which Churchill replied that he had created more bishops than any prime minister since Walpole.[28]

ABCA AND THE 1945 ELECTION

The sharpest and most enduring point of friction during Adam's time as AG was based on the fiction that the ABCA and the AEC had brought about the general election result in 1945. The Conservative politician Alfred Duff Cooper, in his autobiography, was patronising:

> The result of the 1945 election came as surprise to many. It should not have done so. The votes of men serving in the Forces were decisive. Such votes are never likely to be on the side of the party that is in power. To the private soldier the Government is the War Office, and the War Office is the sergeant-major. The exercise of the franchise gives to the private soldier a brief and blessed opportunity of expressing his opinion of the sergeant-major [...] In 1945 there had not been a general election for ten years, and for fourteen years the same party had been dominant.[29]

In fact, the kernel of the problem for the Conservatives after the coalition government was dissolved in May 1945 was distrust of the party that Churchill now led. Reviled by Chamberlain loyalists in the late 1930s he had been threatened with deselection by his own constituency association at that time. His early months as prime minister were marked by the continuing enmity of the Chamberlainites. However, by 1945 he was not only the saviour of the nation but also – it was hoped – the saviour of the Conservative Party. But the war had shown that government action could achieve things that pre-war governments had maintained were not possible: state intervention to ensure full employment (achieved, however, through military and industrial conscription); adequate diets and health care for children, expectant mothers and the population at large; a degree of 'fair shares'. True, it was done at a time of great suffering with external causes, but the state's ability to assuage the suffering was clear. Many asked why, if there can be a fairer distribution of resources in wartime, why not in peacetime? From the very introduction of rationing in January 1940 the warfare state began to mutate into the welfare state.

As labour minister, Ernest Bevin used his wartime powers to ensure that industries subject to control and direction in fulfilling government contracts introduced better working conditions. Better social conditions for (but also closer control over) seamen, dockers and miners, whose contribution to the war effort was clear, were widely accepted. But many Conservatives could not accept as a necessary war measure Bevin's proposals for regulating pay and conditions in the catering trade. This was the largest industry in the country, where there was no statutory regulation and, because of its fragmented nature, little unionisation and no collective bargaining. That it was a coalition bill did not reassure many Conservatives, and 116 MPs voted against the measure. An electoral truce did not mean a political truce. Conversely in 1942 there was a Labour revolt over the level of increase in old age pensions. Younger Conservatives recognised the need for post-war change. Bickersteth recorded a meeting in 1943 with Conservative MP Hugh Molson, who told him about the Young Tory Group, which included Quintin Hogg, Irene Ward and Peter Thorneycroft, who would achieve prominence in the 1950s and later. He wrote:

> Their general attitude is that the public demands great changes but does not wish any radical upheaval in our system of government – but the Conservative Party must be prepared to initiate and tolerate changes. For instance, this group […] supported Bevin's catering bill, and succeeded in forcing the House to accept it – this in the face of […] the more blue-nosed Tory opposition.[30]

Many Conservatives' reluctance to face the nascent post-war world was not helped by Churchill's refusal to consider in Cabinet any discussion of future domestic policy. Military historian Max Hastings noted how, 'despite the urgings of ministers, [he] refused to address himself to "war aims", a post-war vision. Instead, he held out to British soldiers the promise of martial glory […] In supposing such things to represent plausible or adequate incitements to soldier citizens, Churchill was almost certainly mistaken.'[31] Bickersteth complained how Churchill in August 1944 was blocking the distribution of the leaflets on demobilisation and the pre-release education facilities.[32]

The insistence on first things first was not unreasonable: too much emphasis on the post-war world risked diminishing the fighting spirit in the army. But stress on immediate needs obscured deeper issues. The first was that it failed to recognise that buoying up the spirits of the nation required some jam for tomorrow. Something as popularly sentimental as Vera Lynn singing, 'there'll be bluebirds over the White Cliffs of Dover, tomorrow when the world is free', recognised that hope for a better future had to be satisfied. Second, there was already much thinking about the post-war world in government circles. Under the coalition, the Butler Education Act and family allowances were introduced. Five major official reports prepared for the coalition government laid the basis for the rebuilding of London, for new towns around London, for post-war agricultural policy, and for town and country planning. It was not simply a matter of conservatism against progress. The Beveridge Report would have animated to some degree any post-war health and welfare policy of any government. There was a tide of popular determination that this time round the post-war world would be a better place. And not just at home: many were determined that the nascent United Nations Organisation should be an improvement on the League of Nations. (Adam's chairmanship of the United Nations Association in the late 1950s showed his own commitment.) The ABCA poster – 'In war – prepare for peace' – that Paget suppressed was the reversal of the Latin tag *si vis pacem, para bellum*. In the 1930s Britain had ignored this until it was too late: it had wanted peace but failed to prepare for war. Yet it is clear that many of those, whether civilian or military, who stressed the importance of immediate war objectives were also those who feared change in that post-war world.

Although a member of the pre-1914 Liberal government the prime minister had never been particularly liberal. On the Left he was still remembered for suppressing the Tonypandy miners' strike with soldiers (when a Liberal) and his aggressive role during the General Strike in 1926 (when a Conservative). His devotion to the gold standard had proved disastrous. During the war years Churchill's thoughts were elsewhere: on trying to maintain the British Empire and the position of an impoverished Britain in the post-war world. Understandable and desirable though these objectives were, most Britons had their focus on more personal and more immediate needs.

WHICH WAY? WHICH PURPOSE?

There was an inherently deep problem in using education as a booster to fighting morale. Chosen to boost national morale, the very title *British Way and Purpose* for the pamphlets about British social, political and economic life opened the way to dispute. Which 'way' and to what 'purpose'? What in later years would be called the Establishment could see this in straightforward patriotic terms. Patriotism for them meant the defence of the monarchy, the Empire, the Church of England, the City of London, the public schools, the social order and cricket. For those in whatever station who did not identify with these institutions, wartime patriotism included a good measure of hope of change. When the mass of the British people were called to arms against invasion, 'yes', they said, 'we'll defend this country against the dictators, but we will ensure that with victory the way and purpose of this nation meets our needs much more than in the past'. Patriotism was not enough. Those who saw army education as having the narrow military purpose of raising fighting morale found out that they had opened a Pandora's box; hence the baffled fury at the result of the 1945 election. Bickersteth's mother, Ella, was perceptive about the election:

> The return of a Labour government was the result, partly, of the determination of the armed forces to have a government which would promote their interests, it being widely held that Churchill, though an incomparable war leader, was not genuinely interested in social betterment. There was also, perhaps, the feeling that Churchill's power was becoming that of a dictator. The Conservative campaign was badly conducted, the PM's broadcasts being particularly unconvincing.[33]

The fact was that the sense of national unity during the war had grown from different roots. Social historian Jean Freedman discerned how different sections of society were motivated by their own needs and aims:

> trade union leaders recognized that a Nazi victory would mean the end of free trade unions, while property owners realized that their property might be confiscated and their privilege destroyed. Many different paths came to the same conclusion: Nazism was a threat and a danger that had to be stopped. In order to fight against a threatening political 'they', it was necessary to form a strong political 'we', a collectivity strong enough to defeat an extremely powerful military force.[34]

The social kaleidoscope of Britain was shaken up by war and did not settle back into the same pattern. Men and women were called on to undertake tasks and responsibilities that neither they nor society had previously expected of them. Perhaps the office-boy who came back as a colonel was mythical, but he represented a change affecting many. Women in particular took on new roles that some later dropped with relief, others abandoned reluctantly. Once the danger was over, that 'we' began to fragment and British society – in 1939 one of the most highly stratified in the developed world – reverted to its peacetime character, although its strata were more blurred than previously. Sectional interests reasserted themselves.

SIMPLE ARITHMETIC

In emotionally less fraught times historian Jeremy Crang applied simple arithmetic to the assertion that Left-wing indoctrination of the forces won the 1945 election for Labour. The electorate of 30 million included 4.5 million servicemen and women over 21 years of age. Although efforts were made to encourage registration among the forces, there were great difficulties. Only 2.9 million – or fewer than two-thirds – applied for ballot papers. Men in the Burmese jungle, on ships at sea, in transit from one posting to another, or busily disarming Germans had problems in getting their names on the register. Holding back the count for three weeks after election day got many votes by air from India and points nearer home, but nearly 200,000 service votes arrived too late. Service personnel in Australasia were disenfranchised. Of those eligible to vote, 1.7 million did so, directly or by proxy: a 58 per cent turnout, compared with the national figure of nearly 73 per cent.[35] So overall, fewer than two-fifths of the potential service voters cast their ballots. Some service personnel were angry that an election was being held at all while the fighting was still going on.[36] On that score, Labour can be blamed for ending the coalition, and the

Conservatives for holding an early election on a poor register instead of waiting for the autumn.

If the service votes had divided like the national average – 48 per cent for Labour – there would still have been a Labour government; if the proportion was higher (which seems likely), it merely reinforced the national trend. So the service vote, contrary to Duff Cooper's opinion, was not decisive; J.G. Ballard's grandparents' belief in a 'putsch' was even wilder. No doubt many service personnel wrote to their relatives and friends about the surge of opinion in the ranks (and in the officers' mess in many cases) and urged them to vote with their proxy votes. But that cannot explain away all the wave of Leftward opinion. Apart from the experience of the government's wartime measures, specific agents that might be identified were the weekly illustrated *Picture Post* – probably as influential as any ABCA discussion. With a Left-wing slant and a peak sale of almost 2 million copies, it was a potent force. The *Daily Mirror* also had a strong role. Noted for its 'Jane' strip cartoon – in two senses – the paper provided serious reading matter in a popular style. It too was Left-wing. But most daily papers supported the Conservatives.

The electoral truce observed by the three national parties since 1939 meant that they did not contest parliamentary vacancies, leaving the incumbent party to put up a candidate. But that did not hamper other candidates standing, causing a by-election. Left-wing independents and candidates for the newly formed Common Wealth Party sometimes triumphed in unexpected constituencies. Some public opinion was more Left-wing than the Labour Party. D.N. Pritt, standing in the 1945 general election as Independent Labour in west London, showed that his wartime activities gave him enough personal support to defeat an official Labour candidate, and a sitting Labour MP lost to a Communist in London's East End.

Rational analysis does not convince the zealot, whatever his colours. Nothing is more satisfying than a conspiracy theory to explain unwelcome events. Lord Croft added his own twist. In his memoirs he wrote that, 'after close examination', he had come to the conclusion that the army had been subject to:

> a most remarkable propaganda which reached all units to the effect that the only way back to 'Civvy Street' by Christmas was to 'vote Socialist', for their Socialist friends would immediately demobilise the Army, Navy and Air Force [...] Servicemen were speedily disillusioned.[37]

Exactly so, but not for the reasons Croft supposed. It was thanks to the dropping of the nuclear bombs that many more service personnel were released by Christmas 1945. Only 24 per cent of Labour candidates and 19 per cent of Conservatives mentioned demobilisation in their manifestos.[38]

Woodrow Wyatt, elected in 1945 as a Left-wing Labour MP and who moved steadily rightwards in later life, wrote forty years later:

The Army Bureau of Current Affairs was set up to give soldiers education in the workings of the society for which they were fighting. It was a noble gesture, worthy of Periclean Athens fighting the Persians. 'Neutral' background material was supplied for the young officers who conducted such sessions with the troops. Neutral in this context inevitably emerged as anti-Tory. Whoever dreamed up ABCA in the War Office was in part responsible for Labour's landslide victory in 1945.[39]

'In part' is a reasonable interpretation. On the other hand, Michael Howard questioned whether the AEC had much influence over tough young squaddies who wanted to get home and get on with their lives.[40]

The decision to introduce army education was not Adam's alone, nor did he invent the civilian and military structure of army education. It was already in place when he became AG. ABCA and *BWP* were created under his aegis, but (as Croft conceded) he was too busy with other concerns to supervise its day-to-day activities. He certainly championed the structure, which from the start opened up opportunities for debate among the troops. He believed that soldiers should be treated as adults. Other senior officers approved. Once launched neither he, nor Croft, nor anyone else could control the outcome. Adam recalled a meeting at the Treasury a week or so before the 1945 election when Harold Macmillan said that Labour would easily win the north of England. As ever, Adam did not reveal his own opinions, but reported that all the information from the services was that Labour might get in. But he later wrote that, 'The most absurd attack was when a politician told me that ABCA was blamed for the loss of the 1945 election by the conservative [*sic*] party'.[41] This mild show of asperity was an exceptional display of emotion on the part of this controlled man. Was Adam being ingenuous? Was his apparent political neutrality a fig leaf for his satisfaction at the outcome of the election? He knew the political sympathies of both Williams and Bickersteth, and how Croft and other politicians and soldiers of conservative mind resented their influence. Adam was in regular if not consistently close contact with both. He had found nothing to object to in, for example, the first Beveridge pamphlet. Although Grigg had been concerned about 'Leftish tendencies' of certain members of the AEC and its lecturers,[42] he nonetheless also resented the suggestion that the WO under his charge had led to the loss of so many Conservative seats (including his own). Yet the gibe about the AEC's only battle honour being the 1945 election was one that lasted many years.

Adam certainly favoured Labour in 1945, and possibly later. His daughter Isobel described him as having been 'Attlee Labour'. That would have been enough to label him a 'socialist'. Whether he was 'Gaitskell Labour' is less certain, 'Wilson Labour' less still. Yet one enduring achievement of the Wilson period in government is the Open University, which fitted in perfectly with Adam's concern for lifelong learning and bringing out the intellectual capabilities of as many citizens as possible.

Adam's brother-in-law Lt-Gen. Sir Noel Mason-Macfarlane had gone much further, standing as a Labour candidate in 1945 and beating Churchill's protégé Brendan Bracken. 'Mason-Mac' may have been motivated by animus against Churchill, with whom he had many clashes over relations with the Badoglio government and the Italian monarchy, for which he had been responsible in 1943–45. The timing of his move to the Left is questioned, although his antagonism towards the Conservatives was long-standing. After a year in Parliament, ill-health forced his retirement.[43]

In his memoirs Grigg complained that Labour in 1945 gained only 47.8 per cent of the votes, yet won nearly two-thirds of the seats. That was the result of the electoral system.[44] Early in 1945 he had been invited to stand as independent candidate for what would have been a safe seat at Cambridge University. He had declined, as he considered that it would be 'ungrateful and cowardly to run away' from the East Cardiff constituency that had elected him in 1942 when he became a minister.[45] This honourable stand cost him a longer parliamentary career. There was no peerage for Grigg, despite his years of service at the WO, whether as mandarin or minister, nor any honours beyond those awarded in his Indian civil service days in the early 1930s. There were honours for senior officers for their war services. Among them, Adam, a CB since 1939 and a KCB in 1941, was dubbed GCB in 1946. Paget was close behind, gaining the same honours in 1940, 1942 and 1946. Brooke was a little ahead: his dates were 1937, 1940 and 1942, and he was awarded a KG in 1946. Promoted to field-marshal in January 1944, he was created a baron in 1945 and a viscount a year later, taking the title of Alanbrooke.

OVER HERE …

The popular and idealised view of the Red Army's achievements was largely the result of the remoteness of the Soviet Union; the close proximity of other allies contributed to some friction. In 1940 Canadian, Australian and New Zealand units formed part of the British defence forces against invasion. The first remained and the others were soon shipped out to the Middle East where they played a major role in the Eighth Army. Canadian troops were better paid than the British. The contrast increased when US troops began to land in Britain from 1942. Some British women found the freer-spending, smartly dressed and less inhibited Americans more attractive. The Yanks were, in a popular saying, 'overpaid, oversexed and over here'. One of Adam's tasks was to try to reduce the friction. In a film to be shown to US troops posted to Britain, the Hollywood actor Burgess Meredith (a captain in the United States Air Force) played a GI learning about rationing, the blackout, pubs, the Blitz and so on. Comedian Bob Hope, visiting his country of birth, was roped in to explain pounds, shillings and pence. During the filming, Adam and a US general had to say short pieces to camera, but kept fluffing their lines until Meredith took them in hand. The filming started in Dean's Yard, Westminster, but they and the crew were expelled by order of the Dean, so all moved to Hyde Park. It provided an opportunity for Adam to display a sly wit: 'I told Burgess Meredith that there was a statute of Queen Elizabeth that stated that mumming in Dean's Yard was a crime punishable by death, though I made this up in the spur of the moment. He was suitably impressed.' [46]

Difficulties arising from GIs billeted with British landladies were sorted out with the aid of a booklet, and most local differences were settled amicably, Adam recorded. Two weeks before the war ended it was found that US troops were sending 700,000 letters a week to British civilians they had met, which Adam found astounding, given most soldiers' reluctance to write letters. There was another side to the Yanks being over here – the estimated 100,000 British women who married Americans, and thousands more who married Canadian and other Allied servicemen. During his last days as AG, Adam, visiting Germany to meet Eisenhower, found his return plane almost empty. When he saw US men and women at the airfield waiting to hitch a flight to Britain – they had promised British families that they would spend their last leave in Europe with them – he filled the plane.

After the war, Adam received an appreciative letter from the US government: 'his keen and sympathetic understanding of the needs of the American forces, his constant liaison, and his drive for maximum assistance, both in fact and in spirit, were of the greatest value in developing harmonious relationships between the military personnel of the two nations'. [47]

13

THE LEGACY

Between 1939 and 1945 there were major advances in war technology: airborne radar, guided missiles, jet propulsion, computerised code-breaking and atomic weaponry are the most obvious examples. Also among the new 'hardware' were new pharmaceutical products, notably paludrine and penicillin, which would benefit millions. Once invented these could not be uninvented. But it was possible to halt or reverse the improvements in the 'software' introduced to the British Army under Gen. Sir Ronald Adam, such as scientific personnel selection, better welfare provision, improvements in the treatment of battle neuroses and education. During his time at the WO, he recalled in 1960, he suffered from a great deal of well-intentioned and not very valuable advice from retired officers; he determined that when he retired, he would keep away. Neither his 1960 nor 1961 texts comment on what happened to the army after he retired. So we do not know what he thought of his successors' treatment of his reforms, some of which were downgraded or even reversed.

Adam's immediate successor as AG was Gen. Sir Richard O'Connor, an able and gallant soldier who had escaped from imprisonment after capture in the Western Desert in 1942, and who went on to command VIII Corps in the 21st Army Group. His time as AG was not happy. His biographer wrote, 'Like many great soldiers he was politically unsophisticated, and his simple outlook and shining integrity were often a handicap when "fighting his corner" amidst the intrigues of Whitehall.'[1]

In 1946 the army was reverting from a wartime to a peacetime role, but, unlike the situation after the First World War, there was no opportunity to revert to routine practice and comforts. In these post-1945 years several international tension points demanded significant British garrisons and, in some cases, open hostilities: Trieste, Greece, Palestine, Egypt, Malaya, Korea, Kenya and Cyprus. From the very end of the European war, difficulties and distrust increased between the Western Allies and the Soviet Union over the nature of successor regimes, not only in Germany and Austria, but in countries in eastern Europe that had come under Soviet control. So there was no simple return to the status quo of 1939 for the British Army. It could not revert to being that agreeable occupation and a haven of escape from the outside world that Michael Howard discerned after the First World War. The demands on the army were much heavier than after 1918. The major difference was that the army continued to rely on conscripts to fill its ranks, seen by successive governments as a necessary means to meet the international commitments that they had accepted.

Once Adam was out of the way, the WO began to reverse his reforms. First under attack was the WOSB: psychiatrists and psychologists were excluded from the normal selection procedure. The justification for this was that both were in short supply, for the wartime staff had mainly returned to civilian life. So, although in 1946 each WOSB in theory included both specialists, in fact only one in ten had a psychiatrist attached to it and only three in ten a psychologist.[2] But was it chicken and egg? Did the shortage of experts (evident in the war anyway) provide an excuse for excluding them from direct involvement, or were there few specialists available because of the hostile attitude in military circles? If the authorities had wanted the services of psychiatrists and psychologists they could surely have employed them from civilian life on a part-time basis. They simply did not want them. In November 1946 a committee under Lt-Gen. Sir Neil Ritchie recommended that psychologists should not sit on regular commission boards (RCBs), which otherwise retained the form of the WOSBs. Psychiatrists had in fact not sat on these boards since 1943, when permanent commissions were again granted after being suspended in 1939. This had been justified at that time because, unlike raw recruits facing a WOSB, the candidates were already officers or NCOs, with an army record to take into account. After the war most regular commission candidates did not have such a record of prior army experience: they were straight from school, university or drawn from the National Service contingent.

As was shown in the first trials in Scotland, the value of the psychological input to WOSB selection was that it gave a speedy indication of a candidate's ability and character. Nonetheless, any specialist involvement was now to be excluded, except for consultation in certain cases, which risked creating a stigma for the candidate concerned. The Ritchie Report gave no facts in support of its opinion.

Another change in 1946 affecting regular commissions was that, as had been decided before the war, the military academies at Sandhurst and Woolwich were merged and centred on the former. Fees were abolished, and cadets for regular commissions were beginning to be drawn from a somewhat wider social origin than pre-war. But David French has noted how the public-school ethos remained dominant.[3]

Regarding temporary, conscript officers, there was concern in the WO about low standards among the candidates. A committee under Lt-Gen. Sir John Crocker proposed that both psychologists and psychiatrists be limited to supervisory and consultancy duties, so here too the experts were not to interfere in the actual selection, while the role of the COs was reinforced. The committee also concluded that men of potential officer material were picked out too early during training, too great reliance was placed on psychiatrists and psychologists, and sergeant testers were given too much authority in recommending men for the OCTU.

BLUFF COMMON SENSE

The director-general of Army Medical Services, Gen. Sir Alexander Hood, argued in vain that follow-up studies had shown the superiority of the role of specialists over the pre-1942 boards' methods, for the latter had rejected one out of every three potentially above-average cadets. Further studies had shown that the psychiatrists' findings discriminated better than final WOSB gradings. Also, among officers and cadets who later developed psychiatric illness, the psychiatrists' gradings had shown a better predictive value than that of the other board members.[4] The director of army psychiatry was even more forthright: the Ritchie and Crocker reports 'put the clock back [...] the former to the cavalry age and the latter to the Lewis gun age'. All over the world, he continued, the WOSB system had been imitated and its repudiation now would have many repercussions: 'To discard the assessment is clearly a retrogressive step. The recommendation implies that the psychological assessment can be eliminated without seriously affecting the Board.'[5]

So scientific evidence was just not wanted. Out went the experts. Robert Ahrenfeldt, a senior army psychiatrist during the war, concluded:

> It seems clear that opposition in the Army came, if not exclusively, at least preponderantly, from certain senior officers and administrative quarters, whose influence eventually brought about a reversal of the progressive policy which had been so successfully introduced under Sir Ronald Adam, during the crucial years of the war.[6]

It was one thing to have psychological testing of other ranks; to introduce it into the officers' mess was insidious and dangerous. 'Bluff common sense' prevailed and the army went back to the hit-and-miss system prior to 1942. The intrusion of psychological testing threatened what in later years would be called the macho culture of the army. The core of the problem was senior officers' own anxiety. Soldier and historian Shelford Bidwell put it this way:

> 'Psychology' was shrouded with myth and its application blocked by subconscious fears. It was confused with psychiatry, and psychiatrists were confused with 'mad' people, and, moreover, were soft on discipline. To allow

them to participate in leader selection, asking awkward questions about sex, was repugnant to many officers and the resistance offered by military commanders to their use was naturally deep and obdurate.[7]

In 1960 Adam gave his own verdict:

> It was difficult to persuade the army that psychiatry and psychology were not new inventions made by some medical officers and being tried out on the unfortunate Army thus enabling a number of men to escape their duties in the firing line. There was also considerable criticism of the use of these specialists not only from Army officers but from some politicians and even from a few eminent medical men. This was due to ignorance, fear of new ideas and what appeared to be a superstition that mental sickness was the work of the devil and should be ignored.

So the dropping of the 'trick cyclists' represented a step backwards. However, such major elements of the WOSB as aptitude tests, the leaderless group and other initiative tests were retained. So there was considerable gain, but a significant backtracking also. No wonder that O'Connor, caught between such opposing forces – and not a few others besides – 'hated every minute of the job' in Whitehall. After 18 months as AG he retired.

BACK TO CARDWELL?

Although in 1942 Sir James Grigg had tried to reassure the army that Adam's proposal for a 'Corps of Infantry' would be a wartime expedient only, the traditionalists' fears were not assuaged. The substitute, the GSC, was as little liked. So after the war Adam's second major reform soon came under attack. In 1948 there was a partial return to the pre-1942 situation, disregarding many of the benefits of his reform. Once more each recruit, whether regular volunteer or conscript, was allocated to a corps or regiment before enlistment, on the basis of tests and a brief interview at the time of his pre-enlistment medical examination. As in pre-war days, volunteers could justifiably say they wanted to join a particular regiment or corps, and were accepted if physically and mentally suitable. But not all the benefit from the wartime experience in personnel selection was rejected. PSOs and assisting NCOs had now received some training, and scientifically established aptitude tests, both before and after enlistment, took place. If the pre-enlistment selection proved inadequate, conscripts were reposted to another unit during their initial weeks of training. This clumsy process had many of the faults found by Adam in 1941. Problematical recruits could be referred to a psychiatrist by medical or selection officers; some were discharged.

Although the GSC was dismantled, infantry basic training did not immediately revert to the responsibilities of the individual regiments. In 1948 the sixty-four line regiments (largely reduced to one battalion) were allotted to seven, mainly regional commands with between three and sixteen regiments organised into brigades. For nearly four years, one regiment (of nominal strength) in each brigade was designated to provide ten weeks' basic training for all the brigade's recruits. In effect, the chosen regiment played the role of the home battalion under the Cardwell system. On enlistment, recruits were badged for one or other regiment in the training brigade, mostly based on the town, county or region from which they came. On completion of their joint basic training they were usually rebadged and posted for further service to one of the regiments in the brigade. After 1951 the Cardwell system was reinstated, although without the second battalion, except for a few formations, such as the Guards and the Parachute Regiment. Infantry basic training of six weeks went back to the individual regimental depots, although some further training was retained on a brigade basis. So the colonels' wish to inculcate men with a regimental identity from their first day with the colours was achieved.

But the spectre of a 'Corps of Infantry' had not been completely exorcised: in 1951 Maj.-Gen. C.M. Barber, the director of infantry, wrote to the CIGS, F.-M. Sir William Slim, that he was 'alarmed by a comment in the Army Council's minutes that the new structure would permit a brigade to be turned into a single regiment at some future date': regimental colonels will 'be up in arms'. Slim agreed to water down the phrase.[8] The CIGS was himself concerned that the cap badge of his own Royal Warwickshire regiment would be threatened by the then current idea of a European Army. However, the victory for Cardwell was brief. From 440,000 men in 1951 (twice the pre-war level), the army was set after 1957 to run down to 167,000, far too small a number to maintain so many regiments. The first mergers followed in the early 1960s, cutting down the line regiments to thirty-five (plus five Guards regiments). The Royal Warwicks were among the victims. By 2012 there were only sixteen infantry regiments, mainly regionally based, including the five Guards regiments and the Parachute Regiment. They comprised thirty-five battalions, some of which retained, at least informally, the names of former regiments. More cuts were announced in 2012. Cardwell was dead and buried and Barber's fears of 1951 were fulfilled.

NO MORE ABCA

The continuation of conscription meant that some of the morale-raising practices introduced in wartime had to be maintained. If during the height of the war years it had been necessary to explain to soldiers why they fought, it was even more important to explain to young men why they were still being conscripted in peacetime and, for some, sent abroad to fight and perhaps to die. Between 1948 and 1960 nearly 20,000 British servicemen and women died while serving, although only 1,661 from hostile action; nearly twice as many died in air crashes, with sickness and accidents the main causes.[9] The British public accepted this with remarkable equanimity, a measure of the extent to which they were still inured to submitting to authority and to dying for one's country. The death toll averaged four deaths a day for thirteen years (compared with 105 a day during six years of war). Another change was that regular soldiers were to some degree being drawn from a better-educated population than during the economy-dominated interwar years, and they too now expected better social and psychological support from the service.[10]

The high level of propaganda from ABCA to spur the forces to action and to keep up their spirits during a long drawn-out conflict was no longer considered necessary, and both were abandoned. With the return to 'normal politics', the handling of current affairs as part of army education became even more delicate, and the army shied away as much as possible. What exactly comprised the 'British way and purpose' was now being fought out in the parliamentary arena. A further pointer to the delusionary nature of the belief that ABCA had been a creature of the Labour Party was that it was the Attlee government that abolished it. Late in 1946 the war minister, Frederick Bellenger (who had once favoured a more politicised ABCA), told the House of Commons that army education needed precautions against both Left and Right-wing partisan politics. Questioned about the implementation of the Beveridge proposals he replied that, as the matter was under scrutiny by the government, it was better to hold off discussion – the same attitude that Grigg had taken four years earlier.[11]

W.E. Williams left the WO in late 1945 to set up a civilian Bureau of Current Affairs (BCA) to offer a service akin to ABCA to industry, schools and other bodies with an interest in encouraging their employees, students and members in the study of current affairs. The War Office wound up its own publications and bought material from the BCA until once more controversy arose over Williams's interpretation of current events, and the BCA folded. Paradoxically the (now Royal) AEC increased in strength, reaching some 2,000 officers, warrant officers and sergeants – double its wartime maximum. Most of the sergeants were conscripts en route to university. The emphasis in army education was on the practical, lest the spectre of the 'Cairo Parliament' reappear. RAEC personnel were severely warned against introducing any 'political' attitudes. Most national service conscripts were 18 years old, knew that their service would be normally limited to two years, and were much more malleable than the men in their twenties (and older) who served during the war years.

However, the post-war army recognised that if it was to attract enough long-term regular recruits it had to offer conditions of employment comparable with those in civilian life. Some of the more petty restrictions and unnecessary parades were abolished and men were treated more as adults. Moreover, the army had to take them with it and regimental officers were still expected to hold weekly current affairs sessions with their men and were trained to explain why it was engaged in operations in, for example, Korea and Cyprus. So the emphasis on maintaining morale introduced under Adam's stewardship remained an enduring part of army life.[12]

The Labour government was conservative about the armed forces. Talk of a 'people's army' vanished when faced with the reality of the post-war world. It was no time to risk impairment of military efficiency. The government did, however, inherit the changed social attitudes incorporated into welfare provisions during the war. It made some further changes: fairer court martial procedures, the ending of compulsory church and some other parades, a new pay code, officer cadets from a somewhat wider social spectrum, improved uniforms, more attention to the needs of families, better accommodation (the Wehrmacht barracks taken over in Germany set a high standard), freedom to wear 'civvies' while off duty in Britain, better vocational training before regulars left the service, and a modest 'humanisation' of service life. (Sixty years later the pastoral care of ex-soldiers is still poor.) The introduction of means to voice collective grievances was discussed although never implemented, as it was deemed too radical. Adam's flirtation with the ranks proposing their fellows as officers by Regimental Nomination was forgotten like a disturbing dream. A Conservative government might not have gone quite so far, but when the party returned to power in 1951 it did not reverse these reforms. In these respects Adam's tenure at the WO did leave a long-term, if attenuated legacy.

COUNTERPOINT

The spats that Gen. Sir Bernard Paget had with Adam during the war years suggest unbridgeable differences between them. Paget's side is partly on record; Adam characteristically remained silent. Paget believed in discipline as a means to morale; the son of an Anglican bishop, he was a devout Christian – 'a crusading general', in his own son's term. Adam, through deeds rather than announced opinions, reflected his father's Liberal background. His open-mindedness to innovative ideas was rare in a career officer of his background and era.

Paget, after some caution, took up the cause of army education with enthusiasm. Like Grigg, he was hesitant about the open-ended aspects of ABCA. But, unlike some other senior officers, he did not limit his interpretation of education as being merely a means to short-term military objectives, although these had to have priority. He accepted the need for an informed citizenry, within fairly conservative parameters. Like Adam on retirement, he espoused adult education: for three years he was principal of Ashridge College of Citizenship. This institution had been founded in memory of the former Conservative prime minister A.J. Balfour, and was under the direction of senior figures in the Conservative Party. But Paget took on the post only on condition that the college should not be too close to the party. To some disquiet among the college's trustees, he interpreted 'citizenship' widely enough to include trade unionists, socialists and even communists among the thousands of students who attended courses each year. In 1949 financial pressures forced the college to close.[13]

The reality was that Adam and Paget played counterpoint to each other. They were much closer in purpose than the recorded differences suggest. Both made crucial contributions to remoulding Britain's army for the years of victory. As C-in-C Home Forces, Paget benefited from Adam's reforms, whether he acknowledged it or not. The improved classification and training of recruits gave him a much better basis for his own major contribution to the war effort: realistic battle training. For this, Grigg judged Paget among Britain's six outstanding generals of the Second World War, ranking him with Alexander, Brooke, Dill, Giffard and Montgomery. The former minister saw Paget's quality in two elements. First − in a light infantry tradition going back to Sir John Moore at Corunna − his constant stressing to his officers the need to look upon their men as human beings and citizens as well as soldiers (not differing from Adam's position). Second, following an initiative at divisional level, Paget − encouraged by Brooke − took up the concept of the battle school, where more stringent training, including the use of live ammunition, hardened soldiers to the reality of the battles they would face. Initially this raised the fighting capacity of contingents going to the Mediterranean and the Far East, and later in 21st Army Group. Paget also organised many exercises in combined operations, army-air co-operation and the manoeuvring of large forces, all of which proved vital in Normandy and beyond. Like Adam he made a largely unrecognised contribution to remoulding Britain's army after Dunkirk.

Although neither Adam nor Paget would perhaps have publicly expressed their intentions in such stark terms, the fundamental aim of their several reforms was to make British soldiers more proficient killers. The difficulty for the British Army in the Second World War, as Col Sparrow noted, was that 'a very large proportion of those who served as soldiers remained civilians at heart, in the sense that they regarded military service, into which most of them had been conscripted, as an interlude in a civilian career'.[14] This was the dilemma for all the twentieth-century democratic societies fighting with conscript armies: how to teach peaceable civilians to become effective and determined fighters, and how to do it quickly. By 1939 Germany had been preparing for war psychologically and materially for six years; Japan even longer. Moreover, both German and Japanese societies had a tradition of authoritarianism stretching over generations. (It is to the credit of Italians that they took to totalitarianism much less devotedly.)

Following the disasters of 1939–42 the British Army had to learn fast and hard, not least because it needed a good eighteen months in which to produce a fully trained and confident man in a 'teeth' arm. As a foot soldier Paget, as Grigg wrote, had 'no truck with the heresy that the infantry had been relegated to the back of the stage' in favour of armour and artillery, although the human material with which he was supplied was not all of the highest quality'.[15] Wavell's hopes of 1933 – of infantrymen 'fit, active, inquisitive and offensive – confident of making ground with their own weapons', and not just adjuncts to artillery and armour – were not in general achieved. Historian Harrison Place conceded that in 1944–45 the 'artillery-dominated tactics [Montgomery] favoured, a preference shared by his army and corps commanders, were the only practicable ones given the fragility of morale and dwindling reserves of manpower.'[16] Although far from faultless, a 21st Army Group trained to higher standards was not the only benefit that Paget bequeathed (unacknowledged) to Montgomery: his 'Skyscraper' plan for the invasion of Normandy provided much groundwork of the final invasion plan, 'Overlord'.

THE LORD PROTECTOR

Oliver Cromwell held a fascination for British soldiers three centuries after his death. 'Cromwell' was the code word chosen in 1940 as the signal that an invasion was imminent. A tank was named after him. Sir James Grigg described Paget as having a 'Cromwellian spirit [...] serious, not all glum, ascetic, brave, pious', with a deep desire for the welfare of his men.[17] Gen. James Marshall-Cornwall agreed that Paget was 'a dedicated soldier of Cromwellian type', although not agreeing entirely with Grigg as he found Paget 'perhaps somewhat lacking in a sense of humour'.[18] Of Cromwell himself, A.C.T. White, in his history of army education, wrote that he 'believed that victory would go to the side with the higher ideals' and that, in training soldiers, he believed that: 'The mind is the man.'[19] Grigg and Paget would not have disagreed with this; nor Adam.

Others saw a quite different parallel between Britain in the 1940s and England in the 1640s. W.E. Williams more than once quoted Cromwell's approval of 'the plain russet-coated captain who knows what he fights for and loves what he knows'. Both he and A.D. Lindsay compared ABCA with the Putney Debates of 1647. Others were worried by a parallel with the debates in the Russian Army in 1917. However, open discussions of army matters organised by the Levellers had been a step too far for Cromwell, and he arrested the leaders, amongst whose demands was universal manhood suffrage (not achieved for another 300 years).[20] Despite the presence of military police at the first meeting of the 'Cairo Parliament' it was not dispersed by force (as were the Putney meetings). However, the 'chancellor of the exchequer' of the parliament who moved the successful motion for the nationalisation of the Bank of England, was arrested and shipped home: aircraftman Leo Abse, later a lawyer and campaigning Labour MP. (The post-war Labour government did nationalise the Bank of England.) Croft and Grigg, however much they might secretly have envied Cromwell his authority, could not have Pritt and other irritants arrested, let alone hanged. The pulping of the first Beveridge pamphlet was the equivalent of Cromwell's burning of the Levellers' pamphlets. White – no desk-bound theorist, for he held a VC from the First World War – concluded that, 'It is one thing to generate enthusiasm, and quite another to sustain it. The Parliamentary generals, in consolidating morale, took a step that gave them a decisive advantage in striking power and made them the founders of Army education.'[21]

Just as the Cromwellian army had difficulty in limiting debate within its ranks, so did the British Army 300 years later. In an age of limited literacy, the original New Model Army had an important role in spreading the ability to read among its soldiers. *The Soldier's Pocket Bible* and *The Soldier's Catechism* were the seventeenth-century equivalents of the secular *Current Affairs*, *War* and *BWP*. The main purpose of the Civil War tracts was to convince the parliamentary soldiers of 'the inevitable and absolute necessity of fighting', and it recommended all ranks 'to read and observe what hath been written by eminent soldiers'.[22] Second World War soldiers were more sophisticated than Cromwell's Ironsides and less susceptible to official propaganda. Nor did they go into battle singing hymns; their songs were secular, frequently sentimental, often ribald, in some cases obscene. When the fight was over, a fair demobilisation system, gratuities and full employment ensured that the problem of the lawless, disbanded soldiers of the 1650s did not recur, nor the distress of the 1920s and 1930s.

White added a cautionary note that, 'More than anything else, it was these organized debates of the Cromwellian troops that account for the hostility shown in the eighteenth century, and the apathy of Victorian times, towards many proposals intended to bring about a well-informed rank and file in the British Army.' This problem was not dead in the 1940s: witness the divisional commander who did not care how the chaps were kept quiet, so long as they weren't educated.

ADAM'S NEW MODEL ARMY

Adam was Cromwellian up to a point: stalwart in the field and determined to create a New Model Army of well-motivated men. He was convinced of the need for an educated army, but did not fear open-ended discussion by the rank and file. This is where he differed from the Lord Protector and from many of his own contemporaries. Adam showed little evidence of intellectual originality, but well before he was AG he showed a willingness to recognise the value of ideas. In his final address to officers passing out from the Staff College in 1937 he had said:

> It is given to very few of us to think original thoughts, but it is given to all of us to be receptive to the new and original thoughts of others, if we will. We can encourage originality [...] It isn't done nearly enough. Man is a conservative animal and the Army is a conservative assembly of men. To be original and receptive of originality we must think.[23]

Adam was not driven by a conscious or articulated ideology. He makes no mention of Cromwell in his texts. He was no Col Rainsborough, no Leveller, certainly no Ranter, although some would have counted him as an agitator, stirring up undesirable attitudes and actions among the common soldiery. What is striking about Adam is that he displayed no predisposed ideas about the nature of the soldiers with whom he served. He was pragmatic, finding ability in all ranks and all origins. This motivated his attitude towards education in the army and his promotion of adult education after leaving it. He was much concerned that the British educational system of the time had done so little for so many.

F.D. Goode approved of the quartermaster's department, 'wisely' taking in men from industry and commerce, and was appalled that Adam should have brought back many retired officers and promoted many of his soldier clerks to be staff officers.[24] But it is a credit to Adam for his perceptiveness compared with Goode's snobbery. When assembling III Corps late in 1939 Adam considered his batman Robb as too good for the job: he had come home to enlist after being footman to the Ambassador to Chile. He returned Robb to the Buffs to try for a commission, which he achieved, and later became a staff captain in a brigade: from footman to staff officer.[25]

ADAM A 'DOER'

In the distinction between those who wish *to do* something and those who wish *to be* something Adam was a 'doer', to the detriment of tradition if it stood in the way of military efficiency and of positive citizenship. Many of Adam's colleagues were content just to *be*, encompassed within the physical, mental and emotional framework of the army. Adam, however, rose above the army as an institution and moulded it to what he saw as the wider aims of the nation both in war and in peace, and what had to be done to achieve these aims.

Superficially Adam appeared to have left only a limited legacy to the British Army. His successors speedily dispensed with psychologists and psychiatrists, they tried to return to the Cardwell system, and restricted education largely to practical needs. However, the post-1945 army was leavened for nearly two decades with conscripts who, although young and in junior roles, did serve to connect the army with the wider society (its great weakness in earlier generations). Moreover, even when from the mid-1960s it was again wholly composed of regulars, it could not just slump back to the interwar inertia and the resistance to challenge and change that Michael Howard noted after 1918. The army did not suffer from the distrust of the interwar years: it had acquitted itself well in the latter half of the Second World War and although many post-war conscripts were disgruntled they were not generally embittered.[26]

Apart from an unacknowledged legacy from Adam in terms of a new openness to society there were external forces in play after 1945. The uncertainty of purpose – the Empire or Europe? – which had hampered interwar soldiering was fading. Apart from a few scattered islands, the Empire vanished in the 1960s (although the imperial cast of mind lingered on). The Cold War concentrated minds on the need for constant technological and doctrinal change. Close association with other NATO armies less encumbered with tradition and ritual kept British officers on their intellectual and psychological toes. Armies are hierarchical and distinction between ranks inherent, but the requirements of increasingly complex 'kit' demand higher levels of education and training in all ranks. The extent of the social revolution discerned during the war years was later recognised as more limited than it appeared at the time. Nonetheless, after 1945 Britain was becoming a less deferential and class-riven society, and the army reflected this over the following decades. Inter-service rivalries survived, but attenuated by common defence studies and combined action. Three generations on from the reforms Adam introduced – against such fierce resistance – appear to be just common sense.

14

CULTURAL DIPLOMACY

On retirement many old soldiers go off to live in the countryside, tend their roses, and in their minds refight old battles. Not so Sir Ronald Adam. He and Dorothy did go to live in the country, at Faygate, near Horsham, in Sussex, in a house left to him by his great-aunt Hetty with whom he had enjoyed deep mutual affection since childhood. There was indeed a garden with roses, although his special passion was growing soft fruit – strawberries being a favourite. He kept up his marksmanship shooting grey squirrels (there were no panthers in Sussex). But he was immediately taken up with new interests that required almost as much travel in Britain and abroad as had his duties as AG. Although he avoided giving advice to his successors, he did not entirely end his military associations. The appointments in 1940 as colonel-commandant of the Royal Regiment of Artillery and of the now Royal Army Education Corps he retained until 1950, and that of the Royal Army Dental Corps through 1945–51. He also served as president of the Dunkirk Veterans' Association. In an entirely different vein, he was president of the MCC in 1947 and sat on the committee until 1955.

An early foray into the civilian world was, rather improbably, to take the chair of a Board of Trade enquiry into the linoleum industry in 1946, which took up three days of his week for some months. Usually made from compressed linseed oil and cork dust on a burlap backing, linoleum was the basic floor-covering in a great many British households, offices, hospitals and other premises. Linseed oil was in short supply and substitutes were unsatisfactory. Adam applied the personal and organisational skills he had acquired in his forty years as a soldier to examining the state of the product's manufacture and distribution. Like much British manufacturing, the industry was spending less than 1 per cent of its turnover on research and design.[1] The conclusions of the report are now of little interest. What is of interest is how Adam described one aspect of the experience:

> The manufacturers told the committee that their floor coverings had to be of certain traditional colours and patterns to suit the taste of the housewives in particular areas. The committee thought the designs and colours were horrible

and to test the truth of the statement, invited representative working class wives to give evidence. With one accord they said that they disliked both colours and patterns, but owing to rationing, which was still on, and the shortage of stocks, they were forced to take what they were given. Several told us that they took the best household magazine and longed to furnish their homes with good designs. The above sample shows how tradition can stop progress.[2]

So the banal subject of linoleum could not, in fact, better show Adam's quality of questioning conventional opinion and practice – and of respecting the intelligence of the general public.

COUNTERING AXIS PROPAGANDA

Certainly more intellectually stimulating and longer-lasting than the lino enquiry was the major appointment that he took on in the same year: the chairmanship of the British Council, which he held until 1955. For most of this time he doubled up as director-general. The British Council had been set up in 1934 to counter the growing propaganda campaigns of the fascist powers, notably in the Middle East (Italy) and in Europe and Latin America (Germany). Up to the First World War, the British had stood aloof from official cultural or political promotion, until the need to keep on friendly terms with neutral states led the government to carry out propaganda – initially that word was without the negative meaning it soon gained. This activity had faded out with the return of peace, although some distribution of British books and the granting of a few scholarships for overseas students continued. In the 1930s the political threats were a spur to more coherent action. The Foreign Office hoped that private business would finance the operations of the new body, which was formally established under Royal Charter the following year. Business mostly proved unresponsive, and the council relied on small annual grants from the Foreign Office. Hopes of co-operation with the BBC, which had established an Empire Service, were disappointed. During the war years, with Europe cut off by enemy occupation, there was a significant expansion in three areas of political sensitivity: the Middle East, Iberia and Latin America, with added effort also in the Commonwealth and Empire. From £5,000 in 1935 and £330,000 by 1940 the budget reached £2.5 million at the end of the war. In neutral Turkey £300,000 was spent, with 10,000 attending English-language classes. During these years the council also became active at home, fostering contacts with the many Allied servicemen and women stationed in Britain, including language teaching for the free European forces.

The creation of the council at arms-length from the Foreign Office was always subject to criticism. A proposal on the outbreak of war that it be merged with the new Ministry of Information was successfully resisted. The activities of the council were, however, more closely linked with British war aims. In 1944, a report by a Whitehall mandarin supported the quasi-independent role, noting that, 'The British "way of life" is not a comprehensive descriptive catalogue of every aspect of the U.K.: it is selection of the elements of our living and thinking and achievements of which we are proud and which are characteristic of our aims.' But, he continued, the council's work indirectly contributes to the ends of the Foreign Office and the Board of Trade, although 'any attempts to implicate it in them can only prejudice its success [...] broadly speaking, the Council should be left to do its own work in its own way.'[3]

So there was no doubt that the aims of the council's 'cultural diplomacy' were to supplement the more concrete political and commercial objectives of these two Whitehall departments. The following year, a different mandarin wrote a much more critical report, which was not available to anyone at the council for thirty years.[4] He deplored the quality of the overseas representatives; indeed, finding good quality in wartime had been difficult. He proposed that the London HQ be absorbed into the Foreign Office's foreign publicity department, and local representation handed over to the embassy cultural attachés. This fate was avoided, but the incoming foreign secretary, Ernest Bevin, was initially little inclined to favour the council. He finally agreed to extend its mandate for five years, when he thought some of its functions could be taken over by the consular service and the council itself abolished.[5] So the council had both political and bureaucratic enemies at home. Yet while Foreign Office bureaucrats at home were denigrating the council, British embassies abroad were eager for a council presence as an extra arm in fostering good relations with the foreign governments and societies to which they were posted. Frictions and rivalries continued: on a visit to eastern Europe early in 1948 Adam found that embassy information officers were involved in magazines and exhibitions and in other ways were 'poaching on British Council preserves'.[6]

Adam had not been an obvious choice as chairman. Also considered were Patrick Gordon Walker, an Oxford don turned wartime broadcaster and now a Labour MP, writer Harold Nicolson, and Prof. T.S.R. Boase, director of the Courtauld Institute of Art and formerly the council's Cairo representative.[7] On the face of it, Adam was an odd choice to lead Britain's politico-cultural offensive overseas. He had no pretensions to high culture, no interest in art or music, and his reading, apart from matters of professional interest, was decidedly lowbrow. He tackled the 'Ximenes' crossword in *The Observer* (until illness in his mid-seventies slowed him up – and affected the later pages of his memoirs); he enjoyed American thrillers, especially those of Erle Stanley Gardner.[8] Paradoxically, these characteristics show what a shrewd choice he was for the post. The fact that he had no pretensions to high culture was in fact a major asset, for he was unlikely to get embroiled in the politics of the British cultural establishment. Compared with the other names in play, Adam's cultural and political neutrality stands out. Since the death of Lord Lloyd in 1941,[9] the forceful chairman since 1937, the council had been drifting ('in the melting pot', as Adam put it in 1961). Its aims had become diluted and diverted, supervision from London had loosened, its outstations had pursued their own ends, and its budget had multiplied to meet immediate political objectives. Adam could bring to this situation proven administrative skills, diplomatic facility and experience of working to a brief; as a soldier accustomed to taking orders he could be relied on to pursue the government's objectives more closely than might a figure from outside Whitehall or Westminster. Ernest Bevin, with whom Adam had got on well during the war, wrote to the prime minister in May 1946 proposing Adam as chairman. Clement Attlee in a handwritten letter invited Adam to take up the post, which he did on 5 June 1946. For a year, A.J.S. White continued as secretary-general until Adam took on more day-to-day powers by becoming both chairman and director-general from 1947 until 1954, with another year as chairman only. He was then president, an honorary role, until 1969.

By March 1947 the council had re-established representation in twenty-two European countries, but the renewed emphasis on the Continent was at the expense of, in particular, Latin America, where there were complaints that they had been favoured when it was in Britain's immediate wartime interest but were now being neglected. The changing priorities were due to two influences. The first was Britain's economic situation and the shortage of hard currency, dollars especially. This led to economies in overseas activity and was partly offset by bringing more students and other visitors to Britain. The second development was the onset of the Cold War. Initially eastern European countries had welcomed the council's activities after 1945. In April–May 1948 Adam visited Poland, Hungary and Czecho-Slovakia. In the first he found a broad general acceptance of what the council was doing, but that the signature of an overall cultural convention was dependent on British recognition of the country's new western frontiers. In the second the reception was good, with a strong demand for books in English. The Czech visit took place two months after the communist takeover and was overshadowed by the British reaction to this event, including the cancellation of a visit by the Hallé Orchestra and a boycott by British universities of the sixth centenary celebrations of the Charles University. The cool atmosphere was reinforced by the reluctance of a number of prominent invited guests to meet the British party. The only relief was a village festival in Moravia. Later, as Stalin tightened his grip on eastern Europe even more, taking part in the council's activities became increasingly dangerous for its citizens. In communist eyes it was a capitalist propaganda agency. In 1950 the council's offices were forced to close in all three countries. A belief that the council – perhaps unwittingly – provided cover for the Secret Intelligence Service was not confined to communists: the contacts that council representatives had with influential people in many countries could provide useful political and economic information.

The council's general aims were to win friends and influence people abroad, especially the local elites. This was met by sending ballet companies, orchestras and theatre groups on tour, by holding book exhibitions and arranging lecture tours by British academics, writers and other notables. In the other direction, graduate students, academics, journalists and other opinion formers, together with business and political leaders, were invited to Britain for longer or shorter visits. This policy had in some cases material results: the council's annual report for 1946–47 notes how sponsored visitors spent at least £250,000 in this country, and in some cases their visits resulted in 'substantial orders for equipment' from British firms. So there was acute awareness in the council that it had to serve Mammon in order to please its paymasters in Whitehall. The run-of-the-mill work overseas was carried on through the council's libraries, support for British schools and through language teaching. The question was whether the last should be done directly with classes in British Council premises or indirectly by helping raise the standard of English of local teachers. Cost issues favoured the latter. Higher profile activity generating publicity and prestige was visits from such as Laurence Durrell, Sir Steven Runciman, Rex Warner, Patrick Leigh Fermor, Peggy Guggenheim and Freya Stark, as well as leading conductors, composers, orchestras, ballet and theatre groups, and painters.[10]

ECHOES OF ABCA

One issue that Adam encountered at the council echoed his experience with the ABCA. The director of education, Dr A.E. Morgan, came back from a visit to the Middle East with ambitious ideas to expand the educational role beyond language teaching. As White described it, Morgan reported that:

> the 'have-nots', who in the East were vast in numbers, were beginning to ferment and that in their eyes Britain stood as a buttress of the 'haves'. The Council contended 'should [...] concentrate its energies and resources on interesting the peoples of these countries in the British way of life, by taking an immediate approach to the people down to as low a social and cultural level as possible'. The best method was discussion, the value of which had been rediscovered as an educational method [...] The technique, he said, was familiar to those experienced in adult education classes – the discussion methods used during the past few years in H.M. Forces. Special staff would have to be recruited. The cost would be offset by reduction in English teaching.[11]

Morgan's recommendations were accepted, 'with some reservations', by Adam, and the executive committee approved a statement on educational policy. But this was,

White wrote, 'somewhat dangerous ground for the Council. As Representatives and H.M. Missions were quick to point out, discussions can rarely be kept out of politics and any widespread development of these groups might have brought the Council into disfavour with the authorities'. H.A.L Fisher had linked army education with gunpowder and W.E. Williams ABCA with dynamite – both in a society used to democratic discussion – but open debate in the Middle East and elsewhere could have much more explosive power. If – allegedly – ABCA discussion groups had contributed to the election of a Labour government in Britain, how much more dangerous it would be to encourage the subjects of King Farouk of Egypt, Shah Reza Pahlevi of Iran, and King Faisal of Iraq, to think for and argue amongst themselves. Moreover, might not Britain's strategic and commercial interests be threatened by stirring up ferment? Yet the official aim of the council was to promote understanding of the 'British way of life'. As with *British Way and Purpose*, much depended on interpretation. The new policy appeared far more revolutionary than Adam and the executive had intended, but it led to alarm among British diplomats. On 30 August 1949 Bevin wrote to the executive committee asking for a revision of the policy; Adam replied that proposals were not meant to be rigid. White concluded:

> Curiously enough neither the original version of the statement nor its revised version seemed to have any appreciable effect on the Council's actual work in the field except in one or two countries where Representatives interpreted it too literally.[12]

The new policy was quietly watered down, except in some colonies where an advance towards democracy was the established objective. In any case, the attempt to reduce emphasis on the intelligentsia in capital cities in favour of a new level of provincial audience, such as workers' educational movements and study groups in smaller towns, did not succeed.

Like Britain's national experience in those years, Adam's tenure at the British Council was an exercise in controlled decline. The economic situation led to severe cuts in the budget from £2.5 million in 1945–46 to £1.7 million in 1953–-54. This one-third decline masked a greater fall in real terms as a result of inflation and the devaluation of the pound in 1949. The latter meant that even more reductions in foreign exchange expenditure had to be offset by transferring activities from abroad to Britain. Student scholarships and visits to Britain by opinion leaders cost less in foreign exchange; exporting books earned foreign exchange. Britain offered some 400 scholarships and training courses, compared with some 1,200 by France and 4,000 by the US. In addition the council was responsible for 5,000 colonial students coming to Britain by other means, an equal number from India, Pakistan and Ceylon (Sri Lanka) and the same number from elsewhere. Apart from general support, it helped find accommodation for such students.[13] For Adam, the educational and cultural activities with Allied armed forces in Britain during the war were followed by this this peacetime role.

Any belief that Labour governments were more favourable to the council than were the Conservatives was certainly ill-founded. In Frances Donaldson's book, Bevin was described as not sufficiently enthusiastic to fight for the council, while his successor in 1950, Herbert Morrison, was reported to think the council 'a racket'. Two chancellors of the exchequer, Hugh Dalton and Sir Stafford Cripps, pressed for cuts in a routine way. Hugh Gaitskell, however, was 'obstinately determined to get [cuts]. Above all there is in the record the suggestion of a stoutly philistine attitude which allowed all three Chancellors to dispense with even the ordinary protestations of personal sympathy with cultural propaganda or regret at harsh necessity.'[14]

Apart from the council's enemies in Whitehall, there was always a bitter external enemy in Lord Beaverbrook, owner of the *Express* newspapers. He had abated his animosity during the war years but renewed it with vigour once the dangers were over. His newspapers referred to 'the long-haired lads and lasses' and 'the culture boys' of the council. Did it, they asked, need fourteen cars and chauffeurs in London, twenty in the provinces and forty abroad? It counted over 4,000 staff, as well as another 2,500 locally employed overseas. At a ministerial meeting in January 1951 Gaitskell thought the council's spending was much inflated, and remarked that it had been attacked in the press. Other ministers argued that it was only in the Beaverbrook press, and that most national and many provincial papers were favourable to the council, as were most MPs.[15]

The return of a Conservative government in October 1951 made a little difference. The foreign secretary, Sir Anthony Eden, was as friendly as he had been in the same post during the war. The decline in funding slowed but did not stop during Adam's time. Sir Philip Morris, senior co-chairman during these years, described how the problems in those years 'called for ingenuity and statesmanship of a high order and no man could have succeeded without great personal qualities. It is to Sir Ronald Adam's lasting credit that the Council has survived this period of considerable activity and great difficulty, with an enhanced reputation'.[16] The widespread appreciation of Adam by other close observers of the council reflected the skill and charm with which he steered through the bureaucratic and political reefs. He managed to get a proper staff structure with appropriate grades and at the best salaries as were possible, maintaining morale when policies and priorities somersaulted, and persuaded many very diverse and, in many cases, temperamental personalities to give their best to the council. The slow speed and discomfort of flying long distances in the aircraft of the time – many were converted bombers – appeared to exhilarate rather than exhaust him on his tours of inspection abroad and the other international gatherings that he attended.

UNESCO

By heading the British Council, Adam also served as a British representative on the governing body of UNESCO, which had been set up in London in 1946 to develop educational, scientific and cultural co-operation between the initial forty member states. As in many international organisations, the political and bureaucratic infighting that characterised the British Council was multiplied several fold, complicated by ideological conflict as well as by diverse languages, cultures and national psychologies. A taste of this came with the appointment in 1946 of Sir Julian Huxley, a biologist, as the first director-general. He served for only two years instead of the projected six. Apart from his supposed communist leanings, Huxley's lack of religious belief also fed the opposition. Then national pride asserted itself, with the French being mollified with agreement that the organisation be based in Paris, but without the staff being drawn from the inter-war International Institute for Intellectual Cooperation, as they had initially suggested. Moreover, there was dispute within the Western camp, with the US delegation being divided amongst itself.

The communist states were another source of attack, although this was limited in the early days because the Soviet Union did not take up its proffered seat until after the death of Stalin in 1953. Nonetheless, its satellites in eastern Europe faithfully put forward the Marxist interpretation that culture could not be free from politics. In this they had, in effect, an ally in the United States during the McCarthyite period in the late 1940s and early 1950s. President Eisenhower felt obliged to appoint a committee to examine UNESCO. This refuted the accusations by concluding that the UN body did not advocate world government or citizenship, undermine national loyalties or the American educational system, or show any evidence of atheism or hostility to religion.[17] Nonetheless, Eisenhower issued an executive order that all American applicants for senior posts in UNESCO should undergo 'clearance' by the US authorities. This move gave the Soviet Union splendid grounds for rejecting any complaints about their own more rigid attitude towards appointments to the secretariat.[18] The Western states were quite as determined to keep communist states' citizens out of sensitive posts. Out of 293 senior staff in 1948 almost half were American, British or from other Western European states. Not that the British had cause to be smug about political vetting: this was a time when an MI5 officer had a room in Broadcasting House and checked on would-be and actual employees of the BBC.

Adam's role with UNESCO was as a member of the British delegation, led by government junior ministers. The annual reports to the government from the British delegation stress the need for practical aims in view – notably regarding education, libraries, natural science and the exchanges of persons, coupled with a persistent campaign against an 'increasingly inflated budget'.[19] As a fixture under both Labour and Conservative governments for nearly ten years, Adam was in a good position to be elected in late 1952 to the chair of UNESCO's executive board for a year. Speaking at a Reading University UNESCO books exhibition in 1954 he described the three roles of the body as: acting as a clearing house for ideas in education, culture and science (instancing common methods of compiling statistics, copyright); as the only means of pursuing some issues (human rights, race relations); publicising new developments in such fields as mass education, community development in less developed countries and desertification.[20]

The political squabbles should not detract from the work of UNESCO in these years. This included such diverse activities as research into arid climatic problems; the study of indigenous medicinal plants; the spread of Braille; the origins of CERN – the European Centre for Nuclear Research; the conservation of historic books and documents in adverse climatic conditions; the translation into Arabic of Aristotle, Descartes and Cervantes; the International Copyright Convention; the exchange of scientific and other personnel; improving educational methods in less developed countries; the promotion of theatre.

15

LIFELONG LEARNING

Apart from his virtually full-time occupation with the British Council, Sir Ronald Adam was in high demand in other fields. In 1945–53 he was a member of the council of the Tavistock Clinic, continuing his association with Hargreaves, Rees and others who had established the army's personnel selection system. In 1946 he was appointed an honorary fellow of Worcester College, Oxford, and attended as many of the related activities as he could until near the end of his life. In the same year he became president of the Marylebone Cricket Club and served on its selection committee for several further years. In 1946–52 he was a member of the Miners' Welfare Commission. Set up by statute in 1920 it was financed by a levy on coal production and royalties to provide better health, educational and recreational facilities for coalminers and related workers (during Adam's time it was passing over its hospitals, medical centres and convalescent homes to the National Health Service). In 1948 Adam sat on a government committee to consider the rules on the political activities permitted to civil servants. In 1947–52 he chaired the National Institute of Industrial Psychology. He had an insatiable appetite for activity.

In parallel with these already multiple interests, Adam for nineteen years from 1948 was on the council of London University's Institute of Education, which was responsible for teacher training in London and much of south-east England after the 1944 Education Act. The work covered establishing training college syllabi and making staff appointments, organising revision and other courses for teachers, and appointing examiners.[1] The day-to-day work of the institute was in the hands of a director, and Adam took the chair in 1948–50 and an active interest in its affairs until 1967, when he was 82. In 1949 he joined the governing body of Birkbeck College, a particularly apt appointment. Established in 1823 as the first of London's Mechanics' Institutions to teach working people (it admitted women from 1830) in the fields of science, art and economics, its founder Dr George Birkbeck had met with resistance for promoting education among the lower orders. He was, some averred, 'scattering the seeds of evil'. The terminology may have changed over a century but some attitudes had not. Birkbeck's view was that it was time to call on 'the universal benefit of the blessings of knowledge'.[2] Adam could not have put it better. On this board, too, Adam stayed until he was 82 years old.

Also in 1949 Adam took on the presidency of the Library Association, having become aware during his time as AG of the role of libraries and of librarians in providing reading matter for the forces. The association had, even in the middle of the war, handled the distribution of books overseas as part of Britain's diplomatic effort to maintain links with neutral European countries and the Middle East. Moreover, the British Council ran fifty-four main and forty-four branch libraries with a total of 220,000 books. The Council was regularly sending abroad consignments of books worth £5,000 for display and sale at book fairs, with the foreign currency earned being used locally for Foreign Office and council needs. The council was also distributing 1,400 British journals and magazines. After a year's presidency Adam stayed on the board (alongside other previous presidents).

BRITAIN'S EDUCATIONAL INADEQUACY

Adam believed that much had to be done to set British society to rights. It was common currency during the war how many hosts and hostesses in evacuation reception areas were shocked at the low cultural and behavioural level of many children from Britain's big cities. The 'two nations' discerned by Disraeli a century earlier still existed and neither knew how the other half lived. There was a parallel reaction in the army, where Sir Ronald Adam and other leaders were surprised by the ignorance of many servicemen and women about the simplest facts about the government of Britain, and in particular why Britain was at war. That was the origin of the army's education effort. 'One lesson was quite clear and that was that our system of state education was inadequate for a great power. We were unable to provide sufficient leaders for the Army for that reason alone. Public education has been regarded as a limited service to be carried out as cheaply as possible', Adam believed.[3] Children who had left school at 14 had been instructed but not really educated, and had had little subsequent opportunity or incentive to make good the deficiencies of their schooling.

The Butler Education Act passed in 1944 under the coalition government did begin to redress the position: in 1947 the school leaving age was raised to 15 and in 1973 to 16. However, the tripartite system introduced by the Butler Act proved unsatisfactory. There was no 'parity of esteem' between the three types of school that its proponents proclaimed as an aim of the new system, and improvements in technical education were limited. The 'eleven plus' system combined rigidity with arbitrariness and was succeeded by the comprehensive system, in turn widely considered to be defective. But, slowly, further and higher education was extended to more and more of the population. Getting a university degree was no longer just a middle-class objective.

At Birkbeck in 1956 Adam gave the 23rd Haldane Lecture. This was fitting: one noted military reformer speaking in memory of another. Adam described Lord Haldane as the 'greatest ever Secretary of State for War'.[4] As well as army reform they had more in common. After being 'shamefully driven' from public office in 1915 for supposed pro-German sentiments Haldane had extended his interest in adult education, already notable with his pre-war contribution to the foundation of Imperial College and the London School of Economics, and to university education in Ireland and Wales. In his address, Adam referred to a report on adult education in 1919 to the Ministry of Reconstruction that had not been implemented at that time, or later. He commented how the Board of Education 'disliked the report' and by 1925 was spending only £75,000 a year on adult education, with an estimated 400,000 men and women involved in one way or another, largely through voluntary bodies.

In the intervening thirty years there had been a considerable advance: by the time of the Haldane Lecture there were nearly 1½ million people on adult education courses, including 662,000 at Local Educational Authority (LEA) evening institutes and 600,000 at Women's Institutes (WI) and Townswomen's Guilds (TG) courses. Expenditure on university extra-mural, WEA, LEA and other courses was an estimated £2.8 million, including £1.6 million from taxes and £700,000 from local rates; the WIs and TGs spent £1.6 million, including £400,000 from national and local taxes. There was an unknown number of adults pursuing 'general' education in 526 technical colleges, evening institutes and other bodies, and in 174 'arts establishments'. Beyond that there were many autonomous societies for music, art, literature and science. Yet such activities reached only about 20 per cent of the adult population – by coincidence the same proportion as those engaged in educational activities in the army before they were made compulsory. This was still a long way from the 1919 report's aim of adult education being both universal and life-long. The main problems that Adam saw were how to reach the 80 per cent untouched by the opportunities available, how to liberalise adult education in a technical age, and how to help spread adult education in underdeveloped areas, especially the colonies.

Through UNESCO there was now widespread knowledge of adult education in other countries. Radio and television offered great opportunities. Yet Adam was still dissatisfied in 1960, for despite the stimulus given to adult education by the Second World War, the following issues remained:

- The idea that education throughout life should be regarded as a whole has not got through to the Ministry of Education nor to the local authorities.
- It is a truth brought out by the war that there is latent in the mass of our people a capacity far beyond that was recognised, a capacity to rise to the conception of great issues and to face the difficulties of fundamental problems when these are visualised in a familiar form.

–   They only require leaders whom they can trust.
–   That the necessary conclusion is that adult education must not be regarded
    as a luxury for the few exceptional persons here and there, nor as a thing
    which concerned only a short spell of life, so that adult education, is a
    permanent necessity and an inseparable aspect of citizenship and should
    therefore be both universal and lifelong.
–   That the opportunity for adult education should be spread over the
    whole community as a primary obligation on that community in its own
    interest and that therefore every assistance should be given to voluntary
    organisations so that their work, now necessarily sporadic and disconnected,
    may be developed and find its place in the national education system.[5]

At the core of the issue, as was implicit in the army's educational programme,
is what the word 'education' means. According to the Oxford Latin Dictionary
it derives from the root of both *educare* and *educere*. The former is defined as
meaning 'to tend and support the growth of offspring, to bring up, to rear'; the
latter is more expansive, in that apart from also meaning 'bring up', 'nurture'
and 'rear', it can mean 'lead out' or 'bring out'. Whatever other remnants of
his schoolboy Latin Adam remembered in his sixties, he clearly understood
education in the second sense. He wanted to bring out, to draw forth the best
in men and women, to develop their human potential, whatever their social
origin or level of formal schooling.

Many of Adam's post-war appointments differed from his senior army and
British Council experience in that they were not in executive but largely in
advisory and guiding roles. As president of the British Council in 1955–69 he
obviously still knew its inner workings well, but was no longer involved in its
general operations, but offering advice as needed. His title of principal at the
Working Men's College in 1956–61 was less concerned with detail than the name
suggests; the vice-principal had the executive role. Established in north London in
1854 under Christian socialist influence, it had maintained a precarious existence,
linked to the wider adult educational movement of University Extension and the
WEA: 'a peculiar blend of Samuel Smiles's middle-class doctrine of Self-Help and
the Owenite teaching of the need for the working classes to attain independence
through their own co-operative efforts'.[6] In the 1930s it had 1,000 students,
devoting spare time and money to self-improvement. Its aim was to give working
men a liberal education, with emphasis on non-vocational subjects. Many of its
older students had left school at 14 or even 13 and found the college's combination
of education and social activities more congenial and less forbidding than evening
institutes full of younger, sharper men working for exams. After the war, two-
fifths of the men were in manual occupations, with over one-quarter studying the
humanities, an equal proportion mathematics and science, rather fewer modern
languages, and one-fifth music, art and elocution. Such men of drive and ambition

(and women at a smaller parallel college) were the sort that impressed Adam and determined him to encourage them. The teachers were mainly volunteers, drawn from the civil service, the professions, the City and former students, although post-war it was more difficult to find men who could spare the time.

PURSUING PEACE

Adam was not only concerned with classroom learning in Britain: there was an especially urgent need to spread knowledge to the whole world about the threats to peace. As chairman of the British branch of the United Nations Association in 1957–60 he was deeply concerned about the proliferation of arms of all kinds. In a manuscript from 1958 he points to the vast sums spent by the powers on weaponry. He scorned the idea that there could be a limited nuclear war: once started it would inevitably spread. In 1954–55 he had hopes from the international talks about holding down American, Soviet and Chinese armed forces to 1.5 million, with 650,000 each for Britain and France, as well as limiting arms. In May 1955 the Soviet Union accepted this proposal, but, Adam noted dryly, the West soon withdrew the offer on the grounds that it was not feasible to verify concealed stocks of missiles or fissile material. So 'the deadlock commenced'.[7]

Two years later, he and Charles Judd, the director of the British section of the United Nations Association (UNA), put their names to a book entitled *Assault at Arms: a Policy for Disarmament.*[8] The text, completed late in 1959, was drafted by Hugh Thomas who had been in the disarmament section of the Foreign Office.[9] It was written at a very fraught period for East–West relations: hopes of relaxation of tension with the coming to power of Nikita Khrushchev after Stalin's death were foiled by the Suez adventure and the Soviet suppression of the Hungarian revolt. Publication occurred during a brief period of relative calm before the erection of the Berlin Wall later in 1960 and the Cuban Missile Crisis two years later. The authors were concerned at public complacency: 'The destructive power of atomic and hydrogen bombs is the most startling fact of the modern world. Yet for most people this power still constitutes a vague threat.' It recalled that at Hiroshima and Nagasaki 140,000 people had been killed outright or died later, 60 per cent of them from burns. Over 200 people a year were still dying from the effects and 150,000 still needed medical care.

The two twenty-kiloton atomic bombs dropped on the Japanese cities were equal to 1,000 of the conventional TNT 'blockbusters' dropped on Germany, and forty times more powerful than all the German high explosive bombs dropped in the heaviest raid on London in 1941. By 1960 nuclear powers were testing megaton bombs that were fifty times as powerful as the Hiroshima and Nagasaki bombs. One ten-megaton bomb on central London would probably kill 4 million people, with another million seriously injured. A Congressional report in 1959 estimated that one day's nuclear exchange could kill 49 million people worldwide and injure another 20 million. Chemical, bacteriological and biological weapons of unknown power were being added to the world's arsenals.

Assault at Arms was balanced concerning the then active controversy about nuclear disarmament: it considered that both the advocates of disarmament and those of the effectiveness of the nuclear had reason on their side. But, it argued, to get rid of Britain's nuclear weapons unilaterally would necessitate also trying to take up a 'Swiss position' in international affairs: 'Any simple abandonment of the hydrogen bomb by the British would bring neither safety nor innocence'. If the unilateralists' arguments were inadequate, Adam, Judd and Thomas had little belief in the deterrent power of nuclear weapons either and were sceptical about the conventional Western interpretation of the international tension: 'It is not certain that the deterrent has really ever deterred anything. Even if America had not possessed nuclear weapons, would Russia have risked another war, even a conventional one, in the year after 1945? Her casualties in World War II had been 14 million. The task of reconstruction had been vast.'[10]

Within two years of the book's publication, the world was on the brink of nuclear war over Cuba – and was much closer to it, it is now known, than was believed at the time. This did cause the rival blocs to pause for thought: on 1 January 1964 Adam was among several prominent signatories of a letter to *The Times* welcoming as a first step the recent agreement to ban nuclear tests in the atmosphere, outer space and under water.

The dangers of nuclear proliferation remain: the four nuclear powers of his day have become eight, one of them with an unstable government, and two more threaten to acquire nuclear weapons. Thirteen years after *The Times* letter, in May 1977, Adam was among 1,800 signatories in *The Guardian* in respect to an appeal to US President Carter to make all efforts towards 'the elimination of nuclear weapons from this earth'. His co-signatories included playwright Arnold Wesker, novelist Iris Murdoch, naturalist Sir Peter Scott, trade unionist Arthur Scargill, actresses Diana Rigg and Mia Farrow, and many prominent scientists and Church leaders. In the same month, *New Scientist* editor Donald Gould wrote of former Prime Minister Lord Attlee's statement that when the first nuclear bombs were developed he knew nothing of the genetic effects, and that, as far as he knew, neither did President Truman or Winston Churchill. If the scientists knew or suspected, they did not inform the people who made the decision. Now, Gould concluded, at least *The Guardian* advertisement offers some reassurance that, in future, politicians would not be able to make such 'dreadful decisions in crass ignorance of the possible consequences'.[11] We hope so still.

Adam's concern for peace was not confined to weaponry: he was a firm supporter of the 'Freedom from Hunger' campaign that he saw as a threat to world stability, apart from the suffering involved. The Bengal famine was not forgotten.

16

HOW RADICAL WAS HE?

This narrative opened by offering a puzzle about the life of Sir Ronald Forbes Adam, a career soldier who after forty years of steady, conventional rise in his profession, suddenly in his mid-fifties revealed a capacity for radical thinking and action that shocked many contemporaries but which he believed was necessary in the interests of war-beset Britain. Adam is outstanding because, despite forty years of institutionalisation in the army, he was mentally able to step outside the military framework to introduce two concepts hitherto wholly alien to the British Army: the scientific selection of officers and men, and open debate on current events.

Adam was a member of 'a closed caste with limited knowledge of other classes', as described in a Staff College lecture on psychology in 1937. But he was untypical of this caste in that he did over the years develop a deep understanding of and sympathy with other social classes. His upbringing, his social and his professional life, and his recreations at different times of his life – polo, riding, hunting (both fox and big game), shooting and fishing – were those of the British upper classes of his time. He was 'the sort of man who is probably a good change bowler and certainly a welcome guest for a week-end's shooting'.[1] In appearance he was a stereotypical army officer: the gaiters, the jodhpurs, the Sam Browne belt, the erect bearing, the moustache, the clipped hair and the reticent nature. With many officers, their uniform appearance embodied their uniform minds. Adam's did not, and his great quality was that he had escaped psychologically from being hidebound by the military milieu. As he told Staff College students as early as 1938: 'To be original and receptive of originality we must think.'

His own originality was clear in that he could think beyond the social conventions of many of his contemporaries:

Some people who ought to know better, consider that those, in what they consider a lower class, have no ideals or aspirations [...] It was clear from our wartime experiences that nearly every person has some creative urge, if he can be given the right opportunities in any of the wide range of subjects in which creative abilities can be exercised.[2]

He was writing about his experiences in the Second World War. This offers a paradox. For during the First World War, as a troop and battery commander, he was in much closer contact on a day-to-day basis with gunners, bombardiers and sergeants, sharing their dangers, their fears, their grief at lost comrades, and their relief at survival. Perhaps, like so many wartime soldiers, he suffered from 'survivor's guilt', that the enemy shell had landed and killed a comrade-in-arms, rather than killing him. Few wanted to recall or to talk of the terrible things they had seen, and done; fewer still wrote of them. His succinct diary entries from that time show concern for the horses but none for his men or his fellow officers.

Once he was a brigade major – and even more during his interwar progress at the WO and as a Staff College lecturer – he was further and further away from day-to-day contacts with the army's rank and file. Yet it is the experience of the later war, when he was a very senior officer that this consciousness began to show itself. As AG he made tours of inspection and took salutes at parades, but such rituals – about which he had reservations – only served to emphasise the gulf between officers and men. Adam was not content with this:

> Much of his time he spent out of the office, among the troops, flying from one war theatre to the next, observing, questioning, breaking bottle-necks and heartening his subordinates in the field [...] He has never been satisfied with the 'usual channels'.

This appreciation by W.E. Williams, head of ABCA and a passionate fan of Adam, is exceptionally warm, but it shows the man: 'When he stops for a chat with a private soldier it is not for the purpose of showing what an unbending general he is, but for the sake of finding out what he can about the man's work and his state of mind.'[3] Adam was no populist, the sort of officer who would gather a group of men round him, take off his jacket and say, 'Well lads, how are things?' That sort of exhibitionism would not have been convincing, either to him or to others. Yet the approachability side of his character only seems to have revealed itself from 1941 onwards, when he was senior enough to be freer of conventional constraints.

Of course, by then he was in a position of high command and able to make decisions with major effect. Many of those he took in the welfare field were of direct benefit to the majority in the army, even if many or indeed most of them were unaware of his role. The changes he introduced trickled down. Yet the unanswerable question about this elusive man is whether the enlightened attitude towards the ordinary man and woman that he displayed as AG, and later in civilian life, had merely been muffled in earlier years. In the interwar army, too free an attitude towards other ranks would have earned him reproof and stifled his professional career. Being thought a 'bolshie' at that time would have been a career killer. Or did he in his mid-fifties suddenly acquire a new realisation of the nature of British – indeed human – society and the need to alter it? Was his social conscience always there, latent, or did it just develop late? Of course, the major army reforms he oversaw were within the context of the war, and their objective was to make Britain's soldiers more effective as fighting men. But his interest in adult education and social progress in the post-war years shows that the reforms had not just been pragmatic acts to achieve victory.

Adam saw ABCA's achievements in a wider cultural and social context. In an address to the 1945 conference of the British Institute of Adult Education he saw four specific achievements:

- It substituted 'the habit of rational discussion for the anarchy of the barrack-room argument'.
- It had 'trained thousands of subalterns in the ticklish art of taking the chair', and he hoped that this experience of man-management would stand them in good stead in commerce, industry or politics.
- The installation and servicing of thousands of information rooms throughout the army had produced 'brilliant visual aids', and introduced documentary drama that rivalled ENSA in garrison theatres.
- It brought home to 'thousands of women, for the first time, the realisation of their responsibilities as citizens'.

Furthermore, Adam mentioned the widening of many servicemen's and women's cultural horizons: he had seen soldiers queuing to spend half a week's pay for a ticket for the opera; the significance of ancient history was understood: ABCA produced posters of the antiquities of Egypt, Iraq and Palestine. With the post-war optimism that was felt by many, Adam concluded by hoping that the army's inclusion of compulsory education 'in the King's time' would be followed by its inclusion in "the employer's" time' in peacetime.[4] It rarely was, however, as it made no obvious contribution to 'the bottom line'.

TOTAL WAR

Since 1945 historians have disputed whether the often-described sense of national unity from 1940 onwards did in fact occur and, if it did, whether it endured and for how long. The First World War took place 'out there', across the Channel, even though the guns in Flanders could be heard in south-east England, and Londoners at least saw the ambulance trains arriving every day, and they suffered from the bombs dropped by zeppelins. But apart from them, and the inhabitants of a few coastal towns bombarded by German warships, the experience of the civilian population of war, terrible though it was, was mainly second-hand. But in 1939–45 the whole population of the United Kingdom – men, women and children – was liable to suffer directly from enemy action. This war was not just 'over there', in France and points south and east; it was 'over here', on the north side of the Channel. Not only did the second war call on millions of civilians to undertake disciplined tasks in Civil Defence and the Home Guard, and managing rationing and evacuation in their own home towns and villages, it also called far more on civilian brains to develop new weapons and new methods of warfare. Adam's reforms of personnel selection and education depended largely on civilian staff, many of them on a voluntary and unpaid basis, or on wartime engaged experts; the regular soldiers were often obstructive. Apart from the 7 million (and more) men and women who at one time or another served in uniform, three-fifths of civilian workers were in controlled employment. There was also an unprecedented degree of social fluidity. Unlike Churchill, Croft and Grigg, Adam — and the Young Tory Group — recognised it was indeed a 'People's War', and that there was a consequent demand for a 'People's Peace'. The Labour landslide in 1945 was not simply the result of ABCA or other Left-wing propaganda but the rejection of the Conservative Party and the elite that was seen to have so poorly served Britain in the 1930s. Michael Howard was more perceptive than Alfred Duff Cooper. This time round, the slogan, 'a Land fit for Heroes' could not again be used in a cynical electoral bid. Nor this time would the heroes spend their later days standing in the gutter selling matches as a shallow cover for begging.

THREE FORMS OF RADICALISM

Adam's radicalism can be seen most markedly on three principal occasions. First of all there was his attempt to introduce Regimental Nomination to find good wartime officers. This demonstrated his belief that ordinary soldiers had the capacity to recognise which of their comrades had the qualities that would make them officers under whom they would willingly serve. In this, they proved more perceptive than those old stalwarts of British Army lore, the senior NCOs, on whom generations of officers had depended for an interpretation of how the squaddies felt – if such interpretation was indeed sought. But Adam was no revolutionary. He had entered and spent four decades in a hierarchical and authoritarian organisation and he had a strong sense of its discipline. He had joined an organisation whose *raison d'être* was based on force, to be used at best to deter, at worst to kill. His reforms were not aimed at overturning the British Army.

Second, when undertaking the Board of Trade enquiry into the linoleum industry in 1947, Adam and his fellow enquiry members thrust aside the conventional (un)wisdom of the manufacturers and drew more reliably on the views of 'representative working class wives' for a common-sense attitude. More than anything in all Adam's years as a gunner in peace and war, in adjutancy, in soft diplomacy and in life-long education, this episode in such a banal field as the manufacture and marketing of linoleum displayed his most outstanding and precious characteristics: scepticism about received ideas, his respect for the scientific method and his lack of class prejudice. When on the Miners' Welfare Commission, he visited a miners' pub in the North, and noticed that the stools were made of cast iron and chained to the floor. The reason, he was told, was that otherwise the miners would break them up. In contrast with this attitude, he had concluded from the establishment of service clubs in North Africa that when ordinary men and women were offered good facilities they appreciated them, whatever disdainful view their 'betters' may take. In 1960 he wrote:

> I suppose the definition of a Colonel Blimp is a man who has made himself a slave to tradition. My experience since leaving the Army has convinced me that there are just as many Blimps in the professions and not least in academic circles.

Third – and the most radical attitude of all – was his conclusion in the early 1960s that the only way to bring home to the governing elite the inadequacy of the British educational system would be to abolish all private schools. Such a step has always been too drastic for the Labour Party, and little has changed in the half-century since Adam wrote this. Britain is unique among developed countries in that the children of the elite – professional, commercial, administrative, legal, cultural, military, academic, or whatever – are mainly educated in a manner quite different from and quite isolated from over 90 per cent of the population, and the distinction and privilege so gained lasts all their lives.

Was Adam a socialist? Only by the most superficial interpretation that, as in Herbert Morrison's view, 'socialism is what a Labour government does'; a view found also on the Right. However, a less facile definition is that socialism involves the transformation of property relationships, whereas social democracy implies merely their modification. The post-war Labour governments modified property relationships in British society through nationalisation of various industries and services and the continuation of the heavy taxation rates imposed to finance the war. But they were not transformed; there was, for example, no workers' control. Yet Adam's most radical opinion, on ending private schools, would be transformational by removing commerce from education. But he was not a social democrat, even less a socialist, and essentially he represented the radical strain of British liberalism, drawing on the Victorian doctrines of self-help and self-improvement by the masses. However, it is unlikely that he ever paused to reflect on his own ideology, or indeed imagine that he had an ideology at all.

NO SOLID BRASS BRAIN

As for Adam's character in relation to his colleagues and seniors, the former generally found him congenial.[6] Sir John Slessor, Marshal of the RAF, wrote of his usually cheerful countenance; Percy Hobart found him 'charming'. Adam obviously impressed his seniors in such a fashion that – admittedly with vital outside support from Basil Liddell Hart – he was fast-tracked to the post of DCIGS over the heads of colleagues more senior in service. Resentment on their part can be imagined but is not recorded. His advancement owed a lot to his not making enemies, or at least not powerful ones. We get contradictory views about his willingness to delegate. Bridgeman in the harassed circumstances at Dunkirk found that Adam laid down what he wanted done and then let his subordinates get on with implementing the instructions. But Hobart before the war thought him a great 'centraliser' who upset his immediate subordinates by directly contacting their own subordinates, creating both confusion and irritation (coincidentally, a charge also levelled against Leslie Hore-Belisha). Paget when C-in-C Home Forces complained of Adam's interfering in his command and his nagging of COs – again implying some degree of micro-management. The enthusiastic appreciation of his character by British Council and other post-war associates has a ring of authenticity uninhibited by the formality of military chains of command.

Chance played a crucial role in getting Adam to his highest positions and greatest achievements. Minor chance led him to the Staff College in 1920. If not in that year, he would have got there soon after. A greater element of chance was how in the mid-1930s he impressed Basil Liddell Hart. Chance again led Duff Cooper to introduce the military writer to Leslie Hore-Belisha, which led to the 'partnership' that proved so important to the army and in particular to Adam. If his appointments as commandant of the Staff College or as DCIGS had been blocked, the services to his country that he made in and out of uniform could have not occurred in the way they did. He might have gone on to be a competent field commander, but probably too painstaking and cautious for real battlefield success. His ability lay not in originality of thought but in his capacity to recognise a problem, to seize on a solution, drawing on others' ideas as necessary, and to push it through by some means or other, whatever, wherever, and however long the opposition. As AG he impressed Ernest Bevin, who subsequently proposed him for the British Council. His championing of army education led him into the adult educational world in peacetime.

Apparently an austere and taciturn soldier, and every inch a general, Adam was noted for his geniality, notwithstanding 'his brow like thunder and tongue like whiplash'.[5] He did not take himself or his profession too seriously. He skylarked with his children. He teased Burgess Meredith. Among his papers is an anonymous document that opens:

> A Clerk is one who knows a great deal about very little and goes on learning more and more about less and less until finally he knows everything about practically nothing

WHEREAS

Staff Officer is one who knows very little about a great deal and goes on learning less and less about more and more until finally he knows practically nothing about everything.

It goes on to offer satirical interpretations of common military jargon, such as:

Under consideration = Never heard of it

Snowed under = Unable to take more than 2 hours off for lunch

Putting him in the picture = A long, confusing and inaccurate statement on a subject to a newcomer

Kindly expedite your reply = For God's sake try and find the papers – the General is creating [6]

Here was no stiff brass-hat with a solid brass brain to match. He could laugh at his position and so at himself. Adopting a fig leaf and an apple as insignia for his commands showed no danger of pomposity.

In his eighties Adam took it easier: in 1967 he ended his formal association stretching over nearly two decades with both the Institute of Education and Birkbeck College. He was not involved with the foundation of the Open University, which was established two years later in 1969, but he would certainly have welcomed it as providing an up-to-date facility for lifelong learning open to all. Its claim to be the first institution 'to break the insidious link between exclusivity and excellence' summed up Adam's own aims.[7]

When his wife Dorothy became ill in the late 1960s his sister Hetty moved to Faygate to help out, and stayed on after 1972, when 'Doff' died, until her own death five years later. Then housekeepers moved in. Adam was energetic to the last, with lengthy walks each day. His army records record his nationality as 'Scottish' and his religion as 'Church of England'. He was not driven by overt faith any more than ideology, although in retirement he went weekly to the village church, where his grave now lies. Apart from fishing holidays he had few direct connections with his father's land of birth.

The Adam archives contain a draft of a letter, written in that same precise hand, although larger than in earlier years, explaining to Worcester College that, as he was now 96, he could not get about so much and would not be able to attend the next Fellows' Dinner.[8] He died a few months later, on Boxing Day 1982. He was aged ninety-seven years, one month and twenty-seven days, as the Royal Military Academy, Woolwich, would no doubt have recorded it. Obituary notices and personal appreciations were warm and widespread, although most of his contemporaries had already gone. 'Brookie' had died in 1963.

In an address at the memorial service on 23 February 1983 in the Chapel of The Royal Hospital Chelsea, Lord (Asa) Briggs – Bletchley Park boffin, social historian, provost of Worcester College and chancellor of the Open University – said:

> He was a soldier, but a soldier with a difference. Who else as President of the Dunkirk Veterans' Association would have sent the Association an annual Presidential Message in 1963 with the title 'Freedom from Hunger' beginning with the words '60 per cent of the world's population does not get sufficient to eat'? In this message he urged Dunkirk veterans to do all they could locally to support the Freedom from Hunger Campaign which was 'so important for the peace of the world'.

This was a long way from that hedonistic youth in Edinburgh and India.

The Times obituary was especially appreciative: he had 'a warm and generous heart, a notable gift for fellowship and, above all, complete integrity'.[9]

Thirty-six years earlier 'ABCA Bill' Williams had already provided a text apt for an epitaph:

> There may have been among our senior generals men of higher intellectual gifts than Ronald Adam. But none can surpass him in the sterling endowments of character. He is pre-eminently a good man, and a man of the most liberal mind.[10]

At the memorial service, a RA bugler blew *The Last Post*, and then *Reveille*.

NOTES

Sir Ronald Adam provided four main primary sources, all of which are in the Liddell Hart Centre for Military Archives at King's College, London. The first two are his diaries for 1911 (filed as Adam accn. 2011) and 1916–18 (Adam 1/1). The third, 'Lessons of the Second World War', written in 1960, is in LHCMA, Adam 3/13. In the Notes this is indicated as 'LHCMA, Adam 1960'; in the text it is referred to by such a phrase as 'Adam wrote in 1960'. The fourth, in LHCMA, Adam 3/10, is a manuscript memoir written in 1961 and later. In the Notes this is recorded as 'LHCMA, Adam 1961'; in the text by such phrases as 'Adam recalled in 1961' or 'Adam wrote in 1961'.

Abbreviations used in the Notes:

CAB	Cabinet Office papers
CAC	Churchill Archives Centre, Churchill College, Cambridge
ECAC	Executive Committee of the Army Council
FRAM	Firepower – the Royal Artillery Museum
HC	House of Commons
IWM	Imperial War Museum
JRUSI	*Journal of the Royal United Services Institute*
JSCSC	Joint Services Command and Staff College
LHCMA	Liddell Hart Centre for Military Archives, King's College, London
PREM	Prime Ministerial papers
TNA	The National Archives
WO	War Office papers

1: THE PUZZLE

1. Ballard, J.G., *Miracles of Life: Shanghai to Shepperton* (London: Fourth Estate, 2008), p.131.
2. Howard, Sir Michael, *Captain Professor* (London: Continuum, 2006), pp.113–14.
3. Peter, Laurence, *The Peter Principle* (London: Allen & Unwin, 1985), *passim*.

2: FROM INDIA TO INDIA

1. Pevsner, Nikolaus, & Hubbard, Edward, *Cheshire* (Harmondsworth: Penguin, 1971).
2. Author's interview with Isobel Forbes Adam, 26 October 2011.
3. Apart from Adam's 1911 diary sources (at LHCMA 1/2), as indicated, the recollections of his early life are mainly drawn from his interview in April 1976 with Peter Liddle, of Sunderland Polytechnic, held in the Special Collections, Brotherton Library, University of Leeds.
4. Eric (1888–1925), a First Secretary in the Foreign Office, died of illness in Istanbul; Colin (1889–1982), on returning from India, was in 1934–39 District Commissioner for Durham and Tyneside for the Commission of the Depressed Areas.
5. Liddell Hart, Basil, *Europe in Arms* (London: Faber & Faber, 1937), p.52.
6. FRAM, *Gentlemen Cadets Register*.
7. Butler, Ewan, *Mason-Mac: The Life of Lieutenant-General Sir Noel Mason-Macfarlane* (London: Macmillan, 1972), p.6.
8. Pile, Sir Frederick, *Ack-Ack: Britain's Defence Against Air Attack during the Second World War* (London: George Harrap, 1949), p.13.
9. FRAM, file 427 a/c8304-11.
10. LHCMA, Adam 1/1.
11. Siepmann, Harry, *Echo of the Guns: Recollections of an artillery officer 1914–18* (London: Robert Hale, 1987), p.39.
12. *ibid.* p. 161.
13. Bidwell, Shelford, *The Royal Horse Artillery* (London: Leo Cooper, 1973), p.7.
14. Interview with Bridget and Isobel Forbes Adam, 12 July 2011.
15. *Field Service Manual: Royal Horse Artillery* (HMSO, 1908).
16. LHCMA, Adam 1/5. Document from E. Tremlet, HQ, 1 AA Group, to Maj. Hardinge, 8 June 1943.
17. LHCMA, Adam 4/4, *A Short History of the Eagle Troop Royal Horse Artillery* (1955), ch.3. The honour title 'Eagle Troop' was formally granted by Army Order in 1926.

18. Allen, Charles (ed.), *Plain Tales from the Raj* (London: Futura Publications, 1975), p.185.

19. Kipling, Rudyard, *Barrack-Room Ballads, and other verses* (London: Methuen, 1892).

20. Fraser, D., *Alanbrooke* (London: HarperCollins, 1997), p.30.

21. LHCMA, Adam 4/4, *Eagle Troop*, ch.4.

22. Siepmann, p.173.

3: THE SOMME AND THE ASIAGO

1. Liddell Hart, Basil, *Europe in Arms* (London: Faber & Faber, 1937), p.271, cites Haig as believing two machine guns a battalion to be enough; Kitchener conceded that four might be useful but anything above that a luxury. By 1918 each infantry battalion had forty heavy or light machine guns.

2. Bidwell, Shelford, & Graham, Dominick, *Fire-Power: British Army Weapons and Theories of War 1904–1945* (London: George Allen & Unwin, 1982), p.2.

3. From 1976 Adam interview with Peter Liddle. The other personal memories in this chapter are from the same source. Diary entries are LHCMA, Adam 1/3. Adam's postings are drawn from his military records.

4. Farndale, Gen. Sir Martin, *History of the Royal Regiment of Artillery: Western Front 1914–18* (Woolwich: The Royal Artillery Foundation, 1986), p.341, Annex B.

5. LCHMA, Adam 1/1, 1916-18 diaries.

6. LHCMA, Adam 1/1.

7. Farndale, pp.142, 144.

8. Fraser, D., *Alanbrooke* (London: HarperCollins, 1997), pp.72–73.

9. JSCSC, 'Camberley Red', 1919, vol.1, no. 64, Artillery No. 4, Lt-Col Lindsell.

10. Farndale, pp.146–47.

11. Siepmann, Harry, *Echo of the Guns: Recollections of an Artillery Officer 1914–18* (London: Robert Hale, 1987), p.49.

12. LHCMA, Adam, 1/2.

13. Siepmann, p.80.

14. FRAM, MD/183, 119 Austrian attack, 15 June 1918, RA, HQ, Plateau Army, No.3102 di Prob.OP., 22 June 1918.

15. Dalton, Hugh, *With British Guns in Italy* (London: Methuen, 1919), p.223.

16. *ibid.* p. 261.

17. In all British forces (excluding Indian) 8,981 DSOs were awarded for service in the field and 3,310 Military Division OBEs; 141,000 men and women were mentioned in despatches. *Statistics of the Military Effort of the British Empire in the Great War 1914–1920* (HMSO, 1922), p.554.

4: RISING STAR

1. Bond, Brian, *British Military Policy Between the Two World Wars* (Oxford: The Clarendon Press, 1980), p.67.
2. *Statistics of the Military Effort of the British Empire in the Great War 1914–1920* (HMSO, 1922), pp.237, 339.
3. Howard, Sir Michael, 'The Liddell Hart Memoirs', *JRUSI*, February 1966, p.61.
4. Liddell Hart, Basil, *Memoirs of Captain Liddell Hart* (London: Cassell, 1965), vol.1, p.87.
5. JSCSC, 'Camberley Red', 1919, vol.2, no.334.
6. Strachan, Hew, *The Politics of the British Army, Manpower and Society in the Twenty-First Century* (London: Frank Cass, 2000), p.211.
7. Bidwell, Shelford, *The Royal Horse Artillery* (London: Leo Cooper, 1973), pp.80–81.
8. French, David, '"An extensive use of weedkiller": Patterns of Promotion in the Senior Ranks of the British Army, 1919–39', in French, David, & Holden Reid, Brian (eds), *The British General Staff: Reform and Innovation c.1890–1939* (London: Frank Cass, 2002).
9. FRAM, *1926 Service Digest*, 72nd Field Bty, 16th Bde, RA.
10. Sir Ronald was succeeded by his brother Eric's son Christopher (1920–2009), who was succeeded by his uncle Colin's son Stephen (Timmy) (1923–).
11. LHCMA, Adam 2/1, Report on conference at the Staff College, on 13–16.01.30 (HMSO, 1930). See also Holden Reid, Brian, *J.F.C. Fuller: Military Thinker* (Basingstoke: Macmillan, 1989).
12. Holden Reid, Brian, *Studies in British Military Thought* (Lincoln: University of Nebraska Press, 1998), p.180.
13. Bond, p.215.
14. Liddell Hart, *Memoirs*, vol.1, p.261.
15. See Howard, Sir Michael, *The Continental Commitment: the dilemma of British Defence Policy in the Era of the Two World Wars* (London: Ashfield Press, 1989), p.106, quoting DC(M)(32)120.
16. HC Debates, vol.292, col.2339, 30 July 1935.
17. Liddell Hart, vol.1, p.313.
18. LHCMA, Adam 2/2/1-2. 'M.O.I' stand for Military Operations and Intelligence.
19. HC Debates, vol.270, col.632, 10 November 1932.
20. LHCMA, Adam 1961 see introduction to Notes. On 10 December 1941 HMS *Prince of Wales* and HMS *Repulse* were sunk off Malaya by Japanese torpedo bombers: 840 men died, including Admiral Phillips. The aircraft carrier with the flotilla had been held up by repairs in South Africa.
21. LHCMA, Adam 1961.

22. Alexander, Martin S., *The Republic in Danger: General Maurice Gamelin and the Politics of French Defence, 1933–40* (Cambridge: Cambridge University Press, 1992).
23. LHCMA, Adam 2/2/1-2.
24. LHCMA, Adam 1961.
25. Liddell Hart, vol.2. p.17.
26. R.J. Minney (ed.), *The Private Papers of Hore-Belisha* (London: Collins, 1960), p.70.
27. LHCMA, Adam 1961; Liddell Hart, op.cit., vol.2, p.44.
28. French, David, *Military Identities: the regimental system, the British Army and the British people, c. 1870–2000* (Oxford: Oxford University Press, 2005), p.169.
29. JSCSC, 'Camberley Red', Junior Division. vol. 1, file 9/3, March 1937, Lt-Col T.B. Nichols.
30. LHCMA, LH 1/4/2, 16 September 1937; LH 1/1/4, 17 November 1937; LH 1/1/5, 26 November 1937.

5: STUMBLING TO WAR

1. R.J. Minney (ed.), *The Private Papers of Hore-Belisha* (London: Collins, 1960), p.17.
2. Ironside, Sir Edmund, *The Ironside Diaries* (London: Constable, 1962), p.24.
3. CAC, The Papers of Lord Hore-Belisha, HOBE 5, file 5/10, doc.4, letter of 29 October 1937 from Chamberlain to Hore-Belisha.
4. Bridgeman, Robert, *Memoirs* (ed., Robin Bridgeman) (published privately, 2007), pp.94, 112.
5. Harris, J.P., 'The British General Staff and the Coming of War, 1933–39', in French, David, and Holden Reid, Brian (eds), *The British General Staff: Reform and Innovation, 1890–1939* (London: Frank Cass, 2002), p.180.
6. CAC, HOBE 5, file 5/10, doc. 3.
7. Postan, M.M., *British War Production* (HMSO, 1952), p.28.
8. French, David, *Raising Churchill's Army: The British Army and the War against Germany 1919–1945* (Oxford: Oxford University Press, 2000), p.162.
9. Liddell Hart, Basil, *Memoirs of Captain Liddell Hart* (London: Cassell, 1965), vol.2, p.38, 19 October 1937. Note J.P. Harris's view that Liddell Hart's memoirs were 'intended primarily to establish the author's reputation as the prophet, neglected in his own country, whose advice may have saved it from many disasters'. 'Two War Ministers: A Reassessment of Duff Cooper and Hore-Belisha', in *War and Society,* No.6, May 1988, p.65.
10. Liddell Hart, *Memoirs*, vol.2, p.55, 13 November 1937.
11. Minney, p.70.
12. Author's interview with Isobel Forbes Adam, 26 October 2011.

13.   CAC, HOBE 5, file 5/10, doc. 76.

14.   Liddell Hart, vol.2, p.15, 4 September 1937.

15.   Brownrigg, Sir W.D.S., *Unexpected* (London: Hutchinson, 1942), p.131.

16.   LHCMA, Adam 1961.

17.   TNA, C.P. 26(38).

18.   Liddell Hart, vol.2, p.115, 23 May 1938.

19.   LHCMA, LH 11/1938/58, 24 May 1938.

20.   Dixon, Norman, *On the Psychology of Military Incompetence* (London: Jonathan Cape, 1976), p.140.

21.   Liddell Hart, vol.2, p.115, 24 May 1938.

22.   CAC, HOBE 5, file 5/10, doc. 35, Cabinet paper CP26(38), 10 January 1938, 'The Organization of the Army for its role in war'.

23.   TNA, C.P. 84(38), 31 March 1938.

24.   TNA, C.P. 94(38), 6 April 1938.

25.   LHCMA, Adam 2/2/2, CIGS BM 35/329, January 1938.

26.   LHCMA, Adam 1960, ch.10.

27.   LHCMA, LH 1/4/7, 9 January 1938.

28.   Liddell Hart, vol.2, 9 January 1938, p.85.

29.   LHCMA, LH 11/1938/7.

30.   LHCMA, LH 11/1938/9.

31.   Liddell Hart, vol.2, p.87.

32.   LHCMA, LH 11/1938/11.

33.   Colville, John R., *Man of Valour: The Life of Field-Marshal The Viscount Gort* (London: Collins, 1972), p.82.

34.   LHCMA, LH 11/1938/19, 14 January 1938.

35.   Liddell Hart, vol.2, p.86, 18 January 1938.

36.   Hamilton, Nigel, *The Full Monty* (London: Macmillan, 1972), vol.1, pp.279, 302.

37.   Bond, *British Military Policy Between the Two World Wars* (Oxford: The Clarendon Press, 1980), p.55.

38.   Liddell Hart, Basil, *The Defence of Britain* (London: Faber & Faber, 1939), p. 359.

39.   LHCMH, LH 11/1938/11.

40.   Colville, p.96.

41.   Liddell Hart, *Memoirs*, vol.2, p.87, 21 January 1938.

42.   *ibid.* pp.106–08.

43.   HC Debates, vol.332, cols.1561–2, 7 March 1938.

44.   Bond, p.111.

45.   Colville, p.74.

46.   Richardson, Charles, *Send for Freddie: The Story of Monty's Chief of Staff Major-General Sir Francis de Guingand KBE, CB, DSO* (London: William Kimber, 1987), p.38.

47. Adam 1961.

48. *ibid.*

49. Colville, p.99.

50. Pile, Sir Frederick, *Ack-Ack* (London: George Harrap, 1949), pp.75–85.

51. LHCMA, Adam 1961.

52. Colville, p.91.

53. Feiling, Keith, *The Life of Neville Chamberlain* (London: Macmillan, 1946), p.400.

54. Slessor, Sir John, *The Central Blue; Recollections and Reflections* (London: Cassell, 1956), p.183.

55. TNA, CAB 23(39), 19 April 1939.

56. During the 1939–45 war they were to be ironically described as 'premature anti-fascists'.

57. CAC, HOBE 1/5, p.58.

58. Alexander, Martin S., & Philpott, William J. (eds), *Anglo-French Defence Relations between the Wars* (New York: Palgrave Macmillan, 2002), p.111.

59. CAC, HOBE 1/5, file 5/10, p.72.

60. TNA, CAB 22(39), 24 April 1939.

61. Colville, p.95.

62. *ibid.* p.135.

63. LHCMA, Adam 1961.

6: RETURN VIA DUNKIRK

1. Divine, David, *The Nine Days of Dunkirk* (London: Faber & Faber, 1959), p.257.

2. Fraser, David, *And We Shall Shock Them* (London: Hodder & Stoughton, 1983), p.29.

3. CAC, HOBE 10/10, appendix 5.

4. Forty, George, *Companion to the British Army 1939–1945* (Stroud: The History Press, 2009), p.60

5. Alanbrooke, Viscount, *War Diaries 1935–1945,* (eds Danchev, Alex & Todman, Daniel), (London: Weidenfeld & Nicolson, 2001), 21 October 1939, p.9.

6. TNA: WO 197/8.

7. General Henri Giraud was prominent later in the war. He escaped from German captivity and reached North Africa at the time of the British–American landings. President Roosevelt's intense dislike of de Gaulle led him to try to put Giraud, who was militarily senior to de Gaulle and more acceptable to ex-Vichy soldiers and officials, at the head of the Free French. De Gaulle outwitted both.

8.   Dixon, Norman, *On the Psychology of Military Incompetence* (London: Jonathan Cape, 1976), p.140.

9.   Macready, Gordon, *In the Wake of the Great* (London: William Clowes, 1965), p.100.

10. Colville, Sir John, *Fringes of Power: Downing Street Diaries, 1939–1955* (London: Hodder & Stoughton, 1985), p.166.

11. LHCMA, Adam 1960, ch.1.

12. Alanbrooke, Viscount, *War Diaries 1935–1945* (eds Danchev, Alex, & Todman, Daniel), (London: Weidenfeld & Nicolson, 2001), p. 38, 16 February 1940.

13. TNA, WO 166/207, WO 166/204.

14. Adam 1961; Bridgeman, Robert, *Memoirs* (ed. Robin Bridgeman; privately published, 2007), p.142.

15. Divine, p.35.

16. Colville, p.151.

17. Liddell Hart, Basil, *Memoirs of Captain Liddell Hart* (London: Cassell, 1965), p.237.

18. Divine, p. 44.

19. Gort, Gen., *Second Despatch of the Commander-in-Chief, B.E.F.,* Supplement to the *London Gazette,* 10 October 1941 (HMSO), p.5915.

20. LHCMA, GB 99, Bridgeman, 1/25.

21. Gort, p.5923.

22. Divine, p.46.

23. *ibid*. p.45.

24. LHCMA, Bridgeman 2/4.

25. Gort, p.5929.

26. Bridgeman, *Memoirs*, p.169.

27. Sebag-Montefiore, Hugh, *Dunkirk: Fight to the Last Man* (London: Viking, 2006), p.261.

28. Sebag-Montefiore, p.262, quoting French archive SHAT T604, *Notes du Général Fagalde: Commandant le XVIième C.A. sur les agissements anglais à Dunkerque, en mai et juin 1940.*

29. Bridgeman, *Memoirs*, p.168.

30. LHCMA, Adam 2/6/2/, Liddell Hart lecture in November 1959.

31. TNA, WO 197/118, Account of operation of Adamforce, 17 June 1940.

32. Bridgeman, *Memoirs*, p.172.

33. Lord, Walter, *The Miracle of Dunkirk* (London: Allen Lane, 1983), pp.80–81.

34. Sebag-Montefiore, p.406, quoting Fagalde.

35. LHCMA, Adam 2/3, 2/6/2, 1/5.

36. LHCMA, Adam 1/5.

37. TNA, WO 197/118.

38. Abrial served the Vichy regime and died in an air crash in 1941. Fagalde was imprisoned by the Germans but after the war was tried for passing information to the enemy and condemned to five years' imprisonment. He died in 1966 aged 87.

39. Sebag-Montefiore, p.506.

7: GUARDING THE NORTH

1. Collier, Basil, *The Defence of the United Kingdom* (HMSO, 1957), p.124.

2. Lindsay, Donald, *Forgotten General: A Life of Andrew Thorne* (Salisbury: Michael Russell, 1987), p.141.

3. Collier, p. 127.

4. Edgerton, David, *Britain's War Machine: Weapons, Resources and Experts in the Second World War* (London: Allen Lane, 2011), pp.59–62.

5. Lowry, Bernard, *British Home Defences 1940–45* (Oxford: Osprey, 2004), pp.11–14.

6. TNA, WO 166/40, WO 166/41, WO 199/87, WO 199/1414, WO 199/1422, WO 199/1485.

7. Alanbrooke, Viscount, *War Diaries 1935–1945* (eds Danchev, Alex & Todman, Daniel), (London: Weidenfeld & Nicolson, 2001), 23 July 1940, vol.1, p.95.

8. TNA, WO 166/41.

9. Sheffield, G.D., 'The Shadow of the Somme: the Influence of the First World War on British Soldiers' Perceptions and Behaviour in the Second World War.' In *Time to Kill: the Soldier's Experience of War in the West 1939–1945*, (eds Addison, Paul and Calder, Angus), (London: Pimlico 1997), p.31.

10. Ahrenfeldt, Robert H., *Psychiatry in the British Army in the Second World War* (London: Routledge & Kegan Paul, 1958), p.32.

11. Piggott, Maj.-Gen. A.J.K., *Manpower Problems* (WO, 1949), in WO 277/12.

12. Fraser, David, *And We Shall Shock Them* (London: Hodder & Stoughton, 1983), p.97.

13. French, David, *Raising Churchill's Army: The British Army and the War against Germany 1919–1945* (Oxford: Oxford University Press, 2000), p.66.

14. LHCMA, Adam 3/13, Ch.2.

15. Set up in in London in 1920, the clinic had, inter alia, explored battle neurosis on a psychoanalytical basis.

16. LHCMA, Adam, 3/13, Ch.2.

17. LHCMA, Adam, 2/6/2 CRNC No 2/14140/G/Edn.

18. Alanbrooke, *Diaries*, vol.1, p.160.

8: PEGS AND HOLES

1. TNA, WO 32/9814, 27 General/2800.
2. Dicks, H.V., *Fifty Years of the Tavistock Clinic* (London: Routledge & Kegan Paul, 1970), p.104.
3. Ungerson, Col B.: *Army: Personnel Selection* (WO, 1953), p.19, TNA, WO 277/19.
4. Hanham, H.J., 'Religion and Society in the mid-Victorian Army', in Foot, M.R.D. *et al.*, *War and Society: Historical Essays in Honour and Memory of J.R. Western* (London: Elek, 1973), p.165
5. French, David, *Military Identities* (Oxford: Oxford University Press, 2005), pp.58–59.
6. Holmes, Richard, 'Five Armies in Italy', 1943–45', in *Time to Kill: the Soldier's Experience of War in the West 1939–1945*, Addison, Paul and Calder, Angus (eds), (London: Pimlico, 1997).
7. French, *idem,* Chapter 4, *passim.*
8. TNA, WO 32/9814: Note of 13 June 11941 from DAG(B) to Director of Operations.
9. TNA, WO 32/9846: 20/Infantry/3307 of 1 July 1941 from PUS to S/S.
10. TNA, WO 32/9846: Document Marked 11A, 'Memorandum by Adjutant-General: Formation of a Corps of Infantry', 19 July1941.
11. French, *idem*, p.283.
12. Montague, C.E., *Disenchantment* (London: Chatto & Windus, 1922), p.56.
13. See chapter 11.
14. TNA, WO 32/9814: Document 11A, 'Memorandum by Adjutant-General: Formation of a Corps of Infantry', 19 July1941.
15. French, *idem*, p.77.
16. Liddell Hart, Basil, *Memoirs of Captain Liddell Hart* (London: Cassell, 1965), p.222.
17. Wavell, Brig. A.P., CMG,MC, 'The Training of the Army for War', *RUSI Journal*, vol.78 (1933), p.252.
18. Horrocks, Sir Brian, *A Full Life* (London: Collins, 1960, p.252.
19. LHCMA Adam 1960, introduction.
20. Parker, H.M.D., *Manpower* (HMSO, 1957), p.154.
21. LHCMA, Adam 1960, ch.7.
22. LHCMA, Adam 1960, ch.2.
23. LHCMA, Adam 3/4/2, Serial no.2.
24. Ahrenfeldt, Robert H., *Psychiatry in the British Army in the Second World War* (London: Routledge & Kegan Paul, 1958), pp.184, 251.
25. Natzio, Georgina, 'British Army Servicemen and Women 1939–1945: Selection, Care and Management.' *RUSI Journal,* vol. 138, 1993, p.38.
26. Natzio, p.39.

27. WO 32/11519.

28. Ahrenfeldt, p.65.

29. WO 32/11519, Branch Memorandum (BM) Cover No.34A, 29 May 1942.

30. WO 216/66: Reg. No. BM 15/5034, AG(B) to VCIGS, 17 August 1942.

31. *Army Quarterly,* vol. 55, Oct–Jan 1947–48, p.191.

32. Pile, Sir Frederick, *Ack-Ack: Britain's Defence Against Air Attack in the Second World War* (London: George Harrap, 1949), p.187.

33. LHCMA, Adam 1960, ch.1.

34. Paget, Julian, *The Crusading General: The Life of General Sir Bernard Paget, GCB, DSO, MC* (Barnsley: Pen & Sword Books, 2008), p.87

35. Both menus are in LHCMH, Adam 1/5.

36. WO 277/19: *Army: Personnel Selection*, compiled by Col B. Ungerson (War Office, 1953), p.48.

37. French, *Raising Churchill's Army*, p.147

38. Ahrenfeldt, pp.107–112.

39. Foreword to Treneman, Joseph, *Out of Step: A Study of Young Delinquent Soldiers in Wartime* (London: Methuen, 1952).

40. LHCMA, Adam 4/10, brochure published on the 50th Anniversary of the Highland Fieldcraft Training Centre 1943–44 (HFTC Association, 1972).

41. LHCMA, Adam 3/4/1.

42. TNA, W. Temple 40, ff.86–368, 417–55.

43. LHCMA, Adam 1960, ch.5.

44. LHMCA, Adam 4/1, BBC 'Postscript' broadcast, 27 September 1941.

9: OFFICER-LIKE QUALITIES

1. Smart, Nick (ed.), *Dear Grandmother: the Bickersteth Family's Second World War Diaries* (Lewiston: Edwin Mellin, 1999 and 2001), vol.1, pp. 163, 263.

2. LHCMA, Adam 3/4/1.

3. 'Boomerang', (Alan Wood), *Bless 'Em All* (London: Secker & Warburg, 1942), p.51.

4. TNA, WO 216/61, document of 28 January 1941 by Capt. P. M. Studd.

5. TNA, WO 163/161, Morale Committee report for November 1942–January 1943.

6. TNA, WO 216/61, document dated 4 January 1941, headed: SECRET.

7. TNA, WO 205/1c, 13 August 1942.

8. Turner, E.S., *Gallant Gentlemen: a Portrait of the British Officer 1600–1956* (London: Michael Joseph, 1956), pp.301–02.

9. Smart, vol.1, pp.269, 274.

10. 'Cassandra' (William Connor), *The English at War* (London: Secker and Warburg, 1941), p.78.

11. Ahrenfeldt, Robert H., *Psychiatry in the British Army in the Second World War* (London: Routledge & Kegan Paul, 1958), p.52.

12. Crang, Jeremy, 'The British Army as a Social Institution 1939–45', in Strachan, Hew (ed.), *The Politics of the British Army, Manpower and Society in the Twenty-First Century* (London: Frank Cass, 2000), p.19.

13. Ahrenfeldt, p.54.

14. Natzio, Georgina, 'British Army Servicemen and Women 1939–1945: Selection, Care and Management.' *RUSI Journal*, vol. 138, 1993, p.40.

15. Vernon, Philip, & Parry, John B., *Personnel Selection in the British Forces* (London: University of London Press, 1949), p.23.

16. Ahrenfeldt, pp.55–56.

17. Trist, Eric, & Murray, Hugh (eds), *The Social Engagement of Social Science: A Tavistock Anthology*, vol 1. (Philadelphia: University of Pennsylvania Press, 1990), p.3.

18. LHCMH, Adam 1960, introduction.

19. Dicks, H.V., *Fifty Years of the Tavistock Clinic* (London: Routledge & Kegan Paul, 1970), p.310.

20. Piercy, House of Lords Debates, 5th series, Lords 155, col. 1065, 26 May 1948:

Candidates' grading	Old method	New method
Above average	21.2%	34.5%
Average	41.3%	40.3%
Below average	36.6%	25.2%

21. TNA, WO 32/11519: 31A, Minute by P.J. Grigg to the AG, 10 May 1942.

22. LHCMA, Adam 1960, ch.4.

23. *Army Quarterly*, 55 (1948), p.146.

24. Vernon & Parry, p.38.

25. Ahrenfeldt, p.64.

26. Trist & Murray, p.54.

27. LHCMA, Adam 1960, ch.2.

28. LHCMA, Adam 3/4/1.

29. Trist & Murray, p.59.

30. TNA, WO 163/51/A.C./M(42)5.

31. LHCMA, Adam 1960, ch.2.

32. Baron, Alexander, *From the City, from the Plough* (London: Jonathan Cape, 1948; London: Black Spring, 2010).

33. LHCMA, Adam 1960, ch.2.

34. Turner, p.303.

35. TNA, WO 32/11519, document DSP BM/182 of 11 September 1941.

36. Turner, p.303.

37. Murray, in Trist & Murray, p.62.

38. LHCMA, Adam 1960, ch.2.

39. Fraser, George MacDonald, *The General Danced at Dawn* (London: Barrie & Jenkins, 1970), pp. 11–18.

40. Anderson, Dudley: *Three Cheers for the Next Man to Die* (London: Robert Hale, 1983), p. 186.

41. Bowlby, Alex: *Recollections of Rifleman Bowlby* (London: Leo Cooper, 1969), p. 109.

42. LHCMA, Adam, 1960, ch. 2: Education of officer cadets: from 8 November 1942 to 19 December 1942 the record showed:

Educated at:	% successful from	% of successful candidates	
Public school	15	70	= 10.5% of all candidates.
Secondary	61	69	= 42.1% of all candidates.
Elementary	24	40	= 10.5% of all candidates.

43. Sparrow, Lt-Col J.H.A., *Morale*, (War Office, 1949), p. 21, in TNA, WO277/16.

44. Trist, in Trist & Murray, p. 1.

45. Quoted by Crang, Jeremy, *The British Army and the People's War* (Manchester: Manchester University Press, 2000), p. 52.

46. French, David, *Raising Churchill's Army* (Oxford: Oxford University Press, 2000), p. 74, quoting Maj.-Gen. J.A.C. Whitaker, DMT, in WO 231 /8, DMT, 'General lessons from the Italian Campaign', 18 December 1943.

47. Captain 'X' William G.C. Shebbeare., *A Soldier Looks Ahead* (London: George Routledge & Sons, 1944), p. 17.

48. French, p. 66.

49. See Broad, Roger, *Conscription in Britain 1939–64: The Militarisation of a Generation* (London: Routledge, 2006), chs. 9, 10.

50. Trist & Murray, p. 66.

10: DYNAMITE

1. LHCMA, Adam 3/6/3/, ECAC/P(43)137, 23 December 1943.

2. LHCMA, Adam 1960.

3. Sparrow, Lt-Col J.H.A. , OBE, *Morale,* (WO, 1949), in TNA, WO277/16.

4. 'Boomerang' Alan Wood., *Bless 'Em All* (London: Secker & Warburg, 1942), p. 19.

5. Captain 'X' William G.C. Shebbeare, *A Soldier Looks Ahead* (London: George Routledge & Sons, 1944), pp. 20–21.

6. However, universal military service did not prevent the rise of an arrogant officer class, as the Dreyfus issue in France and the Saverne incident in Germany illustrated.
    Alfred Dreyfus was a French officer falsely accused of treason in 1894 for selling secrets to Germany, and was convicted and sent to the Devil's Island penal colony. Partly because of his Jewish origin the French military and

political establishment strongly resisted admitting error until a vigorous public campaign gained him a pardon in 1906. At Saverne in 1913 a German officer made insulting remarks about the inhabitants of Alsace-Lorraine, which had been taken from France by Germany in 1870, and subsequently badly it injured a civilian with his sabre. There were protest against the military throughout Germany. In 1919 Alsace-Lorraine was returned to France.

7.   Mackenzie, S.P., *Politics and Military Morale: Current-affairs and Citizenship Education in the British Army 1914–1950* (Oxford: Clarendon, 1992), chap. 2.

8.   Williams, W.E., *Political Quarterly*, vol. XIII (1942), pp.248.

9.   Hawkins, T.A., & Brimble, L.J.F., *Adult Education: the Record of the British Army* (London: Macmillan, 1947), p.95.

10. Mackenzie, p.57.

11. White, Col A.C.T., *The Story of Army Education* (London: Harrap, 1963), p.87.

12. TNA, WO32/10462, 43 Education 1296.

13. Croft, Lord, *My Life of Strife* (London: Hutchinson, 1949), p.323.

14. CAC, Papers of Lord Croft GBR/0014/CRFT,V/1/1.

15. CAC, Croft, GBR/0015/2, 2/6 Welfare and Education. ABCA,V/15/2.

16. Mackenzie, p.79.

17. Hawkins & Brimble, p.106.

18. *ibid.* p. 301.

19. White, p.89.

20. Hawkins & Brimble, p.299.

21. White, p.96.

22. Quoted by Mackenzie, p.90–91.

23. Wilson, N.S., *Education in the Forces 1939–46: The Civilian Contribution* (The Year Book of Education, 1948), Appendix.

24. Mackenzie, pp.181–83.

25. 'Boomerang', p.22.

26. Wilson, p.91.

27. Hawkins & Brimble, p. 147.

28. Major Antony Cotterell who wrote for *War* and, with official approval, an enthusiastic book on army life – *What! No Morning Tea?* (London: Victor Gollancz, 1941).

29. Mackenzie, p.94.

30. CAC, Croft papers, Section 2/6, Welfare and education: ABCA,V/11/6.

31. Williams, W.E., *Political Quarterly*, vol. XIII (1942), p.254.

32. Smart, Nick (ed.), *Dear Grandmother: the Bickersteth Family's Second World War Diaries* (Lewiston: Edwin Mellin, 1999 and 2001), vol. 2, p.81, 15 December 1942. The diaries and letters of the Bickersteth family provide valuable insight into the experience and attitudes of a politically well-connected upper-middle-class family during the war years.

33. Smart, Nick (ed.), vol.2, p.355.

34. Mackenzie, p.111, quoting Pritt's papers.
35. TNA, PREM 4/14/13.
36. Adam, Gen. Sir Ronald Adam, 'Problems in Adult Education', 23rd Haldane Memorial Lecture, Birkbeck College, 1956, p.12.
37. LHCMA, Adam 1960, ch.7.
38. CAC, Croft papers, Section 2/6, Welfare and education: ABCA, V/8. Note of 3 December 1943 to Grigg.
39. Longhurst, Henry, *My Life and Soft Times* (London: Collins, 1983), p.83.
40. Mackenzie, pp.121-24.
41. TNA, WO 32/1455.
42. LHCMA, Adam 1960, ch.7; note in Adam 2/6/2, file 1.
43. Croft, *Life*, p.325.
44. Smart, vol.2, p.86, 27 December 1942.
45. *ibid*. p.91, 3 January 1943.
46. Extracts from *The Week* in Croft papers, CAC, GBR/0014/CRFT, Section 2/6, Welfare and Education: ABCA.
47. H.C. Debates, vol. 5s, cols.10–14, 19 January 1943.
48. Smart, vol.2, p.201, 19 January 1944.
49. CAC, Croft papers, V/11/6, Section 2/6, pp.1–7; CAB 123/50 Grigg to Anderson 3 June 1943; Anderson to Grigg, 5 June 1943; Mackenzie, p.161.
50. Mackenzie, p.116; TNA WO 165/85. Pt 1, Item 148, citing WO letter 43 Education 1034, 11 May 1942.
51. White, p.100.
52. LHCMA, Adam 1960, ch.7.
53. WO 32/10462, 43 Education 1296.
54. WO 32/10462, 43 Education 1296, ECAC/P(43)98.
55. Davison, Peter (ed.), *The Orwell Diaries* (Penguin, 2010), p. 327, n.17.
56. Marshall-Cornwall, James, *Wars and Rumours of Wars* (London: Leo Cooper, 1984), p.199.
57. Mackenzie, p.221.
58. Goode, Capt. F.D., 'A Worm's Eye View', *RUSI Journal*, vol.138 (1993), pp.30–35.
59. Natzio, Georgina, 'British Army Servicemen and Women 1939–1945: Selection, care and Management.' *RUSI Journal*, vol. 138 (1993), pp. 36–43.
60. Croft, *Life*, p.224.

11: THE HUMANE TOUCH

1. LHCMA, Adam 3/6/3, ECAC/P(43)137, 23 December 1943.
2. Sparrow, Lt-Col J.H.A., *Morale* (WO, 1949), p.9, WO 277/16.
3. Bridgeman, Robert, *Memoirs,* (ed., Robin Bridgeman; published

privately 2007), p.277; TNA, WO 43/Education/1296, ECAC/P(43)98, Appendix A. Bridgeman had left the army in 1937 and taken his seat as a Conservative in the House of Lords until recalled to service in 1939.

4. Entertainments National Service Association.

5. LHCMA, Adam 1960.

6. Howard, Sir Michael, *Captain Professor* (London: Continuum, 2006), p.113–14.

7. TNA, ACM(AE) 24, AG/Gen/94441, 22 October 1940.

8. Grigg, P.J., *Prejudice and Judgement* (London: Jonathan Cape, 1948), p.347.

9. LHCMH, Adam, 1960, ch.7.

10. TNA, 43 Education 1296.

11. LHCMA, Adam 1960, ch.7.

12. White, Col A.C.T., *The Story of Army Education* (London: Harrap, 1963), pp.156–67.

13. Smart, Nick (ed.), *Dear Grandmother: the Bickersteth Family's Second World War Diaries* (Lewiston: Edwin Mellin, 1999 and 2001), vol.2, p.254, 22 August 1944.

14. LHCMA, Adam 1961.

15. *ibid*.

16. *Annual Register*, 22 October 1945, p.82.

17. TNA, BW 1/191, lecture at London University, 6 December 1949.

18. LHCMA, Adam 1960, introduction.

19. *ibid*., ch.9.

20. *ibid*., ch.9.

21. Wilson, A.T.M., Trist, Eric & Curle, Adam 'Transitional Communities and Social Reconnection', in Trist, p.88.

22. LHCMA, Adam 1960; ch.10. Only twenty RCUs were established, according to Trist, Eric, and Murray, Hugh, *The Social Engagement of Social Science: A Tavistock Anthology* (Philadelphia: University of Pennsylvania Press, 1990), vol. 1, p.89.

23. Nichol, John & Rennel, Tony, *The Last Escape: The Untold Story of Allied Prisoners of War in Germany 1944–45* (London: Viking, 2000) p.397.

24. Natzio, Georgina, 'British Army Servicemen and Women 1939–1945: Selection, Care and Management,' *RUSI Journal*, vol.138 (1993), pp. 36–43.

25. Recent research offers different figures but the same order of magnitude. See: Oram, Gerard, *Death Sentences by Military Courts of the British Army 1914–1924* (Francis Boutle, 2005); Puttkowski, Julian, *British Army mutinies 1914–1922* (London: Francis Boutle, 1998).

26. French, David: 'Discipline and the Death Penalty in the British Army in the war against Germany during the Second World War', JCH, vol. 33(4) (October 1998), p.531–45.

27. WO 32/15774, Grigg to Churchill, 5 June 1942, quoted by French, *ibid*., p.542.

28. LHCMA, Adam 1960, ch.10.

29. LHCMA, Adam, 3/4/3, 'Serial No.3, Administration and Discipline', 3.1943.

30. Ellis, John, *The Fighting Man in World War Two* (London: David & Charles, 1980), p.262.

31. Strachan, Hew, *The Politics of the British Army* (Oxford: Clarendon Press, 1997), p.212, quoting Craig Forsyth, 'The 51st Highland division from Saint-Valéry to El Alamein', (Glasgow U., M.Phil. thesis).

32. After the war Russell was a prosecutor at the Nuremburg trials. He was noted for his relentless attitude towards the Germans. His *Scourge of the Swastika* (London: Cassell, 1954) led to his resignation from government service.

33. David, Saul, *Mutiny at Salerno: An Injustice Explored* (London: Brassey's, 1995), p.153.

34. LHCMA, Adam 3/6/3, ECAC/P(43)137, 23 December 1943, Appendix A.

35. IWM, The Papers of Field-Marshal Lord Montgomery of Alamein, Reel 11, BLM 120/7 and BLM 120/8.

36. David, p.195.

37. LHCMA, Adam 3/6/3, ECAC/P(43)137, 23 December 1943. Famine deaths in Bengal were estimated at between 1.5 million and 4 million.

38. LHCMA, Adam 1961.

39. LHMCA, Adam 3/6/4, A.C./G(45)4, marked 'Secret'.

40. LHCMA, Adam 1961.

12: FRICTIONS

1. Goode, Capt. F.D., 'A Worm's Eye View', *RUSI Journal*, vol.138 (1993), vol.138, pp.30–35.

2. LHCMA, Adam 1/5.

3. Croft, Lord, *My Life of Strife* (London: Hutchinson, 1949) p.224.

4. *ibid*.

5. Mackenzie, S.P., *Politics and Military Morale: Current Affairs and Citizenship in the British Army 1914–1950* (Oxford: Clarendon Press, 1992), p.158.

6. Author's interview with Bridget and Isobel Forbes Adam, 12 July 2011.

7. Smart, Nick (ed.), *Dear Grandmother: the Bickersteth Family's Second World War Diaries* (Lewiston: Edwin Mellin, 1999 and 2001), vol. 2, p.23.

8. LHCMA, Adam 1960, ch. 5.

9. See Crang, Jeremy, 'The Abolition of Compulsory Church Parades in the British Army', *Journal of Ecclesiastical History*, 56 (2005), pp.92–106. But the army still had ways of making you pray. As a conscript in early 1950 this author fell out with the 'Other Denominations' from a church parade. The

'C-of-Es' were marched off to church; the Roman Catholics, Methodists, Jews, Presbyterians and one agnostic were marched off to the cookhouse to peel potatoes. On a subsequent occasion he took a hint from Henri of Navarre that, '*Paris vaut bien une messe*', and went to church.

10. Paget, Julian, *The Crusading General: the Life of General Sir Bernard Paget, GCB, DSO, MC* (Barnsley: Pen & Sword Books, 2008), p.89.

11. TNA, HF/1625/C.-in-C. Minutes of meeting at GHQ, 13.08.1942.

12. V. Sullivan, *Leicester Evening Mail*, 27 April 1946.

13. TNA, ACI 626/43.

14. TNA, WO 163/51/A.C./M(42), meeting of AC, 29 October 1942.

15. CAC, Papers of Sir James Grigg, PJGG/9/7/13.

16. Paget, Julian, *The Crusading General*, (Barnsley: Pen & Sword Books, 2008), p.55.

17. Colville, John R., *Man of Valour: The Life of Field-Marshal The Viscount Gort* (London: Collins, 1972), p. 153.

18. Alanbrooke, Viscount, *War Diaries 1935–1945* (eds Danchev, Alex, & Todman, Daniel) (London: Weidenfeld & Nicolson, 2001), p. 405, 17 May 1943.

19. LHCMA, Adam 1960, ch.7.

20. CAC, Grigg, PJGG9/7/17(6), 'Address to Army Education Course', Beirut, 11 July 1944.

21. Grigg, P.J., *Prejudice and Judgement* (London: Jonathan Cape, 1948), p.350.

22. *ibid.*, p.352.

23. LHCMA, Adam 1960, ch.1.

24. TNA, CAB minutes, WM941, 20th mtg, item 6 of 24 February 1941.

25. TNA, PREM 4/6/2 of 30 July 1943.

26. Churchill, Winston S., *The Second World War* (London: Cassell, 1948–54), vol.5, p.581, Appendix C, PM to Lord President of the Council, 2 August 1943.

27. Alanbrooke diaries, p.514, 17 January 1944; p.600, 6 October 1944; p. 631, 1 December 1944.

28. LHCMA, Adam 1961.

29. Cooper, A. Duff, *Old Men Forget* (London: Rupert Hart-Davis, 1954), p 359.

30. Smart, 27.07.43, vol.2, p. 149.

31. Hastings, Max, *Finest Years: Churchill as Warlord 1940–45* (London: Harper, 2009), pp.317–18.

32. Smart, 25 August 1944, vol.2, p.254.

33. Smart, 27 July 1945, vol. 2, p.306.

34. Freedman, Jean R. *Whistling in the Dark: Memory and Culture in Wartime London* (Lexington, KY: University of Kentucky Press, 1999), p.33.

35. Crang, J.A., *History*, vol. 81, no.262, 1996, 'Politics on Parade: Army Education and the 1945 General Election'.

36. McCallum, R.B., *The General Election of 1945* (Oxford: Oxford University Press, 1947), p. 19, p.153.

37. Croft, *Life*, p.325.

38. McCallum, p.103.

39. Wyatt, Woodrow, *Confessions of an Optimist* (London: Collins 1985), p 92.

40. Howard, Sir Michael, *Captain Professor* (London: Continuum, 2006), pp.113–14.

41. LHCMA, Adam 1960, ch.2; Adam 1961.

42. Smart, 31 October 1943, p.174.

43. Butler, Ewan, *Mason-Mac: The Life of Lieutenant-General Sir Noel Mason-Macfarlane* (London: Macmillan, 1972), p.144, p.222–23.

44. The vagaries of the British electoral system are such that in 1951 the Conservatives gained a working majority with 48.6 per cent of the vote, less than Labour's 49.2 per cent. Labour's 13.95 million votes that year were more than ever before or since.

45. CAC, Grigg, PJGG/9/7.

46. LHCMA, Adam 1960, ch.10.

47. TNA, WO 373/148.

13: THE LEGACY

1. Baynes, John, *The Forgotten Victor; General Sir Richard O'Connor Kt, GCB, DSO, MC* (London: Brassey's, 1989), p.259.

2. TNA, WO 32/12134, 1000/Misc/1722.

3. French, David, *Army, Empire and Cold War: The British Army and Military Policy, 1945–1971* (Oxford: Oxford University Press, 2012), pp.60–65

4. TNA, WO 32/12134, ACS/229.

5. For Ritchie and Crocker sources see TNA, WO 32/12134.

6. Ahrenfeld, Robert H., *Psychiatry in the British Army in the Second World War* (London: Routledge & Kegan Paul, 1958), p.72.

7. Introduction to Dixon, Norman F., *On the Psychology of Military Incompetence* (London: Cape, 1976), p.13.

8. TNA, WO 216/35.

9. Letter to the author from the Armed Forces Personnel Administration Agency, Joint Casualty and Compassionate Centre, ref. AFPAA(CO)/14/22/3, of 1 June 2005.

10. Broad, Roger, *Conscription in Britain 1939–1964: The militarisation of a generation* (Abingdon: Routledge, 2006), ch.19.

11. MacKenzie, p. 198.

12. French, *Army, Empire and Cold War*, Ch.3.

13. Paget, Julian, *The Crusading General: The Life of General Sir Bernard Paget, GCB, DSO, MC* (Barnsley: Pen & Sword Books, 2008) pp.143–45.

14. TNA, WO 277/16, Sparrow, Lt-Col J.H.A., *Morale* (WO, 1949), p.17.

15. Grigg, P.J., *Prejudice and Judgement* (London: Jonathan Cape, 1948), p.366.

16. Place, Timothy Harrison, *Military Training in the British Army 1940–1944: From Dunkirk to D-Day* (London: Frank Cass, 2000), p.174. See also: French, David: 'Tommy is no soldier': The Morale of the Second British Army in Normandy, June–August 1944', in Holden Reid, Brian, *Military Power* (London: Frank Cass, 1997).

17. *ibid.*, p.381.

18. Marshall-Cornwall, James, *Wars and Rumours of Wars* (London: Leo Cooper, 1984), p.196.

19. White, Col A.C.T., VC, *The Story of Army Education 1643–1963* (London: Harrap, 1963), p.16.

20. Although all males over 21 gained the vote in 1918 and women over 21 ten years later, it was not until 1948 that 'one person, one vote' became the rule. Until then university graduates had an extra vote to elect the university MPs and in municipal elections business owners had an additional vote.

21. White, p.17.

22. *ibid.*

23. LHCMA, Adam 1/1, Address by Lord Briggs at the Memorial Service for Adam, 21 February 1983.

24. Goode, F.D., 'A Worm's Eye View', *RUSI Journal*, vol.138 (1993), pp.30–35.

25. Adam, 1961.

26. David Lodge's novel *Ginger, You're Barmy* (London: MacGibbon & Kee, 1962) presented a different aspect.

14: CULTURAL DIPLOMACY

1. Board of Trade report, *Linoleum and Felt Base* (HMSO, 1947).

2. LHCMA, Adam 1960, 'Lessons of the Second World War'.

3. White, A.J.S, *The British Council: The First 25 Years* (The British Council, 1965), p.54.

4. Interview with Dr Harriet Harvey Wood, 8 February 2012.

5. Donaldson, Frances, *The British Council: The First Fifty Years* (London: Jonathan Cape, 1984), p.138. Donaldson's book was researched by Harriet Harvey Wood.

6. TNA: BW1/191, GEN/310.20F.

7. Donaldson, p.138.

8. Interview with Isobel and Bridget Forbes Adam, 12 July 2011.

9. As it happened, Colin Forbes Adam wrote a biography of Lord Lloyd, who had also been governor of Bombay and high commissioner in Egypt, and was a firm advocate of Britain's imperial role: *Life of Lord Lloyd* (London: Macmillan, 1948).

10. Cardiff, Maurice, *Friends Abroad* (New York: Radcliffe Press, 1997).
11. White, p.67.
12. *ibid.*, p.69.
13. TNA: BW 82/26.
14. Donaldson, p.164.
15. *ibid.*
16. White, p.103.
17. Maddison, John, UNESCO and Britain (Royston: Museum and Archives Development Association, 1985), p.5.
18. Hoggart, Richard, *An Idea and Its Servants: UNESCO from within* (London: Chatto & Windus, 1978), p.50.
19. TNA: reports on UNESCO: CAB 129/33, 1948; CAB 29/41, C.P. (50) 168 , 7 July 1950.
20. TNA, BW/26, 14 May 1954.

15: LIFELONG LEARNING

1. Institute of Education, London University, files IE/PC/1/1 and IE/2/COM.
2. Birkbeck College, London website.
3. LHCMA, Adam 1960, ch.10.
4. Haldane Memorial Lecture 1956: 'Problems in Adult Education'.
5. LHCMA, Adam 1960, ch.10.
6. Harrison, J.F.C., *A History of the Working Men's College 1854–1954* (London: Routledge & Kegan Paul, 1954), p.xvii.
7. LHMCA, Adam 4/1, handwritten text 'The Arms Race'.
8. Adam, Gen. Sir Ronald Adam & Judd, Charles, *Assault at Arms: a Policy for Disarmament* (London: Weidenfeld & Nicolson for the United Nations Association, 1960).
9. Author's interview with Lord Thomas of Swynnerton on 2 February 2012.
10. Adam & Judd, p.18.
11. *New Scientist*, 12 May 1977, p.346.

16: HOW RADICAL WAS HE?

1. Crang, Jeremy, *Oxford Dictionary of National Biography*, quoting unnamed source in the article on Adam.
2. LHCMA, Adam 1960, ch.12.
3. *Picture Post*, 11 May 1946.
4. *The Times*, 22 September 1945.

5.   Interview with Lord Frank Judd on 2 February 2012.

6.   LHCMA, Adam 1/5.

7.   Open University website.

8.   The college has no record of receiving such a letter in 1982.

9.   *The Times*, 5 January 2012. The newspaper no longer has a record of the author of the obituary notice, but internal evidence suggests that it might have been Williams.

10. *Picture Post*, 11 May 1946.

ACKNOWLEDGEMENTS

The author is above all grateful to Isobel and Bridget Forbes Adam for the loan of documents and photographs relating to their father's career and for their discussions on various aspects of his life. Professor Brian Holden Reid gave helpful advice and most generously read the manuscript and made many valuable suggestions, as did Michael Berendt, Don Hatwell and Robin Bridgeman. Dr Lisl Klein provided valuable material and good advice about Chapters 8–10. Discussions with Lord Judd, Dr Harriet Harvey-Wood, Sir Michael Howard and Lord Thomas of Swynnerton gave valuable insights. Professor David French made generous and lengthy replies to the author's questions, and Professor Martin S. Alexander, Georgina Natzio, Max Schiavon and Professor Brian Bond provided valuable information. The London Library and the British Library have been as invaluable as ever. Special thanks are due to the following for permission to research in and to quote from their archives: Patricia Methven, Lianne Smith and colleagues at the Liddell Hart Centre for Military Archives, King's College, London; The National Archives; Dr Lynsey Robertson and colleagues, Churchill College Archives Centre, Cambridge; Richard Davies, Special Collections, the Brotherton Library, University of Leeds; the Joint Services Command and Staff College; Christine Coates, TUC Collections, London Metropolitan University; Paul Evans, Librarian, Royal Artillery Museum, Woolwich. The author is also grateful for help from Prof. Clare Ungerson; Matthew Wheeler, CILIP; Jessica Womack, London University Institute of Education; Adèle Torrance, Reference Archivist, UNESCO; Mrs P. Hatfield, Archivist, Eton College; Bianca Taubert, Curator, Adjutant-General's Corps Museum; Mark Ogden and Peter Bloor, British Council; Malcolm Harper, United Nations Association; Emma Goodrum, Archivist, Worcester College, Oxford; Dr Alastair Massie and Richard Dabb, National Army Museum; Neil Robinson, Marylebone Cricket Club; the Explore History Centre of the Imperial War Museum; the Wellcome Library; Olivier Entraygues, the Commonwealth War Graves Commission. The author is grateful to the following for permission to quote from their books or for those books and papers of which they are copyright holders: Prof. Brian Holden Reid, Prof. David

French, Dr Jeremy Crang, Dr Georgina Natzio, Prof. Martin S. Alexander, Prof. Saul David, Prof. S.P. Mackenzie, Prof. Brian Bond, Sir Michael Howard, Dr Nick Smart, Lord Bridgeman, David Grigg. The following publishers for permission to quote from their books: Pen & Sword Books, Paget, Julian: *The Crusading General*; Hodder and Stoughton, Sir John Colville, *Fringes of Power*; Harper Collins for extracts from books by J.G. Ballard, Sir John Colville, David Fraser, Sir Max Hastings and Woodrow Wyatt. Among online sources: unithistories.com and generals.dk proved very valuable. The author wishes to thank Jo de Vries, Paul Baillie-Lane and Jay Slater at The History Press for their steering of publication and Amanda Dackombe for her careful editing. Rohan Bolton's preparation of the index is exemplary. As ever Sarah provided support and forbearance.

ILLUSTRATIONS

The author thanks the following for permission to reproduce photographs and drawings: Isobel Forbes Adam (Adam with Northern Command staff; sketch by S. Imogen Browne) and the Trustees of LHCMA, King's College, London (RHA officers, Officers of N Troop, Maxse Redoubt sketch; 1940 Allied officers; Dunkirk map).

FULL CHRONOLOGY

1885 (30 Oct.)	Ronald Forbes Adam born in Bombay
1898–1902	At Eton College
1903 (2 Sep.)	Entered Royal Military Academy, Woolwich
1905 (27 Jul.)	Commissioned as 2nd Lieutenant in Royal Artillery; posted to 54th Bty, 39th Bde, RFA
1908 (27 Jul.)	Lieutenant
1911 (10 May)	Posted to N Bty, RHA, India
1914 (29 Sep.)	Regiment sent to France
1914 (30 Oct.)	Captain
1915 (17 Jan.)	Married Anna Dorothy Pitman
1915 (Mar.)	Second-in-command, 41st Bty, 42nd Bde, RFA
1915 (8 Jul.)	Adjutant, 3rd Bde, RFA
1915 (19 Oct.)	CO of 58th Bty, 35th Bde, RA
1916 (14 Nov.)	Major
1917 (Jan.)	CO of 464th Bty, 174th Bde, RFA, England
1917 (12 May)	Posted with command to France
1917 (15 Jan.)	Father granted baronetcy
1917 (11 Jun.)	Daughter Barbara born
1917 (11 Nov.)	CO of F Bty, RHA, Italy
1917 (11 Nov.)	Temporary lieutenant-colonel
1918 (10 Mar)	Brigade major, RA, XIV Corps
1918 (23 Apr.)	Brigade major, RA, 23rd Division
1918 (Jun.)	DSO
1918 (9 Oct.)	GSO2, RA, XV Corps, Italy
1918 (14 Oct.)	Daughter Margot born
1919	Three mentions in despatches recorded
1919 (3 Jun.)	OBE
1919 (21 Jun.)	Brigade Major, No.5 District, Aldershot Command
1920 (15 Jan.)	Attached 5th Bty, RFA

1921 (22 Jan.)	Passed Staff College
1921 (16 Dec.)	GSO3, WO
1923 (1 Jan.)	GSO2 at Staff College; temporary lieutenant-colonel
1926 (12 Mar.)	Posted to 72nd Field Bty, 16th Bde, India
1926 (1 Jul.)	Brevet lieutenant-colonel
1926 (22 Dec.)	Succeeded father as second baronet
1927 (19 Jan.)	Returned to UK; GSO2, WO
1927 (17 Dec.)	Twins Bridget and Isobel born
1931 (15 Sep.)	Attended 5th course, Imperial Defence College
1932 (18 Jan.)	Posted to 13th Field Bde, RA
1932 (9 Oct.)	GSO1, Staff College; colonel
1935 (19 Jan.)	GSO1 in department of CIGS
1936 (1 Oct.)	DDMO, temporary brigadier
1936 (14 Nov.)	Commander RA, 1st Division
1937 (24 Sep.)	Commandant, Staff College, temporary Major-Gen.
1937 (18 Dec.)	Major-general
1938 (3 Jan.)	Deputy CIGS, temporary lieutenant-general
1938 (25 Oct.)	Lieutenant-General
1939 (12 Jan)	Companion of the Order of the Bath (CB)
1939 (25 Oct.)	GOC, III Corps, BEF
1940 (8 Jun.)	GOC, Northern Command
1940–50	Colonel-in-Chief, RA
1940–50	Colonel-in-chief, (Royal) Army Educational Corps
1940–51	Colonel-in-chief, Royal Army Dental Corps
1941 (3 Jun.)	Adjutant-General to the Forces, temporary general
1941 (1 Jul.)	Knight Commander of the Bath (KCB)
1942 (12 Apr.)	General
1945	Honorary LLD, Aberdeen University
1945–53	Member of Council, Tavistock Clinic, London
1946 (1 Jan.)	Knight Grand Cross of the Order of the Bath (GCB)
1946 (7 May)	Relinquished post of AG
1946 (15 Jul.)	Retired from army
1946–54	Chairman, British Council
1946	Chairman, Board of Trade inquiry into linoleum industry
1946–55	President (1946-47) and committee member, MCC
1946–82	Honorary Fellow, Worcester College, Oxford
1946–52	Member of Miners' Welfare Commission
1947–53	Director-general, British Council
1947–53	Chairman, National Institute of Industrial Psychology
1948	Member of government enquiry into political activities by civil servants

1948–67	Council member, Institute of Education, London University
1949	Chairman, Library Association
1949–67	Member of governing body, Birkbeck College, London
1955–69	President, British Council
1956–61	Principal, Working Men's College
1957–60	Chairman, UK Branch, UNA
1961	Published, with Charles Judd, *Assault at Arms: a Policy for Disarmament*
1972 (2 May)	Lady Adam (Dorothy) died
1982 (26 Dec.)	Died at Faygate, Sussex; buried in churchyard of St Mary Magdalene, Rusper, near Horsham, Sussex

INDEX